EVANS CARLSON,
Marine Raider

Books by Duane Schultz

Wake Island: The Heroic Gallant Fight

Sabers in the Wind: A Novel of World War II

Hero of Bataan: The Story of General Jonathan M. Wainwright

The Last Battle Station: The Story of the USS Houston

The Maverick War: Chennault and the Flying Tigers

The Doolittle Raid

Month of the Freezing Moon: The Sand Creek Massacre, November 1864

Over the Earth I Come: The Great Sioux Uprising of 1862

Glory Enough for All: The Battle of the Crater: A Novel of the Civil War

Quantrill's War: The Life and Times of William Clarke Quantrill, 1837–1865

The Dahlgren Affair: Terror and Conspiracy in the Civil War

The Most Glorious Fourth: Vicksburg and Gettysburg, July 4th, 1863

Into the Fire: Ploesti, the Most Fateful Mission of World War II

Custer: Lessons in Leadership

Crossing the Rapido: A Tragedy of World War II

The Fate of War: Fredericksburg, 1862

Coming through Fire: George Armstrong Custer and Chief Black Kettle

EVANS CARLSON,
Marine Raider

The Man Who Commanded America's First Special Forces

DUANE SCHULTZ

WESTHOLME
Yardley

Westholme Publishing, LLC
904 Edgewood Road
Yardley, Pennsylvania 19067
Visit our Web site at www.westholmepublishing.com

First Printing May 2014
10 9 8 7 6 5 4 3 2 1
ISBN: 978-1-59416-194-0
Also available as an eBook.

Printed in the United States of America.

Contents

8784

Maps

"Many [are] eccentrics and non-conformists" who share a tendency to be "impatient with the petty rules and the micro-management typical of the conventional forces . . . and [are] viewed with suspicion and even disdain by the regulars."

—Historian Max Boot on special forces

Prologue

Jacques Farm, February 1942

Major Evans Carlson stood on a rickety platform built from three wooden crates, the kind their rations were packed in. He said nothing for a moment as he looked out over the group of young marines he and his executive officer had selected, after subjecting them to grueling interviews. These were the elite of the elite; the toughest and most adventurous of the already tough and daring marines. These were the men of the newly formed 2nd Marine Raider Battalion.

They were going to be America's first special-ops team, trained to strike back against the Japanese in the hit-and-run style of the British commandos. But they did not know that. They didn't know much of anything yet, but Carlson was about to tell them.

It was three o'clock in the afternoon on a chilly, rainy day in the second week of February 1942. The marines were assembled in the middle of a muddy field surrounded by eucalyptus trees, which made the whole area smell like menthol cough drops. This dismal place was called Jacques Farm; it was five miles south of Camp Elliott, a rapidly expanding and bustling part of the Marine Training Center near San Diego, California.

It was two months after the Japanese attack at Pearl Harbor, and US forces in the Pacific were being beaten back in one battle after another. Wake Island, Guam, and Bataan were no long unknown names to most Americans. From throughout the nation came angry rallying cries demanding that our forces take action against the Japanese for their attacks on our boys over there. But there would be much more death and loss and surrender before American forces were capable of doing that.

The marines at Jacques Farm would be the first to hit the Japanese and to defeat them on land. But before that happened, there would be Doolittle's raid on Tokyo, on April 18, 1942, which would mark the first victory in the air. The battle of Midway in the first week of June would bring America its first victory at sea. And in August, just two months later, Carlson's Raiders, as the press would call them, would thrill Americans with the first victory on land against a Japanese possession, the tiny island of Makin, two thousand miles west of Pearl Harbor.

Major Carlson and his men would become instant heroes on a huge scale; everyone would know about Evans Carlson and his Marine Raiders. But that fame, and the resentment and jealousy it created, would come at a price that he could not have conceived. At great personal cost, Evans Carlson would achieve what he set out to do: create an elite special-ops force that helped bring about the ultimate victory in the Pacific. The actions of his outfit boosted the morale of the American people when it was at its lowest point. And he accomplished this on his own terms, in his own way, in defiance of the establishment and its strict rules of order and conduct. This is the story of who he was and how he did it.

One

A Test of Honor

E vans Fordyce Carlson had $2.34 in his pocket when he left home
on February 25, 1907. He took the train to Boston, thirty miles
away from his parents' house in Dracut, Massachusetts. From there he
traveled over one hundred miles by boat to Portland, Maine. He was
determined to make it on his own, to get a job and start a new life. He
was eleven years old.

He ended up hungry and cold, sleeping on a pier using empty coal
sacks for a blanket. He got a job the next day at a match factory, running blocks of wood through power saws to make match heads. The
job paid six dollars a week, but a week was long: twelve hours a day
and six days a week. He kept it up for three weeks, existing on a nick-
el's worth of pastries every day until he got so sick he could no longer
work. There was nothing else to do but go back home. But first, he
spent what little money he had left on a new shirt and pants to show
his parents how successful he had been living by his wits.

His mother and father had been frantic with worry, and they were
greatly relieved when he returned, but his mother took his running
away particularly hard. The boy "had hurt her beyond repair," his
friend and biographer wrote years later. "Evans was willful and capri-
cious," she said. "She was right."

His father, a Congregationalist minister, told the boy he had committed a sin by hurting others. "The boy went outside into the cold, snow-
covered night, walked down to his father's church. . . . [N]ot knowing

where he was walking and leaning against the yellow clapboard, [he] wept in shame for the first time in his life. And for the last time."

Evans Carlson was born in 1896 in upstate New York and grew up in a succession of small towns in Vermont and Massachusetts. His father, a devout and pious man, stayed poor all his life, moving from one small church to another. He ran a strict home for Evans and his two brothers and one sister, with "hymns and grace before meals and Bible reading and Sunday School and sermons and lectures on the Holy Land."

Evans hated it and found it hard to be the model son that the son of a preacher was expected to be. He always felt as though he was letting his father down by not living up to the high standards set for him. No, it was better to leave and go out on his own, before he disappointed his father even more.

He did not like his mother, and they frequently clashed over his behavior. "The aristocratic attitude of my mother irritated and antagonized me," he told a friend. Born to a family of high pedigree dating back to the American Revolution but no money, she often chastised him for not behaving in the right and proper manner. "Evans," she would say, "that isn't the way it's done in the best of families."

The boy had problems in school, too, but he learned a great deal on his own through voracious reading. He pored over *Robinson Crusoe*, the popular children's book of the day, and devoured the writings of Mark Twain, Jack London, and Ralph Waldo Emerson. He also developed a keen interest in hiking and camping and living in the rough, an ability that would serve him well in the Raiders.

When he was fourteen, Carlson left his home for good after being suspended from school for a year. Someone had cut the rope for the school bell, and he was the major suspect. The principal questioned a number of other students, and Carlson listened to the sessions through a heating vent in another room. For whatever reason, whether he actually did it or was just looking for an excuse to get out of school, he confessed to the deed and was given the suspension as punishment.

The freedom from school served as a reason for "cutting away the last excuse for keeping him home. But the father knew that well. He had seen his son's restlessness. 'We can't keep Evans home now,' he told his wife. 'He's going to leave us again.'"

So at age fourteen, Carlson was off to a new life. He would not see his parents again for seven years, and by then he would have gone halfway around the world.

The boy's first stop on his odyssey was seventy miles away, in the little town of Vergennes, Vermont, where he found work on a farm and enrolled in the local high school. This time on his first night away, he told his parents where he was and said they should not worry about him. He even promised to keep in touch and let them know how and what he was doing. But he also said that he would not return home for at least seven years. He was determined to make something of himself, to live up to the high standards his father had set for him, and to see the world. He thought seven years would be enough time to do that.

While still in Vermont, Carlson worked as a freight handler for a local railroad and also learned on his own how to send and receive telegraph messages, a valuable skill in those days. When he finished the second year of high school, he wondered what to do next. He thought he might become a writer and wrote a long novel, but he found it too derivative of one of his favorite Jack London books. Then, too, his father had once told him that a college degree was a requirement for becoming a writer. Since he had neither the desire nor the money to go to college, he would have to find something else to do.

He moved to New Jersey, stayed with old friends of his mother's, and began working on a surveying crew and going to night school in Newark. He quit that school after only one month, which marked the end of his formal education. He worked hard at his job and tried to be "one of the guys" by going out with them one night to a bar and ordering whiskey.

It was the first drink he had ever had in his life, and he all but passed out—he was still only sixteen—and had to be carried out of the saloon by a fireman. When he sobered up the next day he took stock of his life. He decided that being a writer was out, going back to school was not attractive, and he no longer liked surveying or the prospect of becoming a civil engineer. There was only one possibility left as far as he was concerned. He would join the navy and see the world, and work his way up to become an admiral.

But a funny thing happened on his way to the navy recruiting office near the Hoboken Ferry. His walk took him past the army recruiting office, and he stopped and looked in the window. He was intrigued by the colorful recruiting posters of cavalry charging across open fields and soldiers in exotic places like China and the Philippines.

There was one little problem: the minimum age for joining any of the services was twenty-one. Certainly not for the last time in his life, Carlson bluffed his way through, telling the sergeant on duty that he was twenty-two. He stood almost six feet tall, weighed 150 pounds, and might have passed for twenty at the most.

Perhaps the sergeant was behind on his quota for the month, but whatever the reason, he signed the boy up and suggested he go into the field artillery. When the friend of his parents on whose farm he had been staying found out what Carlson had done, the husband sent a telegram to his father: "Evans enlisted U.S. Army, underage. Can cancel enlistment. Advise."

His parents agonized over what to do, but in the end reluctantly decided that it was time their son learned that there are consequences to his decisions to be borne, and so they did not interfere. "The boy has to learn from his mistakes," his mother said.

Carlson liked being a soldier, and he quickly found out that he was good at it. But he still could not hold his liquor. He found that out in a bar on his first leave when he was trying once again to be one of the boys by drinking as cavalierly as they did. He got deathly sick again, and when he came to, he found himself in a dilapidated hotel room somewhere in the Bowery in New York City. Years later he told a friend, "At first, I tried to drink with the boys. Then I noticed they were a lousy bunch and that the few who got ahead were sober and reliable. I must settle down and get a reputation for reliability. I began to study." In less than a month he was promoted to corporal and not long after that made sergeant, an unusually rapid rise.

He felt awful, and as he forced himself to get up and make his way back to camp, he realized that his leave had ended the day before. He was AWOL. It did not take him long to decide what to do about it. He had to turn himself in and take the consequences. He faced a summary court-martial, which found him guilty and sentenced him to a fine of five dollars. From that day on, he resolved to be less concerned about fitting in and trying to be accepted by others, and to become a model soldier.

In 1913, at age seventeen, Carlson went overseas for the first time when he was sent to the Philippines. Not long after he arrived, he wrote a letter home. "I know now, father, that the army will either make me or break me, and I think you need not fear for me anymore."

He adapted to the discipline and the way of life well. And he also had his first intimation that Japan might someday be an enemy of the United States. In 1913, California passed a highly discriminatory law preventing primarily Japanese from owning or even leasing agricultural land. The nation of Japan was incensed, and fiery speeches were made threatening war against "fascist America." Carlson was excited at the prospect of going to war and was keenly disappointed when the threat of military action by Japan died down.

Not long after that, Carlson was transferred to Hawaii, and his troop transport stopped in Nagasaki for coal. He walked the streets of the city and was both fascinated and repelled by the sights, particularly the cruel exploitation of women and young girls in prostitution and heavy manual labor. His grievances against the Japanese would grow in years to come.

A test of honor awaited Carlson at his next duty station, Schofield Barracks in Hawaii. He had become a model soldier by then and was quickly promoted from the rank of private to assistant sergeant major. His commanding officer was so impressed with him that he told him he would recommend him for a commission as a second lieutenant.

There was only one problem: at nineteen, he would have been too young for a commission. He decided that the only honorable thing to do was confess to his commanding officer that he had lied about his age when he enlisted. The man was impressed with Carlson's integrity and kept his secret. Had he turned him in, Carlson would have been given a dishonorable discharge. Nothing more was said about getting a commission.

Carlson decided that if he could not become an officer, he would learn as many skills as he could in his off-duty hours. He worked hard to learn how to type and take shorthand, and he took correspondence courses in military tactics, administration, and surveying. He was trying to be ready for whatever opportunities might come his way.

He left the army in 1915 as a sergeant and arrived in San Francisco with a grand total of eighty dollars, all he had been able to save during his three-year enlistment. He quickly found that his money did not last long when he had to go back to paying for his meals and lodging again. He ended up in a small town of three hundred people outside of San Bernardino.

He got a job with a construction company working both the day and night shifts for thirty cents an hour. He slept a half hour at a time between shifts, putting in twenty-to-twenty-two-hour workdays. He wrote to his sister that he desperately needed money in order to get ahead in the world.

In the meantime, in the short periods between shifts, he met and courted the daughter of his landlord. Her name was Dorothy Seccombe, and she was "beautiful, clever and resourceful. 'And practical too.' He thoughtfully wrote to his mother." He was in love for the first time, but they decided to wait until he could become a civil engineer and get a better job before getting married.

Unfortunately, Pancho Villa, the bandit turned revolutionary leader, interfered with their plans when he crossed from Mexico into New Mexico and killed some two dozen American ranchers and soldiers. Carlson had stayed in the army reserves and was called back to active duty. On the spur of the moment, they decided to get married anyway just before he was sent to El Paso, Texas, as part of a five-thousand-man force under the command of General John J. "Black Jack" Pershing.

Carlson stayed at Fort Bliss as an instructor in field artillery and so missed the fighting in Pershing's punitive expedition into Mexico.

Carlson turned out to be an excellent instructor. His artillery batteries were always sharper than the others. That experience, which involved teaching many men who were college graduates, also helped him deal with his continuing sense of intellectual inferiority brought on by his lack of a college degree. As usual, he put his feelings in a letter to his father, whom he was still trying to please: "It is curious that during these last months with the militia, I have constantly come in contact with college men from all over the country, and always I have been received as one of them and have held my own. Unless I told them otherwise, they have taken it for granted that I was a college man."

The experience provided a much needed boost in self-confidence.

The United States entered World War I in April 1917, and in July, Carlson was offered a commission as a second lieutenant in the regular army. This meant a permanent job; he could now count on a stable career on active-duty status, along with promotions, ever higher pay, and job security with the prospect of a secure retirement.

Two months later, Carlson was promoted to first lieutenant and also became a father. "Evans Junior," he wrote to his parents, "born at 5:30 A.M. With ten fingers and ten toes, a full crop of hair, and the strength to hold onto his father's finger with the grip of a python."

In November 1917, he was promoted to captain. He found that he had the requisite military presence, the ability, style, and look of a leader who commanded his men's obedience and respect. They would have followed him anywhere because they knew he would lead them well and not ask anything of them he would not do himself.

When his outfit, the 345th Field Artillery, moved from Texas to Fort Dix, New Jersey, ready to sail for France, Carlson took a rare leave to go home. It was his first visit in seven years. The son who had left home at age fourteen with dismal prospects in view was now a captain in an impressive military uniform with a bright future ahead of him. And with a wife and a child. Dorothy and Evans Jr. were not with him on his parental visit; they had returned to California.

The visit was all Carlson could have hoped for. His proud father preached a special sermon to his congregation with his son in the church in his uniform. When Carlson was getting ready to leave, he asked his mother if she could forgive him for running away. "It's all past now, Evans," she said. "There's nothing to forgive."

Carlson was attached to the 87th Infantry Division, which sailed to England on the once-elegant Cunard liner RMS *Mauretania* and then took a transport to France, arriving on November 8, 1918, ready for war. Three days later, on the eleventh day of the eleventh month, the war was over. Carlson was keenly disappointed not to have the chance to lead his men in combat, to prove himself as a warrior.

In addition, the career he thought was clearly marked out for him was now in doubt. The army would be drastically reduced in size, as it was after every war. This would limit his chances for promotion, as he would have to compete for higher rank with those who had compiled successful combat records. Staying in the army could still provide job security, but there would be fewer opportunities for an ambitious young man.

He stayed in Europe for a while and managed, on his own initiative, to get a posting on General Pershing's staff investigating recommendations that had been made for the Medal of Honor. He had a good time, traveling over parts of Germany in a car with a driver, and began to learn French. When that assignment ended and he was shipped back home, he resigned from the army in December 1919. "I didn't like to be in an army in peacetime. I thought I would get out and make some money. War was an adventure or nothing." Not long after, he and Dorothy were divorced. Carlson had not been prepared for the challenges and responsibilities of marriage, and he agreed with his wife that it had been a mistake for both of them.

It was time for him to start over again—in a sense, to run away from home as he had done before, to make it on his own. He had not needed his parents when he was younger, or his wife in 1919, or the protection of a steady job. He felt that they all tried to take away the one thing that mattered most: his independence.

So Carlson went back to California and got a job as a traveling salesman for the California Packing Corporation, or CALPAC, later known as Del Monte Foods. It grew, picked, and canned food products, which it sold to grocery stores. Carlson worked out of California but was on the road most of the time covering his territory, which stretched for hundreds of miles between Texas and Montana. This was long before interstate highways had been developed. Travel by car was a lot slower back then.

And so, unfortunately, was the economy. There was widespread unemployment after the war, with many industries that had thrived and prospered in wartime going bankrupt in peacetime. Carlson worked hard for the next two years, trying to learn the ways of business, but he was increasingly unhappy, bored, and even humiliated at times because of the way he had to behave in order to persuade someone to like him enough to buy what he was selling. "I made money," he said later, "but didn't like it. It was the doldrums. I yearned for adventure and going abroad."

Clearly it was time for another change. But to what? "He had failed," his biographer wrote, "he had drifted; he hated his work; he was getting old. . . . [T]o a New Englander, to Carlson, to grow old without the satisfaction of work and achievement is to die slowly, without having lived." He was twenty-six. He had been on his own for twelve years, and now had nothing to show for it, nowhere to go.

He decided that the business world was not for him, and that he was too old to go to college. He believed he had only one option. He would go back into the army, where he had been a captain. But now he was told that he would only be taken back on active duty as a second lieutenant. The thought of being outranked by those he had served with before was more than he could bear. There was another possibility, however.

On April 28, 1922, Evans Carlson quit his job and joined the Marines.

Two

How's That for Guts?

"Well, I'm back in the service," Carlson wrote to his father, a few days after he enlisted. "And believe me, I'm so happy I'm almost moved to tears. Lord, I've fought off the desire to get back into harness but I'd rather be a buck private in the Marines than a Captain of industry. . . . My heart is in the service."

He did not stay a buck private for long. Not with nine years of experience in the army and the rank of captain. Three weeks after he enlisted he was promoted to corporal and qualified as an expert shot on the firing range with both pistol and rifle. The next step was the examination for Officers Training School, which he passed. By June, just two months after enlisting, Carlson was on his way to the Marine base at Quantico, Virginia, thirty-five miles south of Washington, DC.

He stopped in Washington at Marine Corps headquarters to clear up the matter of his lying about his age when he had joined the army. He wanted to start his new career by setting his record straight. He was relieved when he was told that such matters were a common occurrence in all the services. His records were quietly changed, and nothing more was ever said about it.

He did well at the training school, earning top grades in all his courses. Two days before Christmas 1922, Carlson was once again an officer and a gentleman, a second lieutenant assigned to duty with the 5th Infantry Regiment at Quantico.

Carlson took his meals in Mrs. Mountjoy's boardinghouse, where he met another newly commissioned officer, Merrill B. Twining. Carlson was in charge of the stables at Quantico—somewhere he had learned to ride horses—in addition to his other duties, and he helped Twining learn to ride. Twining remembered him as, "Always friendly and helpful. . . . Carlson was several years older than the rest of us newly commissioned officers and much more mature."* At Quantico, Carlson took part in his first large-scale maneuvers, involving the Marine Corps East Coast Expeditionary Force. He was put in charge of the mule-drawn ambulance train during the long march from Quantico to Lexington, Virginia, 150 miles southwest. They were heading up into the foothills of the Blue Ridge Mountains when rainstorms pelted the area, turning the roads to thick, deep mud.

The food and supply trucks bogged down, which meant they could not keep up their daily deliveries. The troops were getting hungry, and the commanders were worried about how they were going to get their men out of such a mess. "We went hungry," Merrill Twining said, "until Carlson's mule-drawn ambulances came undeterred to our rescue and rations were distributed in abundance throughout the stormbound convoys. Carlson became an instant expeditionary force hero." General Smedley Butler, in command of the exercise, was saved from a humiliating failure by Carlson's initiative and persistence. Butler took an instant liking to the young officer, who would remain a favorite of Butler's for years to come.

Thus Carlson found himself in a desirable position less than a year after his enlistment. It seemed clear he could rise high in rank, perhaps all the way to general, like Butler, who was also something of a maverick. But Carlson knew that if he were to enjoy a successful career, he could not do so alone. In the small, insular world of the military, it was necessary to have a proper wife, one who knew how to advance her husband's career through social graces and playing the appropriate role. It, too, was a demanding job, and not every woman had the interest or ability to take it on.

*Merrill Barber Twining (1902–1996) became a Marine Corps general and received a tombstone promotion to four-star general on retirement. He was the brother of General Nathan F. Twining and the nephew of Rear Admiral Nathan C. Twining.

Carlson took advantage of Quantico being so near to Washington to mingle in the right society, to be seen at all the right places, dressing and acting in ways appropriate to his station. He went into debt to purchase the best clothing and uniforms. "He made his protocol calls, joined the Army and Navy Club in Washington, attended horse shows and dances, squired [a] colonel's daughters, sent flowers, went fox hunting in Virginia, played polo in Chevy Chase, and attended church."

He found many women suitable for boosting his career, but he met the one he would marry at a tea dance in the Hotel Miramar in Puerto Rico, where he had gone for winter maneuvers. Her name was Etelle Sawyer, and she was a graduate of the University of Maine and of Wellesley College. She was in Puerto Rico on a goodwill mission organized by her friend Lou Hoover, whose husband, Herbert Hoover, would become president in five years. Etelle was well connected socially and also beautiful and charming. A friend of Carlson's, Edgar Snow, described her as a "lovely Southern girl whose specialty is tea with raison crumpets."* She was exactly what Carlson had been looking for. One month after they met, he wrote home that they were going to be married:

> I took her over to headquarters at Culebra Island yesterday. In fifteen minutes, every officer, from general down, was her humble servant. And the beauty of it is that she is entirely unaffected. . . . The date of the wedding will be set when I know what is to become of me this summer.

During the exercises and war games held in Puerto Rico that winter, Carlson became impressed with the military value of aircraft. He foresaw the time when airplanes and their pilots could become the most important part of all the services. That was where he wanted to be, and

---

*Etelle Sawyer was born in Maine and so did not come by her Southern accent naturally. Her niece and nephew, Gail and Glenn Everett, remember her as "an excellent hostess who charmed everyone who knew her" and whose "manner gave the impression of being a Southern lady."

so, after his wedding on April 29, 1924, he applied for pilot training at the Pensacola Naval Air Station in Florida. He completed twenty-five hours of flight training before he washed out by failing a flight check. It was a great disappointment for him; just when he was convinced of the direction his career should take, it all fell apart.

"Failure is hard to take gracefully," he wrote to his father. "But perhaps it was my destiny not to fly. Where to now?" He needed something new and challenging at which he might be able to excel and make a name for himself. He chose to go to China—a booming place for ambitious young officers—but his request for duty there was turned down. He faced more than a year of tedious duty in command of a rifle company in San Diego, and then guarding the mail in Portland, Oregon.

The only boost to Carlson's career and morale in those days occurred when General Butler told a reporter that the reason the Marine Corps was more popular and respected than the army was because it had officers like Evans Carlson who put the welfare of their men ahead of their own. "I never took an arbitrary attitude," Carlson said about his leadership style. "I have been an enlisted man and I understood men. I never used my rank or official position to embarrass the men and to their disadvantage. I got satisfaction out of doing things for the men which they couldn't do for themselves. Other officers never bothered."

To pass the time, and to try to compensate for his lingering sense of inadequacy at not completing college, Carlson started an intensive program of self-study. He read the works of Upton Sinclair, Theodore Dreiser, Sinclair Lewis, Walt Whitman, and Carl Sandburg, among others. He was driven to keep improving himself, to live up to his father's high standards.

At the beginning of 1927, Carlson was sent back to San Diego to join an expeditionary force being readied for service in an undisclosed location, known only to Carlson and a few others. Major Alexander A. Vandegrift, commander of the 3rd Battalion of the 4th Marine Division, had chosen Carlson to be his operations and training officer. Everyone wanted to know where they might be going, and one day Etelle Carlson asked if it was Nicaragua. Carlson shook his head but said the orders were secret and he could not say. She knew then where it was to be. "Where else in the world do they send Marines?" she asked. "If it isn't Nicaragua, it's China."

US marines had been stationed in China protecting American companies and citizens since the middle of the nineteenth century. Together with troops from Britain, France, the Netherlands, Italy, Spain, Portugal, and Japan, they occupied the International Settlement along the curving Whangpoo River in Shanghai. The US Navy patrolled the river in specially built gunboats, including the USS *Panay*, fated to be sunk by Japanese aircraft in 1937.

American and European business interests felt threatened by the growing Chinese Nationalist movement led by Chiang Kai-shek and its escalating war against the Communists who were also vying for control. The fighting between these two forces had intensified, and US officials decided that more marines were needed to deal with the Chinese.

Carlson and the 4th Marines docked in Shanghai on February 24, 1927, at the Standard Oil pier. The men were eager to leave the crowded transport and sample the delights that old China hands had told them about—mostly cheap whiskey and women, all for a dollar or two. Unfortunately, all the men could do for the next several days was gaze at the gleaming white buildings of the International Settlement in the distance. The only times they got off the ship were to drill periodically on the pristine green grounds of the Standard Oil Country Club.

Finally, on March 5, the 4th Regiment went ashore and marched smartly through the main streets of the settlement. The Western troops often marched through the area as a show of strength, and the reaction was predictable. The European and American residents cheered heartily, assured by their presence, while the "silent Chinese who no matter what politics they followed, watched this display of foreign power with clear hate."

Carlson settled into the routine of occupation duty. The slow pace of action "combined with the steaming sultry Shanghai summer began to wear him down. He became depressed and even stopped his study and reading; he felt completely without ambition. . . . He read little; he talked less; he let himself slide on the toboggan of slippery days." His health and spirit declined, and he lost fifteen pounds.

When the weather turned cooler in September, he seemed to revive. He was promoted to first lieutenant, Etelle arrived from the States, and he was given a new assignment. He became intelligence officer of the regiment, a position that forced him to develop expertise in Chinese history, culture, and politics. He read everything he could find in English and began to study the Chinese language. "I didn't know anything about intelligence work but I went ahead just the same. I now became interested in politics in China for the first time."

He became so immersed in his studies that he wrote articles for the *Marine Corps Gazette* and book reviews for the English-language publication *China Weekly Review*, as well as a series of articles for the regimental magazine. It was one of the most productive and happiest times of his life. He felt fully involved in his work and believed he might be meeting his father's expectations.

Carlson's twenty-month tour of duty in China ended in 1929. He was hoping to be sent to Nicaragua. Marines had been in that country since 1853, initially to make sure that no other power would attempt to build a canal linking the Atlantic and Pacific Oceans. Whoever controlled such a link would have enormous economic and political power. The marines stayed on in Nicaragua long after the United States completed the canal in 1914, at first to assist in establishing a Nicaraguan National Guard to deal with roving bands of insurgents who kept trying to overthrow various Nicaraguan dictators friendly to American interests.

Marines also became involved in Honduras, Mexico, Haiti, and the Dominican Republic to protect rapidly growing American business interests, particularly the United Fruit Company. In 1935, Smedley Butler wrote the book *War Is a Racket*, condemning the long wars Americans had fought in that region and the lives lost for the sole purpose of helping American companies thrive and prosper.

Marines were still at war with insurgents in Nicaragua in 1930, and in May of that year, thirty-four-year-old 1st Lieutenant Evans Carlson arrived there and was immediately made a captain in the Guardia Nacional. Marines were placed in command of Nicaraguan troops so as to be better able to control the unrest. After nine years in the army and five years as a marine, he was finally going to see combat.

Carlson was sent inland to a remote village to take command of a group of thirty-five Nicaraguan National Guard troops. Fortunately, part of his self-study program while he was in China included Spanish in the hope that he would one day need it. He was not yet fully fluent, but his new troops were able to understand what he had to tell them. Once again he demonstrated his ability to relate to his men, even when they were from a different culture. "I met the Nicaraguans as equals and developed the principles of fair play and justice. The men were shooting their officers. I went to one place where they had just killed two. I had no trouble as I treated the men as I would have liked to be treated myself and won their confidence." For example, Carlson never rode a horse when his men had to walk; if they had to walk, so did he. "We were all equal," he said.

Not long after his arrival, a group of one hundred insurgents attacked a nearby village. Carlson led a force of sixteen men against them. When they caught up with the enemy, he led an attack that lasted ten minutes and killed five insurgents; Carlson lost none of his own men. The action taught him a valuable lesson about guerrilla warfare. When he tried to track down the band, all he could find were men going about their usual activities working on their farms with no weapons in sight. When he questioned them about the armed men, they professed to know nothing. The insurgents had vanished, but he suspected correctly that they had blended in with the local people, or even that they were the locals.

A few days later, Carlson decided to go into the jungle by himself for about twenty miles to look for signs of the guerrillas. It was a dangerous undertaking. Fellow marine Samuel Griffith talked about it in an interview over fifty years later: "So he [Carlson] got himself a mule and started off. He was dressed like a native with a serape covering his body. You know, one of those long waterproof cloths with a slit in the middle for your head; it hangs over your shoulder. And under the serape, he had a Thompson submachine gun. And that's the way, all alone, he rode those twenty miles. How's that for guts? . . . He was kind of like a prophet out of the Old Testament, strong and righteous."

Much of what Carlson learned about fighting insurgents in Nicaragua would later be put to use on Makin and Guadalcanal. He found that it was best to never remain in a static position for long while fighting, to always be flexible and ready to move on a moment's notice to outflank or surround the guerrillas. Always keeping on the move became one of his guidelines for jungle warfare, along with moving rapidly with as little in the way of supply lines as possible. Troops should carry only what was absolutely necessary and be trained to live off the jungle. If they are burdened with extra supplies, they will be more vulnerable because the insurgents can move faster. He concluded that small, mobile forces were much better at fighting that kind of war than large concentrations of troops.

Like so many other marines, Carlson contracted malaria, and a few months later, after recovering, he was transferred to a staff job in Managua. At Christmas, while he and his men lined up in front of headquarters waiting to receive their pay, huge tremors tore through the earth, sending the buildings tumbling to the ground. The earthquake lasted only a few moments, but it killed one thousand people and caused $15 million in damage. Fires broke out all over the city, and Carlson and his men worked around the clock digging people out of the destruction, caring for the injured, carting them to makeshift aid stations, bringing food and water, and burying the dead. When some semblance of normalcy was restored, Carlson was hospitalized with malaria and later sent home.

Letters of commendation poured into Washington from high-level Nicaraguans, lavishly praising Carlson for his heroic efforts. Not long after, in a formal ceremony, he was awarded the Navy Cross, a high honor in times of war and peace.

In March the following year, 1933, Carlson was on his way back to China for a second tour of duty. Wanting to see the real China, not just the Westernized International Settlement in Shanghai, he asked to be sent to the Forbidden City, Peiping (Beijing). He and Etelle rented a house just inside the city's walls.

Carlson's duties as adjutant to the American legation were not arduous or time-consuming, and he immersed himself in the good life.

He played polo and attended teas, formal dinners, and parties, and he resumed his study of Chinese language, culture, politics, and art.

The couple entertained lavishly and opened their home to visitors as diverse as former world heavyweight boxing champion Gene Tunney, the editor of *National Geographic* magazine, and writers and scholars such as Owen Lattimore, later an adviser to Chiang Kai-shek. The writer and reporter John Marquand, who later won the Pulitzer Prize for his novel *The Late George Apley*, said he did not think of Carlson as a typical rigid military man. "When I knew him in Peiping, he impressed me as being a scholar; a man interested in ideas and culture."

Carlson taught classes on Chinese history and culture to Western visitors and expatriates as a way of furthering his own understanding. He found that his teaching altered the behavior of the five hundred marines who made up the legation guard. The unit had been plagued by lax discipline; each month, up to one hundred men were routinely brought up on charges. Carlson was able to make a difference in their deportment by offering them the same courses he was giving to Western civilians. He also wrote editorials in the *Legation Guard News*. "The editorial was 250 words," he later noted, "and I always tried to point to a moral to change the attitude of the men toward the Chinese, to make them see the Chinese as human beings, different but real."

The results of Carlson's program were dramatic. Discipline problems with the Marine guards dropped by 90 percent, with the average number of men who came up on charges every month falling to ten. Carlson concluded that "when soldiers are given information about the situation in which they act and live, they derive from it a sense of responsibility. . . . He would never forget this lesson." He would use it and the lessons he learned about guerrilla warfare in Nicaragua to great effect in shaping his Raiders in World War II.

Carlson's second tour of duty in China ended in 1935. He was promoted to captain and sent back to Quantico. During his stay there he would soon meet the most powerful man in America, who would change his life. Without him, there would have been no Carlson's Raiders.

Three

Direct to the White House

Captain and Mrs. Evans Carlson stood up when the tall, rather ungainly woman entered the room followed by Jack and Jill, two Irish setters. The others who had been waiting for lunch also rose. They included Marine Lieutenant Colonel and Mrs. Lemuel Shepard, Assistant Secretary of State Francis B. Sayre Sr., and Episcopal Bishop Julius Atwood.

"Shall we go into the dining room?" the woman said. "Franklin is already at the table."

Franklin was Franklin Delano Roosevelt, and the woman who showed them to the table was his wife, Eleanor. The luncheon was over in only an hour on that cold day in February 1936, but the bond forged between the US president and the Marine captain lasted years.

The two men became very close over the following months. It quickly became apparent that they shared the same passionate interest in China. They could talk about it for hours and not run out of things to say. One of Carlson's officers in World War II later wrote that "Carlson was prouder of his relationship with President Roosevelt than of anything that had ever happened to him."

Carlson's duty assignment at Quantico was as an aide to the base commander, Major General Charles Lyman. Within a year, Carlson also was serving as second in command of the Marine guard at the so-called Little White House at Warm Springs, Georgia, sixty-five miles southwest of Atlanta. Roosevelt had been visiting Warm Springs for years for treatment of his polio, bathing in the soothing waters there. It was one of the few places he could genuinely relax and reduce his schedule of formal activities and visitors. The Marine guard always went with him, giving him more time to talk with Carlson about China and what they both perceived as the growing Japanese threat.

Another member of the Roosevelt family spent long hours talking with enthusiasm about the same topics with Carlson: the president's twenty-nine-year-old son, James, who would become Carlson's executive officer on the Makin raid. Father and son were passionate about the East, but neither knew as much about China as Carlson—although the president thought he did.

The Roosevelts had deep family ties to China. FDR's grandfather on the Delano side had visited China in 1833 and made a fortune in the tea trade and more in opium dealing. When he returned to the United States, he managed to lose his money, and so he went back to China and amassed an even greater fortune.

President Roosevelt identified strongly with his grandfather's roots in China, which, one historian noted, gave him a false sense of expertise in China's history, culture, and future importance in world history. "I have a background of little over a century in China affairs," he liked to say. And he loved to talk about it with Captain Carlson.

Carlson had another satisfying experience during this tour of duty at Quantico that also added enormously to his self-confidence. Eager to learn more about global affairs and international diplomacy, he applied to take a course in international law taught by professor Charles E. Hill at George Washington University. There was a problem, however. It was a graduate course with strict entrance requirements, seemingly insurmountable for someone like Carlson who lacked even an undergraduate degree. Carlson was turned down in person by Hill, who told him he did not have sufficient academic background. Carlson asked what books he would have to read to be allowed into the course. Hill said there were ten important books in the field, thorough knowledge of which was required for admission.

"In the next two weeks, Carlson read the books, outlined them, presented himself again to Hill and demanded a written examination. The professor, a little frightened by the Marine's vigor and determination, told him he could take the course without such a test."

Carlson was thrilled to have the opportunity and threw himself into the work. The course opened up a new world to him, and the knowledge shocked him. Even though he had participated in the US interventions in Nicaragua and China, he had not understood how much of it was driven not by idealism, as he had naively thought, but by pure economic interests. Carlson learned the true meaning of the phrase "Dollar Diplomacy" as he realized that much of America's foreign policy was dictated by the need to protect its investments abroad, such as Standard Oil in China and the United Fruit Company in Nicaragua. It seemed that the large companies, not the government, were directing American foreign policy.

He was pleased that Professor Hill found him capable of dealing with the subject matter. With evident pride, he wrote that "nothing, not even having dinner with FDR, has happened to me in many a day that has set me up as much as having received a B for my work at George Washington U. Not bad for a non-college graduate, eh?"

Carlson was summoned to the White House on July 15, 1937, days before he was scheduled to return to China for his third tour of duty there. The president had asked to see him personally.

"I understand you are going out to China again, Evans," Roosevelt said. "I want you to do something for me while you're there. I want you to drop me a line now and then—direct to the White House. Let me know how you're doing. Tell me what's going on. I suspect there's going to be a great deal going on this summer in China. I'd like to hear what you have to say about it. . . . Shall we keep these letters a secret? Just between the two of us? Shall we?"

Carlson agreed, excited at the prospect of telling the president everything he could learn in China. Roosevelt suggested that Carlson send his reports addressed to his private secretary, Marguerite

"Missy" LeHand. That way the correspondence would remain unofficial and not be included in formal White House diaries and records of events.

It was, of course, a breach of military protocol; all communications are supposed to flow from the originator of the report to the next person in the chain of command. By sending his reports to the president in the guise of letters to Missy LeHand, Carlson was bypassing his superior officers. He was apparently not bothered about violating standard operating procedure, nor was Roosevelt. As James Roosevelt noted, "Father never gave a hoot about the chain of command."

Over the next two years, Carlson sent a total of seventeen detailed reports on conditions in China as he viewed them. Roosevelt came to depend on Carlson's reports for their openness and viewpoints that differed from the information he was receiving through official channels. He discussed at least one of Carlson's reports with the secretary of the interior, Harold Ickes.

When the president did not hear from Carlson for a while, he would ask LeHand to contact him. "My chief loves your letters," she wrote to him in December 1937. "Thank you ever so much for taking the trouble to write as you do." Several months later, after receiving more reports, the president asked LeHand to write again to tell Carlson how greatly his letters were appreciated. Carlson was so flattered that he replied, "I am devoted to him not only as our President, but also (and primarily) because of the things he stands for as a man."

Word eventually got out that Carlson was writing directly to the White House, bypassing the chain of command. His superiors were annoyed, questioning what a captain could have to say to the president of the United States. People became suspicious and began to keep a discreet eye on Carlson's activities and the people he associated with outside the Marine Corps. In the coming months, he was found to be friendly with a number of people whose loyalty to the United States was questionable. It was the beginning of a growing sense of distrust and suspicion that would follow him for the rest of his days.

Carlson arrived back in China in late July 1937, just in time for war. As his ship, the SS *President McKinley* approached the dock at Shanghai, Japanese planes attacked the city. He watched them release their bombs just beyond the International Settlement. The Japanese, having taken Manchuria from China in 1931 and five northern provinces in 1935, were now ready to conquer all of China. Chiang Kai-shek was more concerned with fighting the Communists for control than he was in actively resisting the invasion from Japan.

Carlson reported for duty to Admiral Harry Yarnell, commander of the Asiatic Fleet. Yarnell, who was angry about Japanese militarism, assigned Carlson to the US Naval Intelligence Unit as an observer. "We need all the trained observers we can find," Yarnell told him. "We've got to find out how the Chinese fight, and what's more important, how the Japs fight."

"It's exactly what I want to do," Carlson replied.

The fighting was taking place within sight and sound of Shanghai's International Settlement. Every morning, Carlson had only to walk a few blocks to watch clashes between several thousand Chinese and Japanese troops, battles that often left blood running in the gutters. Afterward, Carlson, along with the American and British journalists who were covering the conflict, would stroll back to their hotel for a nice lunch.

By November 1937, Chinese troops were being driven out of the city. Even though the Chinese were losing the battle, Carlson had great admiration for their fighting spirit and fortitude. He was also fascinated by the sheer pageantry of it all. "It was a grand scene," he wrote home. "It had drama and excitement and imminent death. To me such a scene is the epitome of life." Carlson often deliberately exposed himself to danger, at least in part because of the problems of his marriage, the nature of which he never explained.

On the final day of fighting in and around Shanghai, Carlson and some newsmen watched from a fragile balcony as the battle took place no more than fifty feet away. After lunch, he and the reporters climbed the ladder part of the way to the top of a water tower at the edge of the French Concession to have a better view. All the while, Japanese machine-gun fire punched holes in the tank above them. A few minutes later, they noticed blood dripping down from above.

While bullets continued to whiz round them, Carlson climbed to the top of the tower, seventy feet above the ground, and discovered the body of a British reporter. The man was wearing a red poppy in his lapel. It was Armistice Day, the eleventh day of the eleventh month, marking the end of World War I on the Western front, but in China, war raged on.

In the days and weeks that followed, as Carlson observed more of the fighting and sent his personal reports to President Roosevelt, he was seen in the company of some Americans who were considered to be the "wrong crowd." These were reporters and journalists who had been labeled Communists or at least Communist sympathizers—Reds—who had traveled among and lived with the Chinese Communist armies. Carlson deliberately sought them out, as they did him, and their ideas changed his worldview. The meetings also fueled the growing suspicion among the American military hierarchy in China that Carlson was one of them.

Among those who became close friends was Edgar Snow, a thirty-two-year-old journalist and suspected Communist sympathizer from Kansas City, whose book about the Communist guerrilla army, *Red Star over China*, was published in 1937. When he gave Carlson a copy of the manuscript before publication, Carlson asked if people like Mao Tse-tung and Chou En-lai, the Communist leaders, really existed or if Snow had made them up. Snow said they were indeed real people and challenged him to find out for himself.

Carlson left Shanghai the day after Christmas 1937, on what would be a two-thousand-mile journey through harsh terrain and weather, to spend fifty-one days behind Japanese lines to study the operations of the Chinese Communist Army. Eventually he would travel by sampan, horseback, and train, but mostly he went on foot through the winter over difficult mountainous territory. He took with him a sleeping bag, tea kettle, chopsticks, one cup, a wash basin, Ralph Waldo Emerson's book *Selected Essays*, and the September 1937 issue of *Reader's Digest*, which contained thirty-two articles, including one titled "Men Do Not Like War."

During his journey he met another suspected Communist sympathizer, forty-five-year-old Agnes Smedley, an American writer from Missouri. She later referred to Carlson as the "firmest" friend of her life, and Carlson's biographer wrote, "They were in love with each other, not as a man and a woman, but as true equal humans, as comrades." Carlson "found Agnes 'grand, attractive, alive, animated, wise, courageous, a wonderful companion'—albeit a little impetuous. Many of Agnes's friends believed she longed for a more intimate connection with him." Snow and Smedley remained friends with Carlson for many years.

One of the highlights of the arduous trip was a night Carlson spent with Mao. Carlson wrote about the meeting in detail, reflecting its importance to him:

"A single candle lighted the room in which he worked, and when I entered I came face to face with a tall man whose leonine head dominated a well-built body. Crowning the massive head was a mane of jet black hair, parted in the center and thrown back carelessly. Kindly eyes regarded me thoughtfully from a face that suggested the dreamer. . . .

"We talked late into the night, and our conversation covered the war, the political situation in Europe and America, the development of political thought down through the ages, the influence of religion on society and the ingredients of a successful world organization. . . .

"It was very early in the morning when I left Mao. . . . [T]he view of him which would remain with me was this picture of a humble, kindly, lonely genius, striving here in the darkness of the night to find a peaceful and an equitable way of life for his people."

Carlson's travels to study the operations of the Communist army took him deeper into the Chinese hinterland. At one point, he marched on foot with a unit of six hundred Chinese soldiers across eight mountains, covering a distance of fifty-eight miles in thirty-two hours. What amazed him was that no one dropped out or lagged behind as they crossed gorges, forests, and icy rivers with little food, thin uniforms, and poor shoes. He described the Eighth Route Army as the "most self-restrained, self-disciplined army in the world. What I have seen is a revelation, an experience I shall never forget."

Carlson concluded that the endurance and success of the Chinese Communist army against the Japanese was due to what he called "ethical indoctrination." Each soldier, Carlson wrote, "knew why he was fighting; he knew why it was necessary to endure great hardships and to make great sacrifices; he knew the value of freedom; there was created within him the desire to do his duty, no matter what sacrifice or effort it entailed."

This willingness to sacrifice, Carlson believed, was engendered by the officers' confiding in their troops and keeping them informed of the details of pending operations. The soldiers understood why they were fighting, suffered no class distinctions or acts of discrimination from their officers, and understood what was expected of them. Officers and men, referred to as "leaders and fighters" in the Eighth Army, worked together as equals to achieve their goals. Carlson found, "The Chinese have two words for working together: *Gung*, meaning 'work,' *Ho* meaning 'harmony.' Gung Ho! Work together! That is the end result of ethical indoctrination."

Carlson decided that if he ever commanded troops in battle, "Gung Ho" would be their motto, watchword, and guide.

Carlson was determined to tell the American people about his experiences, to warn them about his growing certainty that the Japanese military planned to attack the United States. In addition, he believed he had a duty to criticize the American government for continuing to sell vital war supplies to the Japanese. Taking such positions publicly would further damage his reputation among those who already considered him to be a Communist sympathizer. He realized it would also damage his military career, if not end it. "I have a responsibility to tell," he said, "because I know."

His crusade began on August 7, 1938, when he arrived in the city of Hankow. He sought out three American reporters and told them that the US government was sending oil, scrap metal, steel, and other supplies to Japan. American companies, he told them, were making huge profits from these sales, which were aiding Japan in its war against China. Before long, he cautioned, the Japanese were certain to attack

Evans Carlson meeting with leaders of the Chinese Eighth Army during the Sino-Japanese War, December 29, 1938. (*Granger Collection*)

the United States using those same supplies. Two days later, the first article quoting Carlson by name appeared in the *Chicago Daily News*.

A month later, on September 17, Carlson received an official reprimand, warning him that harsh action would be taken if he continued to speak openly to the press. His friends in the Marines and in civilian life also warned him, but he ignored them, even though he realized it could end his career. He was being considered for promotion to major. The Marine Corps commandant, General Thomas Holcomb, admired him, and he had a close relationship with President Roosevelt. His star would continue to rise in the war he was sure was coming, if he stopped talking.

There were also financial considerations. Carlson would be eligible for retirement in less than two years with a guaranteed pension of 75 percent of his annual pay. The country was still in a recession, and he would be unlikely to find a job in the private sector since he was denouncing business interests so strongly. But he knew he could not follow the order to be silent. He told a few friends that he might quit the corps.

"You're crazy, Evans," Agnes Smedley told him. "You're naïve. You're an innocent. You don't know anything about the capitalist system. Do you think it has any use for men of principle? You won't get a job. You'll starve to death!" His wife also tried to dissuade him from resigning from the service, pointing out that when he had quit the army years back, he had not done well in civilian life.

Army General Joseph "Vinegar Joe" Stilwell, who had spent as much time in China as Carlson, said he admired Carlson for his principles but cautioned against resignation. He would be making a big mistake. Admiral Harry Yarnell of the Asiatic Fleet also wanted Carlson to change his mind. He sent a formal report to Washington praising Carlson for his "outstanding service," and held up his resignation to give him time to reconsider. But there would be no backing down.

In March 1939, Carlson wrote to President Roosevelt: "I feel deeply that I can be more useful as a civilian than as an officer. As a civilian, I can help to interpret to the American people the significance of events in the Far East. As an officer I cannot do so without embarrassing the government. This sounds altruistic, but I am very sincere about it, and I feel that I must follow the 'inner urge.'"

Roosevelt expressed his sorrow at Carlson's resignation but wished him well.

His resignation became official on March 17, 1939, and he spent the next two years keeping a busy schedule of speaking engagements to every audience that would listen to his message that America must stop arming Japan. He tried to persuade Congress to embargo the sale to Japan of supplies that could be used for hostile purposes, but he did not succeed.

Carlson's talks and radio addresses were well received, but for the most part he was speaking to those who already agreed with his views. He also wrote magazine articles and two books. *The Chinese Army*, published in 1939, and *Twin Stars of China*, published in 1940, received positive reviews from critics who shared Carlson's concern over the menace of Japan. Raymond Gram Swing, the noted radio commentator, said Carlson knew more about China than any other American. But the publicity only fueled the charges that Carlson was a Communist.

In fall 1940, believing he had done all he could to alert the American public to the Japanese threat, Carlson returned to China.

This was his fourth visit, the first as a civilian. He traveled more than four thousand miles throughout the unoccupied territory, observing factories and meeting with leaders of the Nationalists and the Communists.

In January 1941, he decided to come home. He had a hunch that war would begin sooner than he had anticipated. He stopped in Manila, the Philippines, to warn army General Douglas MacArthur that the Japanese were preparing to attack his forces there and suggest that MacArthur be prepared to wage guerrilla warfare. The imperious MacArthur did not take kindly to advice offered by a former captain in the Marines.

Carlson arrived in the States in late January and told a reporter for the *Los Angeles Times* that America would be at war with Japan in fewer than three months. At the same time, his eighteen-year marriage to Etelle was ending in divorce. He had made his last two trips to China without her, and they had spent more time apart when he was on his lecture tour. It was a mutual decision, his biographer wrote. "If Carlson wanted it, so then did she; if she wanted it, so then did he." A friend saw him in New York not long after and wrote that Carlson seemed depressed. "He cannot see things clearly ahead of him. I think he is very low in funds."

Life changed again in April when he addressed the Army and Navy Club in Washington, DC, about the best tactics for fighting a war in the Pacific. At the end of his speech, a Marine colonel approached him. "Carlson, isn't it about time you came back?" he asked.

He agreed that it was. With the help of the Marine commandant, General Holcomb, and against the spirited opposition of many officers in the corps, Evans Carlson returned to active duty on April 28, 1941, at the rank of major. He was sent to San Diego to join the 2nd Regiment as its operations and intelligence officer. Then, one Sunday morning some months later, the guard at the camp gate stopped his car as he was leaving the base.

"All leaves cancelled, sir," he said. "The Japs attacked Pearl Harbor."

Four

We Give No Mercy

"At last I have received a break," Carlson wrote to his father. It was February 5, 1942, two months after Pearl Harbor. "Today I was placed in command of a special unit with carte blanche to organize, train and indoctrinate it as I see fit. There is nothing like it in existence in the country. Naturally, I am delighted. I will hand pick my personnel. Jimmy Roosevelt is to be my executive officer. . . . Things seem to be moving in a direction I have so long urged and had almost despaired of seeing materialize. But now I have been afforded the opportunity to practice some of the precepts I have been preaching these past years."

Carlson had gotten everything he wanted to wage war on his own terms, even to having the choice of men who would serve in his new unit. He was free to select them himself, an extraordinary opportunity rarely granted in the military. If other marines were jealous of Carlson's special treatment, and many were, they were well advised to keep their complaints to themselves.

Carlson was not the only one who had been pushing for the formation of separate elite commando units to take the war directly to the enemy. President Roosevelt was adamant after the Pearl Harbor attack about retaliating as soon as possible to deflate Japanese pride and lift the morale of the American people during the continuing string of defeats in the Pacific.

On the night of the Pearl Harbor attack, after meeting with his cabinet, a visibly angry Roosevelt spoke with his old friend William J. "Wild Bill" Donovan, an influential lawyer and diplomat who had earned a Medal of Honor in World War I. Roosevelt had recently made Donovan a colonel in the army and charged him with establishing a center for coordinating intelligence information from the armed services and the State Department. Five months later, in June 1942, that operation would become the Office of Strategic Services (OSS), and later, in 1947, the CIA.

In their conversation on the night of December 7, 1941, Donovan proposed that he take a much more active combat role in the war, an idea with which Roosevelt agreed. The president suggested that Donovan switch from the army to the Marines, where Roosevelt would promote him to brigadier general, and set up small commando-style units—like the British ones Prime Minister Winston Churchill had bragged about—to strike at the Japanese. To no one's surprise, the higher-ranking Marine Corps officers objected to the idea of a General Donovan. They did not want an outsider, particularly an army man and friend of Roosevelt's, to become a politically appointed officer in command of "real" marines. They also opposed the concept of small, independent, elite units operating outside the normal chain of command. They would make the same objection when Carlson was later proposed to lead such units.

General Holcomb, the Marine Corps commandant, was caught in the middle, between the president's wishes and the opposition of his own command. "The Donovan affair is still uppermost in my mind," he wrote to a friend. "I am terrified that I will be forced to take this man. I feel that it will be the worst slap in the face that the Marine Corps was ever given [and] be bitterly resented by our personnel."

At the same time the president and Donovan were pushing for commando units, another Roosevelt was promoting the idea. The president's eldest son, thirty-five-year-old James, popularly known as "Jimmy," had been friends with Evans Carlson since 1937 at Warm Springs, Georgia. Now he urged the creation of a unit to make brief commando-like raids based on the tactics used by the Chinese Communist guerrillas, as espoused by Carlson. How closely he and Carlson might have worked together behind the scenes is not clear.

Holcomb and other high-ranking Marine officers were just as opposed to James Roosevelt's approach as they were to Donovan's, but at least Roosevelt was not proposing a political appointee to lead such an outfit. Also, this request was from a marine officer, albeit, in their opinion, one in name only. They did not consider young Roosevelt to be a real marine, and they strongly opposed the command of such a unit going to Carlson.

True, Carlson was a genuine marine, but not one in the orthodox mold; he was too much of a maverick, too radical to be given command. And the brass knew that with the president's backing and James as the link between his father and Carlson, they would have virtually no control. Carlson would have a free hand.

James Roosevelt had been a sickly child, battling a heart condition and lingering pneumonia, and his health remained a problem well into adulthood. In 1938, physicians at the Mayo Clinic in Rochester, Minnesota, removed much of his stomach in an attempt to deal with bleeding ulcers. He had had problems at school, never meeting his father's high expectations. He earned mediocre grades at Groton, the private preparatory school in Massachusetts, as well as at Harvard University. He enrolled in law school but dropped out after a year, and did not do much better in the business world. The president once broke down in tears when told that James had tried to influence him with regard to a business client. "Jimmy!" the president said. "What a problem he is."*

It was impossible for James to be free of the public perception that because he was the president's son, everything came easy. That image was not helped when in 1936, his father chose him to be his aide on a state visit to Argentina and arranged a commission in the Marines as a lieutenant colonel. "It was ridiculous, really," James wrote later. "I was totally out of my depth. I didn't know what I was doing."

---

*The president often introduced James, then in his twenties, as "my little boy, Jimmy." The Raiders called him Jimmy in their interviews and memoirs, and the press frequently used the nickname as well.

He was embarrassed by the rank; he resigned in 1939 and joined up again as a captain in the reserves. This time he participated in the standard training programs like other reserve officers and felt more comfortable in his position. On the day after Pearl Harbor, he confronted his father, insisting that he be given an assignment that would expose him to combat. Reluctantly, both of his parents agreed.

And what better person to go into combat with than Evans Carlson? James knew Carlson well and felt comfortable with him. Further, he was familiar with Carlson's unique approach to combat. And what better person to advance Carlson's cause and to help him organize the fighting unit he wanted than the son of the president? James would be able to cut through red tape and provide Carlson with access to everything he needed. It would be a mutually beneficial arrangement.

Historian John Wukovits wrote that James Roosevelt put his ideas for an elite commando unit in a memo on January 13, 1942, which he sent to the Marine Corps high command. He called it "Development within the Marine Corps of a Unit for Purposes Similar to the British Commandos and the Chinese Guerrillas." He described an outfit based on Carlson's observations of the Communist Eighth Route Army's notion of ethical indoctrination, which called for a policy of close relationships between officers and men, elimination of class distinctions, and full sharing of information to all ranks. It also proposed to do away with military titles; the only distinction being that between leaders and fighters. Thus, James Roosevelt was proposing precisely what Carlson wanted.

General Holcomb had to approve it, like it or not. He agreed to what seemed like an odd compromise in order to establish this new unit, with commanders in place, before Roosevelt could appoint Wild Bill Donovan to the job. He formed one Special Forces battalion on the West Coast, based in San Diego, with Carlson and James Roosevelt in charge, to operate according to Carlson's plan. But Holcomb also established another battalion on the East Coast, at Camp Lejeune, North Carolina, to be run like a traditional Marine Corps unit. It would be commanded by the perfect recruiting poster officer, Colonel Merritt Edson, who considered Carlson a Communist and not to be trusted.

Carlson's outfit would serve the Pacific theater, which was primarily a Marine Corps area of responsibility. The other unit would serve in the European theater whenever that opened up. In accordance with long-standing Marine Corps policy, units on the West Coast were given even-numbered designations; those in the East were assigned odd numbers. And so, to the everlasting anger of Carlson and his men, they became the 2nd Marine Raider Battalion, while Edson's group would forever be known as the 1st.

Still, James Roosevelt had gotten all that he and Carlson wanted. "The plan," he wrote, "was rather revolutionary, but father bought it and helped sell Admiral Nimitz on the idea. We were given a free hand to recruit volunteers from the San Diego Naval Base." Now all Carlson needed was to find men who would fight his war his way. Not just any marine would do.

Carlson's Raiders came from all over the country, from all walks of life and backgrounds. But they were united in purpose—to defeat the Japanese, to avenge Pearl Harbor—and they joined the Marines to do it. And now, in late winter 1942, they were trying to get into the new commando force they had heard about, which held the promise of getting into action soon.

Ben Carson was eighteen years old, the son of a farmer from Henderson, Minnesota. He planned to go to church with his parents on the morning of Sunday, December 7, 1941, but their car would not start. Not even with the horse pulling it. The 1937 Plymouth was in such bad shape that it often had to be hitched to the horse and pulled to get the engine to turn over. Ben decided to do farm chores instead when his mother came running out of the house, carrying their battery-operated Philco radio. She shouted that Ben's brother, George, was in danger. He was a gunner's mate on the USS *Maryland* now based at Pearl Harbor, and the Japanese were bombing it!

Five days later, with his trigger finger wrapped in thick bandages and an aluminum frame as a result of a farming accident, Carson bought a sixty-cent bus ticket for Minneapolis, fifty-five miles away. His father, who had served in World War I, sent him off with one piece of advice: never volunteer for anything. Carson headed for the Marine Corps Recruiting Station. Sixty years later, he said, "I'll never forget my first entry into that place. The sergeant was standing there with a beautiful red stripe down the side of his pants. Just the kind of suit I would like to have. And he said, 'What do you want?' I said, 'Well, I want to join the Marine Corps, too.' And his response was 'What the hell do you mean, too? You're the first guy in three days.' I thought that I would have to choose my words more carefully after that."

When Carson went for his physical, the doctor didn't ask about his smashed finger. Carson said, "Doctor, what about my finger? I smashed it in a corn binder." The doctor never even glanced at it. He was too busy with the paperwork.

"One next to it work?" he asked.

"Yes."

"You're in."

Carson boarded a train for boot camp in San Diego, arriving on New Year's Day 1942, only to find that most of the training staff was hungover from the night before. He completed basic training in four weeks, learning how to march without stumbling too much, how to shift a rifle from one shoulder to the other, and how to put on a gas mask. He was assigned to guard duty with no bullets for his rifle and put in charge of keeping four empty garbage cans safe from the enemy.

Bored and frustrated, he wondered how he was going to help win the war. Then he heard about "some nutty major that was going to start an outfit that promised action pretty shortly. So I thought I would investigate that." The nutty major's name was Evans Carlson.

Dean Voight, of Medford, Wisconsin, joined the Marines at age nineteen. "I just hated the idea of anyone attacking the USA in that way," he said in a 1995 interview. "I thought I wanted to retaliate. Pearl Harbor revenge you might call it." A family friend wanted him to join the navy, but his father vetoed that idea. "He just said that he would rather have a sister in the cathouse than he would a son in the Navy." Voight arrived in San Diego a few weeks after Pearl Harbor "pretty soused," and made it through boot camp. He wanted to get into welding, the job he had done before the war, but was told he would be in the infantry. Disgusted by the way he felt he was being pushed around, he signed up for the new outfit he had heard about, Carlson's Raiders.

Dean Winters grew up in small, isolated towns in Utah, dropped out of school in the seventh grade, and went to work in the Civilian Conservation Corps. The CCC was a popular Roosevelt New Deal program that employed young men on a variety of public projects such as working on roads, national parks, and dams. Winters was paid thirty dollars a month and sent twenty-five dollars home to his parents. He joined the Marine Corps the day after Pearl Harbor, at age nineteen. When asked in 2000 why he chose the Marines, he said he wanted to be, "The first to fight. I didn't think it was very nice what they did at Pearl Harbor, and I thought it was my duty to take care of that situation."

Ordered to guard a California beach against the Japanese, Winters walked his post carrying a broomstick on his shoulder and was told to pretend it was a rifle. He decided that if he was going to do any fighting, he would have to try out for the Raiders. When he applied, he was told "there was a ninety-nine percent chance of us being killed, but I didn't believe that."

Frank Duesler, of Dodgeville, Wisconsin, joined the Marines in 1940 on a bet. A friend insisted that Duesler could not pass the Marine Corps physical. Duesler won the bet, but his friend never paid up. Duesler, who was twenty, became a radioman stationed at San Diego, where he read about Carlson's special unit that promised the chance to see action soon. He signed up right away to try out for it.

After the Pearl Harbor attack, it was not unusual for men to lie about their age, so eager were they to enlist and take revenge against the Japanese. Bill Orrick, who was too old at thirty-five, told the recruiter he was twenty-nine. Walt Kelly, too young at sixteen, said he was seventeen. "We were afraid the war would be over before we got in," he recounted years later. Wilford Patrick quit high school and added a year to his age. "We didn't want to miss it," he said. They were all so eager to fight. And they would soon get their chance.

Clyde A. Thomason was a Marine sergeant at the time of Pearl Harbor. He had enlisted in 1934. A Georgia boy, he had been a top student in high school, a varsity football player, and an actor in school plays. After graduation he worked in construction, then the CCC, and as a door-to-door salesman before joining the Marines.

He served as part of the Marine detachment aboard the heavy cruiser USS *Augusta*, won the ship's boxing championship, and sailed to ports in China and Russia. At six-feet-four and 190 pounds, he was the ideal recruiting poster type. But he was judged too tall for the Raiders and had to ask for a height waiver. Throughout his admirable career, in peace and war, Thomason always wanted to be "where things are happening."

When Victor Maghakian heard about the Pearl Harbor attack, he was not surprised. He hated the Japanese long before the war. The son of poor Armenian immigrants living outside of Chicago, Maghakian enlisted in 1934 at age nineteen, seeking adventure. He served tours in the Philippines and China, where he earned the nickname "Transport," for his uncanny ability to commandeer a car or a truck whenever he felt the need for one. He never liked to walk when he could ride, and so, "I'd scrounge around the area until I saw a vehicle I liked, then I'd steal it. Jeeps were my specialty, although I would take a truck or a bicycle if that's all that was available."

He witnessed the cruelty with which the Japanese treated the Chinese people and once got into a fight in a nightclub in China with five Japanese officers. After Pearl Harbor, Maghakian heard about a so-called suicide unit being formed by Carlson and made up his mind that that was where he wanted to serve.

Jack Miller had it all—good looks, good grades, athletic ability, snazzy clothes, and a generous nature. Everybody liked him. He breezed through high school and Southern Methodist University in his hometown of Dallas, Texas. He had been active in his high school ROTC program and signed up for officers' training after college, receiving his commission in the Marine Corps. He was patriotic and determined to serve his country in the war he was sure would come soon.

While training in California, then age twenty-one, he heard about the formation of Carlson's Raiders. "Jack decided he wanted to be one of them and volunteered," his sister said. "They were very selective and choosy and the assignments they would do would be dangerous, but Jack wanted to be a part of that."

Bill Murphree had a habit of going AWOL, changing his name every time he did so and getting away with it. Born in 1917 in Bold Springs, Tennessee, he joined the army in 1936 and became a skilled radioman and telegrapher. On May 5, 1941, seven months before Pearl Harbor, while stationed at Fort Benning, Georgia, he got drunk and found himself in Tennessee, where he had a girlfriend. "Went AWOL," he told a niece years later. "I just didn't want to go back. I knew I'd be busted and get stockade time." He went to Houston and took a job with a railroad but grew worried when his boss kept asking to see his draft card. He left to head west, working as a ranch hand on an isolated farm. But then came Pearl Harbor. Murphree returned to Houston and joined the Marines, using the name Richard Craven. Sent to boot camp in San Diego, he was chosen as his outfit's Outstanding Marine. He claimed he had learned about military routine from the Boy Scouts.

Things were going well, but he was still concerned about being tracked down by the army. Then, "I saw on the bulletin board that they were looking for volunteers for a Raider outfit. I wanted out of the U.S. badly, so I volunteered for the Raiders." He would remain Richard Craven until 1943, when he went AWOL again, and twice more in 1944, but by then he had been awarded the Navy Cross.

Bill Lansford grew up in Latino neighborhoods in East Los Angeles; he rarely heard English spoken until he was fourteen. His mother was from Mexico, and his father, of English and Irish descent, was mostly absent. Lansford always wanted to join the navy and see the world, but when he tried to enlist in 1940, he was rejected as too short and skinny. He kept trying to enlist, but the navy kept rejecting him. "[They] rejected me over and over until I got to be, uh, like a fly hanging around a gravy bowl there, you know the navy station. And one day I came out and there was this enormous Marine in blues standing there, and he gave me a real pep talk, and he said, 'Why don't you join the Marines. They're the best outfit there is.' And I thought, well, the Navy doesn't want me; I'll try them. So in a way, it had been a second best choice, but it was the best choice I ever made in my life." And so was volunteering for the Raiders.

One Marine lieutenant tried four times to volunteer for the Raiders but was turned down personally by Carlson each time. The fellow did not even get the chance to have an interview, but he kept trying. His name was Evans C. Carlson Jr., and he was Carlson's son by his first marriage. The younger Carlson had joined the Marines in 1938 and received his commission in 1941. He fought on Guadalcanal with the 1st Marine Division. His father kept refusing him because he did not want to be accused of favoritism.

Carlson Jr. missed the Makin raid but did join his father's outfit later. In 1999, he told a fellow marine that he got into the Raiders "by accident," and also with the assistance of Major Roosevelt, who put through the orders for his transfer to the Raiders without telling his father. "Roosevelt had a great sense of humor," Carlson Jr. said, "and wanted to surprise the colonel with the new Raider arrival—and the colonel was *indeed* surprised!" Roosevelt persuaded Colonel Carlson that Lieutenant Carlson had all the qualifications to be a Raider.

The "Old Man" finally gave in and allowed his son to join, but told him, "Expect no favors. If anything, I'll be tougher on you than on anyone else. I won't mean to be, but that's what I'm sure will happen."

Carlson's fiercely independent nature and determination to shape his own outfit led him to reject three of every four marines sent to him from the 1st Marine Raider Battalion being trained on the East Coast. Headquarters had ordered 190 men and seven officers from the 1st Raiders to California to help Carlson's unit get ready for combat. Carlson bristled at the idea of being forced to take anyone he did not personally select, and when the troops showed up, he put them all through the same grueling interview process as the others. The majority of the newcomers flunked Carlson's rigorous screening. This displeased not only the high command in Washington, which had ordered the move, but also the fierce-tempered commanding officer of the 1st Battalion, Colonel Edson, who had spent eight months training his men to be tough fighters.

Edson never forgave Carlson for the humiliation of claiming that his men were not good enough to serve in Carlson's unit. The Marine Corps brass was also angry with Carlson for disobeying their orders to accept Edson's men. But they said nothing about it to Carlson. They thought it unwise to challenge someone with close connections to the president, but they would remember Carlson's actions. And when the time was right, they would have their revenge. Carlson could not be allowed to get away with such insubordination.

The interviews for applicants to Carlson's Raiders were conducted by Carlson or Roosevelt and were notably straightforward. Out of three thousand men who volunteered, one thousand were accepted, and not all would be able to complete the training, which was probably the most demanding of any unit in the armed services. The men lined up for interviews outside a nondescript building at San Diego's Camp Elliott Marine Base. Dean Voight was interviewed by Roosevelt, who was a bit more easygoing than Carlson, at least as Voight recalled it fifty years later. "Jim Roosevelt interviewed me and he asked me if I could do this and that and if I could swim with a 90-pound pack on my back, and I said, 'Can you?' and he says, 'Yup.' I said, 'Well, I can do anything you can do.' He said, 'You're in.' That was all there was to it."

Roosevelt asked Ben Carson what he did for a living and whether he could swim. The third question, Carson recalled, was, "'Can you march thirty miles on a cup of rice?' That kind of stopped me since I had never done that, but I thought if anybody could do that I could.

"And the fourth question really stumped me. I thought he had a trick question. 'How often do you go to Sunday School?' I thought I had better be careful with that one. I finally came up with 'as often as my Mom made me.' And he said, 'Dismissed.' And I marched out of there."

Carlson's questions to the applicants were more pointed. He started out by asking why they wanted to join the Raiders, and then he got more specific. "Can you cut a Jap's throat without flinching? Can you choke him to death without puking? Are you willing to starve and suffer and go without food and sleep?" He asked Sgt. Kenneth McCullough if he could walk fifty miles in one day. "I told him if anybody else could, I could. He asked me if I could cut a man's throat. I had to think a little. I just knew if it was them or me, I'd do it."

Carlson focused, above all, on the volunteers' motivation for fighting the Japanese. "I won't take a man who doesn't give a damn about anything," he told Roosevelt. "But if he has a deep feeling about wanting to fight, even for the wrong reasons, take him. I know I can shape him into wanting to fight for the right reasons."

At the end of every interview, Carlson stood erect, almost at attention, and issued what some took as a promise and others a threat. "I promise you nothing but hardships and danger. When we get into battle, we ask no mercy, we give no mercy." He was not exaggerating.

Five

Closer to War

M ajor Carlson stood on the small raised platform and looked out at the one thousand men he and Jimmy Roosevelt had selected to be Raiders and gestured for them to come closer. Carlson did not look like a hero that day at Jacques Farm, standing on those wooden crates. He was forty-six years old and rail thin; though he stood tall and straight, he appeared somewhat frail. He had piercing blue eyes, a long nose, and a pronounced, chiseled jaw. One historian wrote, "Rarely has a person combined such diverse qualities; an intellectual who loved combat; a high school dropout who quoted Emerson; a thin, almost fragile looking man who relished fifty-mile hikes; an officer in a military organization who touted equality among officers and enlisted; a kindly individual with the capacity to kill."

"As you were, boys," he called out. "Come on up here. Let's get together."

Carlson smiled at the men as they gathered in front of him. The men had assembled in the middle of a muddy field a few miles south of San Diego to begin their training as Raiders.

"The first thing we're going to do," he announced, "is to sing our National Anthem." He reached into his back pocket and took out a harmonica, blew a C note, and began to sing. At first only a few men joined in, then more, but quite a few of them did not know the words. Still, it was loud enough for two marines driving by in a truck a hundred yards away to hear it. They stopped the vehicle, got out, and stood at attention, as regulations required.

When the last words of "The Star-Spangled Banner" rang out, Carlson pulled his pipe out of his pocket and told the men to make themselves comfortable, sit down if they wished, and light up their cigarettes. He had a lot to tell them about how the Raiders would operate, like no outfit they had ever seen or heard of before.

He began by talking about what he had learned in China about the way to fight the Japanese soldiers, along with the notion of ethical indoctrination, and a battle cry he tried out—"Gung Ho!" They would truly work together, he said, just like the Chinese army he had spent so much time with. Also, he promised, the Raiders would be fully informed of everything that was going on at all times and would have the opportunity to express their opinions and objections.

There would be no caste or class differences between the men and their officers, Carlson told them. "We'll live as you live; work as you work; eat as you eat; fight as you fight. [The officers] give up all our privileges cheerfully and willingly." That announcement really got the men's attention, eliciting looks of surprise, amazement, and no doubt disbelief.

Such talk was the opposite of their experience since their enlistment. Some men doubted that such equality—a democracy—could exist in a military unit. Some officers appeared doubtful, too, or at least uncomfortable. They would all soon learn that Carlson meant to keep his word.

The Raiders also learned that they were in for some difficult training in the weeks and months ahead. They would be required to march fifty miles in a day with little food or water. They had to be tough, Carlson reminded them, because the enemy was tough. "The Jap is a wily and rugged enemy experienced in hardships. And so I can promise you nothing but the toughest life while we're in the States and the toughest battles when we're overseas."

But first, they had to get rid of the chicken shit on their new base at Jacques Farm, all two-and-a-half feet of it.

Jacques Farm had been a working farm. When it became the new home of the Raiders, only one building was still standing; it was designated as the mess hall. Unfortunately for the men, it had been a dilapidated chicken house, and it contained the residue of many years of use. Private Ben Carson remembered it being, "Full of manure and rattlesnakes and all kinds of things. My previous farming experience helped a lot when Flannigan, our mess sergeant, said that it was going to be the mess hall. There was about thirty inches of chicken manure. About five days, the privates worked to clean it out."

The men built their own barracks and headquarters buildings. Until those projects were completed, they lived in tents and cooked their meals on gasoline-fueled stoves out under the eucalyptus trees. "We hoped the food would get a little better," Carson said, "but each and every time you belly-ached about something, we were told 'Carlson didn't promise you a rose garden.'" Lieutenant Jack Miller wrote to his mother that he "lived out of a pup tent, ate from mess gear, washed his clothes in a bucket, slept on the ground, and bathed and shaved in cold water, but would have it no other way."

The men worked eighteen hours a day, seven days a week to construct the camp buildings and kept the same hours once formal training started. Their days began at 4:30 a.m. and continued until well after sundown. James Roosevelt, who kept up the pace with the others, believed they marched more than any other American military unit in training.

Sergeant Clyde Thomason recalled "marching five, eight, ten miles and calisthenics to get into shape. Twice a week a thirty-five mile hike, and once a week a seventy-mile overnight hike. We never rode." They soon were able to travel seven miles in an hour, with full gear and little food. Carlson kept them on a restricted diet, limited mostly to rice and raisins. Sometimes they marched along the roads through the small towns near the base, and it was not unusual to see an ice-cream truck tagging along behind. But no one dared stop to buy any.

Always, no matter how great the distance, the Old Man, Evans Carlson, was out front setting the pace. Dean Voight said Carlson would summon them early in the morning and point to a far-off mountain. "'See that mountain over there? We'll be there by evening.' And off we'd go. He would do anything we could do, plus some. He was a gutsy old man. I think he could walk forever."

In the rugged six weeks at Jacques Farm, training also included instruction in how to fire various weapons, kill with bare hands, go on patrol through the jungle, and scout out the enemy without being seen or heard. Nothing was left to chance. There was instruction on using whatever was at hand in a jungle or clearing for camouflage, setting off demolitions, scaling a bare cliff, reading maps, fighting in streets and buildings, and maintaining appropriate hygiene under difficult conditions.

"Gradually," Lieutenant Oscar Peatross wrote, "individuals were converted into units and esprit was born; Marines became Raiders—Carlson's Raiders." "Gung Ho!" became more than a battle cry. It was a spirit that transformed and bound them together.

Carlson also changed the way his men looked, dressed, and armed themselves, and how they were organized to do battle. And every deviation from orthodox Marine Corps procedure made him all the more suspect to those in higher authority. He designed a field jacket that was shorter and less bulky than the regulation jacket. The men called it the "Gung Ho jacket," and soon everything they were issued was "Gung Ho," down to their boots and knives.

The Gung Ho knife was nine and a quarter inches long with a seven-inch blade and was based on a design used by British commandoes. The Marine Corps at that time did not issue knives, and the high command did not believe them to be useful, either as weapons or tools. Under Carlson's tutelage, the Raiders found them useful for both purposes. (They are still displayed regularly at Raider reunions.) For boots, Carlson evaluated a number of designs after rejecting the standard issue type. He settled on Oregon logging boots as the best footwear to get the men through long treks over rough terrain. Ben Carson referred to the Old Man as "a boot nut. Because he would issue us new shoes and he would march us right up to a creek with those brand new shoes. Then you could not take your shoes off until your feet dried. That was the way you formed your shoes to your feet.

Very few people knew that, including me. I would think, 'what a waste.' That made the most comfortable shoe I ever had."

It was Carlson's idea to provide the outfit with greater firepower than was standard in the Marine Corps or the army in 1942. Instead of the old, heavy, 1903 Springfield rifle, the Raiders carried the lighter, more accurate semiautomatic M1Garand .30 caliber, eight-shot rifle. And the Raiders, like all marines, memorized and believed the creed: "This is my rifle. There are many like it, but this one is mine. My rifle is my best friend. It is my life. I must master it, as I must my life. My rifle, without me, is useless. Without my rifle, I am useless."

Since Carlson's focus was on small-unit guerrilla warfare, he abandoned the traditional eight-man squad and instead formed firing teams of three men each. One man carried the M1, another carried a Thompson submachine gun, and the third had a Browning Automatic Rifle (BAR). "We had tremendous firepower," Ben Carson said in a 2001 interview. "We could have taken on John Dillinger and ten like him with just one squad."

Of course, such a significant reorganization of the basic squad unit in the Marine Corps was yet another mark against Carlson to those in command. And some of them did not yet know about his greatest sin: abolishing all formal distinctions in rank.

"We'll live as you live," Carlson had announced during the Raiders' first meeting at Jacques Farm, and he led by example. From the first day, Carlson slept on the floor of his tent, stood in line for meals, and ate the standard rations. He marched with his men, carrying full pack and weapons, and when they were out in the field, he built his own fire, cooked his meager meal, and cleaned up after himself. His officers had to follow his Spartan example and not ask for or expect the perks and privileges of rank.

As Carlson put it, "You can never enforce discipline unless the men believe in you as an officer. And the way to make them believe in you is that you share everything that the men share. Then they will be happy to follow your leadership because you will have demonstrated it."

The Raiders were given no leave during their six weeks at Jacques Farm, not even a Saturday night to go off base. Frank Duesler recalled that "we weren't allowed liberty, but guys would sneak off and then they'd come back carrying bottles of whiskey. And to get back you had to hop from rock to rock to get across the big stream there. . . . It was fun. I think so. We were all young and full of p & v [piss and vinegar]."

Despite the policy on leaves and the intensity of the training, few Raiders dropped out and their spirits remained high. Fifty years later, Dean Voight recalled that "we were close knit and we were just like all brothers. I mean, 'My life is yours, and your life is mine.' We're still like that to this day." Dean Winters remembered the time similarly. In a 2001 interview, he said, "When I was a Raider, I was with friends. I knew they would die for me; I knew that I would die for them. And they knew I would die for them."

Part of what bound the Raiders in spirit was Carlson's "Gung Ho" Friday night gatherings. They were like town hall meetings, open forums in which everyone was free to ask questions and raise concerns without fear of retribution. Also, the meetings became the only truly social time during which they could relax.

Carlson opened the sessions with a tune on his harmonica, leading the Raiders in the national anthem or "The Marines' Hymn" ("From the Halls of Montezuma . . ."). Then he would greet them with a shout, "Ahoy Raiders!" to which they would yell "Gung Ho." Sometimes the men provided their own entertainment. Private Jack Bauer kept the men laughing with his quick, spontaneous one-liner jokes, never repeating a single one. But not all attempts were successful. Lieutenant Peatross wrote about one man who "claimed to be an Eskimo and performed what purported to be an Eskimo dance. It soon became obvious that this couldn't be one. The 'Eskimo' was quickly booed off the makeshift stage and later was transferred from the Battalion." The Raiders proved to be a tough audience.

Later in the war, when Carlson described those Friday night sessions to Robert Sherrod, correspondent for *Time* and *Life* magazines, he said:

> We used to hold discussions. We would tell these men the
> implications of the war. We would show the connections
> between the war in Europe and the war in the Pacific. Then we
> would ask for questions. It was surprising how those privates
> could point out things that hadn't occurred to me, and I had
> studied global war for a long time. I learned as much from
> them as they did from me. . . . I think they knew what they
> were fighting for. Anyway, I tried to teach them.

By April 1942, the Raiders were getting closer to war, and there suddenly seemed to be a heightened sense of urgency. Carlson and his
men wanted to strike at Japan in return for the Pearl Harbor attack, but
they also had a more personal concern. Carlson had learned that
Merritt Edson's outfit, the 1st Raider Battalion, was being reassigned
to the Pacific theater and would soon be leaving the East Coast.
Carlson was not about to be beaten by Edson in the race to be the first
Raider outfit in combat.

Carlson was summoned to navy headquarters in Hawaii to discuss
possible targets for his battalion's first commando raid. The Raiders
reported to San Clemente Island off the coast of California south of
Los Angeles for three weeks of practicing beach landings in rubber
assault boats. While there, they were given strict orders not to shoot
the wild goats, no matter how hungry the men were. But they were per-
mitted to harvest the abalone, a large, edible sea snail, along the shore.
"I had never seen an abalone in my life," said Ben Carson, of
Minnesota. "This was a clam with only one shell; it looked like God
had left before finishing the job."

They completed amphibious training on April 18. Four days later,
Admiral Nimitz, commander in chief of the Pacific Fleet, wrote to
Admiral Ernest J. King, commander in chief of the navy, that the 2nd
Raider Battalion "had reached a morale peak which can be maintained
only by engaging in active operations." Carlson's men were deemed
ready for battle.

Carlson had written to President Roosevelt on March 4 that he
believed the outfit was ready to assume its unique role. "I feel now that

those months of experience with the Chinese guerrilla armies were not in vain." Roosevelt replied on March 12: "I am delighted to have your letter, and to know that all goes so well with you. What you tell me about the new outfit is most interesting and surely there will be a chance to use it."

That was what Carlson and his men hoped when they boarded the USS *Franklin Bell*, on May 8, 1942, headed for Hawaii. Carlson spoke to his men over the ship's loudspeaker on their first day at sea. "This battalion is now headed for the theater of operations in the Pacific. . . . We become the first of our land forces of our nation to carry the war to the enemy. By our faith, our energy, our courage, and our intelligence, perhaps most of all by our willingness to sacrifice comfort and convenience, we shall march on to victory."

Carlson's Raiders arrived in Hawaii on May 18, but instead of seeing action right away, most of them spent nearly two more months training at Camp Catlin, located between Honolulu and Pearl Harbor on the island of Oahu. The only visible changes in the outfit were the insignias of rank worn by Carlson, promoted to lieutenant colonel, and by James Roosevelt, promoted to major.

As they sailed into Pearl Harbor, the terrible destruction from the Japanese attack four months before was shockingly evident. Lieutenant Peatross wrote, "It'll probably take me the rest of my life to erase this picture from memory; but now that we're taking the war to the Japs, this sobering sight might be just what we need to see us through to the end."

At their new camp was another reminder, the remains of a Japanese fighter plane that had crashed into the side of what would become their mess hall. The Raiders quickly cleared the wreckage, stripping off pieces of aluminum to make bracelets and souvenirs to send to the folks back home.

And then it was back to the same old training routine. "A lot of marching," Dean Voight said. "A lot of climbing hills and mountains and sliding down ropes and rappelling and all this stuff." But there was something that lured most of the Raiders into reckless insubordination: pineapples.

Camp Catlin, only half a square mile, was too small to be a training camp in itself. So Carlson sent Roosevelt to persuade the neighboring landowners to open their extensive holdings to the Raiders for training purposes—for the good of the nation, of course. The surrounding land was occupied mostly by pineapple plantations, and the owners received sober assurances that their crops would be safe. Surely no Marine Raider would dare steal the fruit, even though Carlson had taught them to live off the land.

The temptation proved too great. "After a long hike," Peatross remembered, "a ripe, juicy pineapple was a delicacy unparalleled. It was ready-to-eat food that required no cooking, hence no fires to light and no smoke-blackened pots to wallop." Carlson tried lectures and warnings to get the men to stop, but that had the opposite effect, encouraging them to take more risks. It got so bad that men had to be searched whenever they left a pineapple grove; violators were fined or given solitary confinement with only bread and water. That reduced the pineapple stealing but did not eliminate it. The pineapples were still irresistible to some, regardless of the consequences.

Some new arrivals joined the Raiders at Camp Catlin, though they were not put through the exhaustive interviews the others had endured. One was Marine Lieutenant Jerry Holtom, who had grown up in Japan with his missionary parents and spoke Japanese fluently. Three American civilian interpreters were added, along with two Korean civilians, who were given the nicknames "Gung" and "Ho."

On May 22, four days after the Raiders reached Hawaii, two companies were dispatched to Midway, a tiny island at the northwest end of the Hawaiian Island chain, approximately one thousand three hundred miles from Oahu. Their orders were to help defend the beaches against a Japanese invasion force; it was anticipated that as many as six thousand Japanese troops were on their way. One company commander asked at a briefing how long they and the small number of marines already on Midway were expected to hold out against such a large force.

"To the last man and last bullet," said the Marine Corps briefing officer, "but *if* our 'cheese in the trap' plan works, and *if* we sink their carriers, your chances of survival will increase. Any more questions?" No other hands were raised. The Japanese did plan to invade Midway, but American carrier planes sent their invasion fleet scattering with heavy losses.

The Raiders on Midway were safe, but those back at Camp Catlin were disappointed at not being selected to go. The belief surfaced that they had been judged less capable. Why else, they wondered, were they left behind while the others went off to fight? They were put to work guarding the beaches and possible landing sites near Camp Catlin. (In fact, the men who went to Midway were simply chosen at random.)

The Midway companies returned on June 21, just in time to prepare to move out. Because combat destinations were kept secret from all but the top commanders, only Carlson and Roosevelt knew where they were headed, but the men expressed concern when they were issued cold-weather clothing aboard the transport. That could only mean the freezing Aleutian Islands off Alaska, which the Japanese had attacked on June 3. Fighting in that cold, desolate, rocky, and mountainous terrain was not a pleasant prospect for men who had spent two months training to fight and survive in jungles.

But a few hours after departing Hawaii, the ship's captain announced over the loudspeaker that they were heading for Midway. The Raiders turned in their cold-weather uniforms and disembarked more cheerfully. However, the only useful thing they did there was dispose of the remains of hundreds of gooney birds, or albatrosses. The birds, which had a wingspan of more than six feet, had been killed to protect aircraft from crashing into them on landing or takeoff.

Two days later, the Raiders left Midway, heading north again toward the Aleutians, and were once again issued cold-weather clothing. A few days later they turned south, returning to Camp Catlin on July 3. They wondered whether anyone in the high command knew what they were doing. Were the marines ever going to fight the Japanese, and if so, where?

"This time, Carlson, it sticks," Admiral Nimitz said. "We don't know much about what the Japs have there. . . . They've got a seaplane base and a great deal of supplies. As to how strong a force defends the place, we haven't much definite dope. You'll have to make your own estimate. We're allowing you two subs. That'll mean a force of about two hundred men."

The mission was on; the target chosen. Under pressure from President Roosevelt to give Carlson's Raiders an assignment, Nimitz considered a number of possible targets for commando raids. Wake Island was one. The Marine garrison there had held out against the Japanese for two weeks after the Pearl Harbor attack before being overwhelmed. The island of Tinian was also a possibility, as was Attu in the Aleutians. The planners even considered striking at a vital railway tunnel or steel mill in Japan, but those were ruled out as being too far away and too dangerous.

Failure of the Raiders' mission, whatever the target, would be yet another blow to American morale. A victory, no matter how small, was clearly needed, and so an island called Makin was chosen. It was two thousand miles west of Hawaii, measured eight miles long and a half-mile wide, and was part of the Gilbert Islands area.* The raid was intended not only as a morale booster for the home front but also as a diversion to prevent Japan from sending reinforcements to Guadalcanal, which was scheduled to be invaded ten days before the Makin raid.

Makin marked the easternmost penetration of the Japanese Empire, and it was used as a weather station and a seaplane base for reconnaissance patrols. Estimates of the number of Japanese troops occupying the island ranged from 50 to 350. More information was needed.

Lieutenant Holtom was appointed the battalion's intelligence officer. He was sent to Palmyra Island, where a fisherman from the cluster

---

*The main island of the Makin Atoll, on which the invasion would take place, was called Butaritari, but it was easier for everyone involved, including the press and even official government reports, to simply call it Makin. That name made for better and shorter headlines, and we will use it throughout the book instead of Butaritari.

of islands that included Makin had been brought by submarine for questioning. The man, once he was deemed sober, provided a wealth of information. He told Holtom that there were no more than fifty Japanese troops on Makin, commanded by a Sergeant Kanemitsu. He showed Holtom on a map precisely where the defensive fortifications were, as well as the locations of the Japanese headquarters, communications and supply centers, and other facilities. He seemed certain that there were no mines or booby traps on the beaches or inland, and that the Japanese troops on Makin felt so secure that they did not even bother to patrol the beaches day or night.

Despite such thorough intelligence gathering and reporting by Lieutenant Holtom from an eyewitness who was an island native, desk-bound naval intelligence officers at Nimitz's headquarters at Pearl Harbor insisted that there could be as many as 350 Japanese troops on the island, which would give the enemy numerical superiority and a dangerous advantage over Carlson's force of two hundred. "If there really were 350 Japs on that island," Raider Brian Quirk told an interviewer more than fifty years later, "it would have been goodnight sweetheart for us."

In late July, the two hundred Raiders slated for the Makin Island operation moved to the beach at Barber's Point to practice landings in raging surf using rubber boats from a submarine. However, the subs they were supposed to use in the attack were not yet available, so the men set up a couple of buoys two thousand yards offshore and practiced coming ashore from them. The waves were so high, fast, and intense that it was one of the few spots on the Hawaiian coastline that was not strewn with barbed wire and other defenses. The brass believed that Japanese troops could not possibly carry out a landing in such rough conditions.

But the Raiders were expected to do just that in their flimsy rubber boats with old Evinrude outboard motors that frequently stopped dead when the water drenched their exposed ignition systems. Fortunately, each boat had a backup power source—men with paddles rowing as fast as they could. The work was dangerous, and the boats often capsized, throwing the men into the explosive surf. Private Carson was nearly killed when a huge breaker flipped his boat, plunging all hands into the sea. He hit his head on a metal pressure gauge and was knocked unconscious. Another man grabbed Carson before he went under again and dragged him back to the beach. He revived but had a sore head for a while. With practice, the Raiders became so proficient maneuvering their little boats that they were confident they could land on any beach anywhere.

When they would reach the beach in their training drills, they would make their way through a mockup of Makin's dock, roads, trails, and buildings, an exact copy of what they would face on the mission. Each man memorized every detail of the area where they were headed, though they still had not been told the island's name. "We had no doubts," Lieutenant Peatross wrote later, "as to our readiness to handle anything that might await us."

Carlson was also highly confident about the mission, but he harbored lingering doubts about how wise it would be to permit Roosevelt to come along. He did not question Roosevelt's ability or courage; none of the Raiders did. "Jimmy was a hell of a good Marine," Captain Sam Griffith said. What concerned Carlson was the possibility that young Roosevelt might be killed or captured. The result would be an enormous propaganda victory for the Japanese and another blow to American morale, overshadowing any victory the Raiders might achieve. Also, Carlson's own reputation would then be tainted, and he would be known forever as the man responsible for the death of the president's son.

Carlson took his concerns directly to Admiral Nimitz, who seemed to agree. He, too, was worried about losing James Roosevelt on his watch, particularly if he should be captured. That would be a public relations disaster for the admiral and the Marine Corps.

To his great credit, Roosevelt was appalled at the idea that he might not be allowed to go on the raid with his men. He wanted no special treatment and, above all, wanted to prove his courage and value to the Raiders, and perhaps also to win his father's approval.

On July 29, a little more than a week before the mission was due to start, Roosevelt wrote to his mother about his continuing concern over his health. He reported that his insides were producing even more gas, that he felt lousy and was "a liability to my own group. Unfortunately,

I need such things as rest, milk, and good food which is not greasy. . . . Any other officer would not have been given waivers on my defects [flat feet, weak vision, and stomach ailments] and when this next job is done at least inside I'll feel I have stood the test of making it no matter what the odds."

When he learned that the question of his participation had reached Admiral Nimitz, he called his father to plead his case. The president was furious and immediately called Admiral King, Nimitz's superior. "Look, my son's an officer in that battalion; if he doesn't go, no one goes." That settled it.

A few of the Raiders scheduled for the operation were not able to go. One man broke his arm when his rubber boat overturned at Barber's Point. Another accidentally shot himself in the foot, and a few took advantage of Carlson's offer at the final Gung Ho meeting to allow anyone who changed his mind to back out.

A gunnery sergeant in Lieutenant Peatross's group had just learned that his wife, a U.S. citizen born in Japan and living in San Diego, had been arrested and interned as an enemy alien, part of the general roundup of Japanese-Americans on the West Coast. The sergeant told Peatross he could not bring himself to fight the Japanese when his wife had been so mistreated by the American government. The official reason stated in his service record was claustrophobia; he would not be able to stand confinement in a submarine. Peatross consulted his immediate superior, and it was agreed that nothing would be gained by forcing the man to go on the raid under those circumstances. Further, he was too good a marine to damage his reputation by stating the real reason. There was no problem finding eager replacements for those who could not go.

The final days of training ended in a dress rehearsal on August 6, with Nimitz attending, that involved landing at Barber's Point at dawn. Everything went according to plan, a textbook perfect landing. The men of the 2nd Marine Raider Battalion were ready to go to war.

Six

To Makin Atoll

T he trucks came for the Raiders on Saturday, August 8, after midnight. The men hoisted their gunnysacks onto the vehicles and climbed in after them, wondering whether this was it, the attack they had been training for for so long. Or was it just another practice drill? But if it was only an exercise, why were some of the guys staying behind?

Those in charge, who did the counting, checked off 221 names of those slated for the mission. The others had to wonder why. Had they failed in some way? Were they being washed out of the program? They were not told until after the war that it was simply a matter of space. The two submarines could not hold them all.

The men scrambling into the trucks wore their usual khaki shirts and pants, but the clothing had been dyed black. Instead of wearing their helmets and cartridge belts, they had stuffed them into their gunnysacks. The trucks started their engines, and the long line moved out of Camp Catlin, heading for the submarine base at the southern end of Pearl Harbor. The subs were docked at the fifteen-hundred-foot long concrete wharves, which had not been damaged in the December 7 attack.

The USS *Nautilus* was twelve years old, having been launched in 1930. With two diesel engines, it could maintain a surface speed of more than seventeen knots. It was 371 feet long and had a 33-foot sidebeam. The other sub, the USS *Argonaut*, built in 1937, was the only submarine designed as a minelayer. It was thirteen feet shorter than the *Nautilus* and was considered underpowered for its size, with a top surface speed of fifteen knots.

The Raiders made their way in the darkness across wooden gangplanks onto the iron decks. When they reached the open hatches, they dropped their gunnysacks down and descended the ladders after them. Carlson boarded the *Nautilus* with 87 men; Roosevelt went aboard the *Argonaut* with 134.

To accommodate the passengers, the crews of the submarines, which had been reduced in size, had removed all but six torpedoes from both boats. The rubber boats for the landing on the beaches were brought aboard, slathered in grease, and packed into the torpedo loading tubes. Every spare inch had to be utilized to hold the marines and their equipment.

Ben Carson recalled that they were herded aboard the sub and "told to find a place to sit down . . . and shut up! The subs were sunk right at dockside to give the Raiders a feeling of confinement. I remember telling a nearby sailor that the sub had sprung a small leak and his reply shocked me. 'Get used to it. We got the hell blown out of us in Manila Harbor by depth charges and ain't had time to fix 'em yet.'" If news like that did not add to their already considerable apprehension, there was a lot more to learn over the next eight days about life aboard a battle-weary submarine.

"Everything was thrown together in great haste," wrote naval historian Clay Blair Jr. "Living conditions were far from satisfactory. The air conditioning was not adequate. Below decks it was sweltering, and the Marines were either wilting or seasick." The heat was overwhelming, with temperatures soaring above 90 degrees with the humidity at 85 percent.

"You feel like you're in a tomb," said Private First Class Brian Quirk. The men had little to do but stay in their cramped bunks. And before long, with sweaty bodies and no showers available, the odor could not be ignored. "We never did take our clothes off," Ben Carson said, "because there was no place to bathe, no place to wash up. I tell you what, if you have ever walked in a Minnesota chicken house in February when it is 12 degrees below zero outside, that is how that submarine smelled."

Most of the time, they still had the pleasure of smoking. There were few restrictions about cigarettes on the subs, except sometimes when submerged. The navy brass had decided that giving up smoking under the difficult conditions aboard would be bad for morale. There was "barely enough oxygen to light a match or ignite a lighter, but the Raiders still enjoyed their smokes. The glow from dozens of lit cigarettes looked like a swarm of fireflies in the blue light that was standard when the sub was running on the surface."

Sanitation also became a problem. There were not enough toilets for all the extra men on the mission. Wait your turn and don't linger once you got there—that was the unspoken rule. But worse, the subs' toilets were so complex to flush that some men had to be specially trained. Dean Winters was among them:

"They trained me to flush toilets. That was quite a job. I had to flush it for 50 men. . . . They called me a Crapper Cop. . . . [I] had to drop it into a tank so that you could shoot it into another tank, and then you'd need the pressure outside, if you were under, submerged, or something—you had to build up at least twenty pounds [per square inch]. Then you'd open the valve and shoot it out into the ocean. So, they didn't want to teach everybody because if they didn't do it right, it could splash back in their faces." Each flushing required eleven steps.

Winters and the other Crapper Cops had to be constantly vigilant and always available when any of the fifty men in the charge of each cop used the facilities. At least, he said, it helped pass the time, and for the rest of their lives they were proud to remind everyone at Raider reunions that they had once been Crapper Cops.

Another job some of the Raiders took on was Can Smasher. Ben Carson, among others, volunteered to smash empty cans flat to make them as small as possible for the garbage. Every bit of trash and garbage had to be disposed of, and there was no choice but to throw it into the sea. All items had to be crushed, placed in weighted bags so they would sink, and tossed overboard. That way no trail of debris would follow the subs over the empty sea to give away their heading to any aerial reconnaissance.

Carson found that can smashing had certain benefits. "It was a criminal case if you got caught stealing food out of a submarine," he said. "As a can smasher there was a lot of perks in there. When somebody would steal a can of olives, they would always leave two or three in there for the guy to get rid of the evidence. I was learning the perks of the job."

The Raiders tried to help the submarine crews as much as they could as a way to pass time, since they had nothing else to do. The ideal job was to help the sailors on the bridge stand watch, which allowed the men to breathe fresh air. However, the Raiders had no training or experience in standing watch and frequently raised false alarms when their shouts about a flight of Japanese planes bearing down to attack them turned out to be a flock of seagulls. Or when the ship sighting off the port bow was actually a fog bank. Eventually they all learned to laugh about it.

The biggest problem was finding a place to sleep. "The sleeping accommodations were perhaps the worst privation they endured during the trip," wrote historian George Smith. "Bunk space was created by stretching canvas over two-by-fours. They were like bunk beds, four tiers high and four beds deep without any room to turn over. It is a wonder that the men didn't all suffer from claustrophobia or something worse."

"It was hot and humid," recalled Corporal Howard Young. "The guy on the top bunk would perspire, and his sweat would go to the lowest portion of his bunk, which was where his hips were. [Then] it would drip down to the guy below and mix with his sweat, then down to the next until it got to the lucky fellow on the bottom. From there it went onto the deck, where the one with the mop duly mopped it up, day and night."

No more than twelve inches separated a bunk from the one above it. It was difficult even to turn over. And if a man whose bunk was against the wall had to get up to use the toilet, the other three men had to get up and wait for him to return.

"I remember I never did sleep in my bunk," Ben Carson said in a 2001 interview, "because I had to crawl over three other guys and I couldn't stand all the animosity going in and out. I just slept down along the bulkhead. I worked a deal out with a sailor that I could sleep in his bunk when he wasn't in there." A number of Raiders made similar arrangements with other sailors. "We became buddies," Dean Voight said about one crewman, "and whenever he stood night watch, I'd get to sleep in his sack. It was hell of a lot roomier than the one the Raiders wanted me to sleep in."

Eating aboard the submarines also presented challenges. The galleys were constantly busy, preparing food around the clock. Carlson's men ate only two meals a day, but crackers and soup were always available for those who got hungry. But with so many men on board and such limited table space, each meal took three and a half hours to serve. The men had to eat in shifts, and many marines ate standing up, sometimes jostled by others looking for space. They complained about the coffee but were surprised to find the food tasty and abundant, particularly when compared to the diet the Raiders had been on in their training camps.

If the food was one of the few highlights of the voyage, another was the chance to go up on deck and exercise. They were allowed twenty minutes topside daily, and they worked out during that time as vigorously as they could—pushups primarily—being careful not to topple overboard. The decks of the subs were perpetually wet, the boats themselves rolling from side to side and pitching up and down. There were no railings. It took four minutes to get up on deck and three minutes back down. Lieutenant Peatross wrote, "After spending hours packed in the troop compartments like sardines in a can, the few minutes spent on the open decks were spiritually as well as physically rejuvenating. It was a chance to stretch, to be free of the presence of other human bodies, to see the sea and the stars, and enable all to breathe fresh air and clear the lungs of the constantly recycled submarine air."

On August 12, three days after the Raiders left Pearl Harbor, John Haines, who was in command of both submarines, authorized Carlson to inform the men of their destination. Maps and aerial photographs of the target were handed out. They immediately recognized the terrain; it looked just like the mock-up on which they had practiced so many landings. "Hell," one man said, "I know this atoll ass-backwards from the King of Spades."

Carlson and Roosevelt, in their respective subs, distributed copies of Carlson's Operations Order 1-42 and informed the assembled Raiders of their mission. They described the installations and buildings, the beach for their landing, and the way each group would move inland to capture its assigned target. They noted that naval intelligence estimated the size of the enemy force on the island at 250 troops. The Raiders had to be prepared for the worst and hope that the fisherman Lieutenant Holtom found—who said that only fifty Japanese soldiers were on the island—was a lot closer to the truth.

The countersigns to be used once they landed "were typically Carlson," said historian John Wukovits. "If a man needed to challenge someone to determine his identity, he was to shout, 'Hi Raider.' If he did not receive the reply of 'Gung Ho,' the Raider was to open fire."

The overall goals were threefold: to destroy Japanese facilities such as the seaplane base and the weather station, to find any documents that might have useful intelligence information, and to take prisoners.

Carlson had strenuously objected to the last objective, asking how they were supposed to ferry prisoners back to the subs in their small rubber boats. And how were they to keep prisoners fed and under guard during the eight days of their return journey? The subs could barely hold the number of men they had now. Carlson's objections had been overruled. Standard operating procedure at that early stage of the war was to expect to take prisoners. No one in the high command yet realized that the Japanese rarely surrendered, much preferring to die in battle or kill themselves.

The men took a more practical approach to the idea of capturing Japanese soldiers. Ben Carson recalled that his squad leader back at their training camp had said, "'now this thing [about prisoners] ain't going to go over as well with you guys.' And he said that because we were going on the submarines, if we take any prisoners, we have to dispose of them. I remember one of the kids in the squad said, 'well, why don't you just turn them loose after we leave the island?' 'No, that ain't disposing.'"

The Raiders would take no prisoners.

On August 14, Carlson held a full-scale rehearsal. Since they were still at sea, they could not leave the submarines, but they practiced all the complicated steps up to the point at which they would depart the sub for their landing in the rubber boats. They divided into even-numbered and odd-numbered teams. One assembled on the starboard side of the deck, the other on the port side. Merely getting to their assigned places was difficult, with everyone trying to move at once in the crowded quarters. Their movements had to be precise and quick, and performed in a prescribed sequence or the drill would collapse in chaos.

"Not one Raider had a direct route to his debarkation station," Peatross wrote. "Each had to detour to pick up something en route— a machine gun, ammunition, paddles, a radio, whatever. Then he had to help extract his team's boat from the torpedo loading scuttles, unlash it, and drag it to the appropriate air hose for inflating. In the meantime, the outboard motors, having been collected at the foot of the appropriate ladders, were tied to ropes, hauled up over the ladders, and through the hatch, carried to the appropriate debarkation station, and attached to the boats."

Every man and every item of equipment had to operate like part of a well-oiled machine. The boats had to be pulled out of the torpedo loading tubes, dragged and pushed up ladders and through hatches. After the motors were attached, gasoline had to be poured into the tanks and the boats placed in order on either the starboard or port side. Once they were ready, the Raiders would climb into the boats, take their assigned positions, and wait until the submarine submerged, allowing the rubber boats to float. That was the plan—and indeed that was how it went during the practice drill.

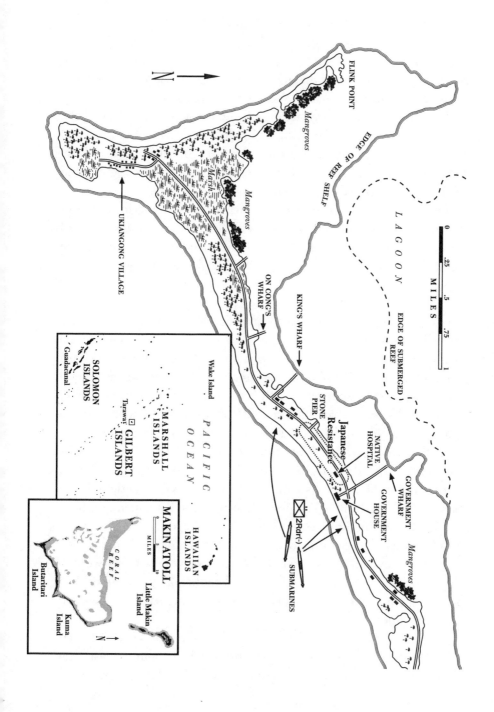

"Even under ideal conditions," Peatross wrote, "the physical complexities . . . were immense, but with the hazards engendered by darkness and a wet, narrow pitching deck, the timing and coordination required easily surpassed that needed to control the movements in the rings of the Ringling, Barnum and Bailey five-ring circus."

But what if a storm was raging off the coast of Makin? Or if the Japanese received warning of the impending attack and were prepared to open fire as the Raiders approached the beach? The men could feel their anxiety rising as they realized the complications that might doom the mission, despite their rigorous training.

Further, the plan depended on having both submarines, one of which was faster than the other, meet at the same time in the midst of the vast Pacific Ocean, and on finding the island, assuming it was the right one, where their maps showed it to be. A lot could go wrong.

On August 16, the night before the mission, Colonel Carlson and Major Roosevelt held their last Gung Ho meeting. They informed the men of the latest intelligence information, but the Raiders had been around long enough to know that much of what was called "intelligence" was really speculation. Still, they had to take it seriously. Carlson told them that "they could expect tank resistance, plane attacks from nearby islands, and even an enemy landing force to strengthen their garrison. They must be off the island before any reinforcements arrived." The threat level had been increased. Tanks, planes, and reinforcements had not previously been mentioned officially. And the size of the Japanese garrison was still an open question. Would 221 Marine Raiders be enough to do the job?

The official policy formally announced at that last briefing agreed with what they had already decided for themselves, that they were to kill enemy soldiers and not be concerned about taking prisoners. The point was emphasized; there was no room to bring back prisoners on the submarines.

Their final meal aboard ship was a dinner of ham and mashed potatoes. They called it "the last supper." Some joked about the last meal given to prisoners before they were executed. "I had thoughts," Brian

View of Makin Atoll through the periscope of the submarine *Nautilus*, August 17, 1942. (*National Archives*)

Quirk said, "that we might be on a suicide mission. Others thought the same thing, too. We knew that it wouldn't take much for things to go wrong. For most of us, we thought it was going to be a hair-raising mission. And that was just about the case."

The submarines were down to periscope depth at seventy feet off the coast of what everyone assumed, and hoped, was Makin. The captain of the *Nautilus* announced that the smoking lamp was lit, even though they were submerged. He knew the men needed to have a smoke at such a time, but when the matches and cigarette lighters came out, none of them worked. The oxygen level was too low.

Ben Carson saw a lot of sailors standing around the periscope waiting their turn to look. "I looked through the periscope and I saw some palm fronds and a lot of water on the lens. I asked where we were and [the officer in charge] couldn't tell me what island. On the way back I went through the officers' country and there were a bunch of officers with a map on the table. On the corner of the map, it said, 'National Geographic.' I thought 'now there is a government agency I have never heard of before.' They were looking at a National Geographic map." That was the best they could find at that early stage of the war.

Peatross also took a look through the periscope and was not happy about what he saw—or, rather, what he did not see. He wrote that his view was of "palm trees, a sandy beach and lots of water, identical to thousands of other islands in the Pacific. But the church steeple, the sole prominent cultural feature and a key reference point in all of our briefings and rehearsals, was not to be seen." Were they about to hit the beach of some place they had not prepared for?

A week before they had left Pearl Harbor, Peatross and Lieutenant William MacCracken, a navy doctor on the *Nautilus*, overheard a conversation between two submarine officers at the Officers' Club. As Peatross recalled, "'At best,' one man said to the other, 'it's going to be a risky trip. Those two old pig-iron, mine-laying boats are just too big, too slow, too difficult to maneuver.'

"'Besides all that,' the other officer said, 'you just can't navigate accurately enough to pop up next to one another after making a 2000-mile trip, and to make it more difficult, they have to arrive after dark.'"

Carlson's marines were about to find out if the officers were right.

At two the next morning, August 17, 1942, the Raiders put on their black uniforms, had breakfast and coffee, and assembled their gear. Each man carried one D-ration chocolate bar, all the food he would have with him. If the men needed more to eat they would have to find it on the island. Carlson made sure he had everything he needed and then stuffed two books into his pockets: the New Testament and *Essays of Ralph Waldo Emerson*.

Several minutes later, Commander William Brockman, skipper of the *Nautilus*, climbed down from the conning tower and approached Carlson. "Colonel," he said, "I've got some bad news for you. Squalls above. Heavy swells, and an onshore wind. It's going to be touch and go getting off the subs and getting on to the beach."

Seven

Everything Lousy

The sea raged, the wind howled, and fifteen-foot waves broke over the decks of the submarines. It was worse than anything the Raiders had encountered during their practice runs at Barber's Point. And it was so dark that it was hard to see the man standing next to you, much less the other submarine only yards away.

"God, it was a mess up there," Ben Carson recalled in a 2007 interview. "The wind was blowing, and the sub was bobbing up and down for about fifteen to eighteen feet."

The captains of the subs had a difficult time keeping their boats from crashing into each other, what with the rising waves and the heavy pull of the tide, which turned out to be far stronger than naval intelligence had predicted. It was a major feat of navigational skill for the ships to have met at precisely that spot. The skippers could barely make out what appeared to be an island off in the distance, and it was impossible to discern any landmarks.

Carlson stood in the conning tower of the *Nautilus*, peering through the darkness. He and the submarine's skippers—Commanders Brockman of the *Nautilus* and Haines of the *Argonaut*—agreed that it was possible they were off some other island, not near Makin. But the more they discussed it, the more they assured one another that they were in the right location. It had to be Makin. Otherwise, all they had gone through would have been in vain.

They agreed that the mission should proceed despite the weather but knew they would have to make at least one major alteration in their plan. The Raiders had been prepared to place the rubber boats along the length of the decks and climb into them. The subs would then submerge, leaving the boats to float free. That would not work in the current conditions.

The rubber boats would have to be lowered into the water, and the men would then have to jump off the decks into them. They would have to do it only when the boats were rising in the swells and not when they were far down. This was a tricky and dangerous procedure that they had never practiced. But there was no other way to get the men into the boats.

First, however, the rubber boats had to be made ready: brought up onto the decks, inflated with air hoses, the outboard motors attached, and gasoline poured into their small tanks. While all that was going on, according to Lieutenant Peatross, "Rain was coming down in torrents, a strong onshore wind was stirring whitecaps all around, seas were running high . . . and the submarine was rolling and pitching heavily. It was truly a time of hard dark and stormy weather, and not a star was to be seen."

Once the boats were lugged on deck—hard, slippery work in itself—they had to be inflated using air hoses like the ones back home in the neighborhood gas station. That was not easy to do, however, on a wet steel deck bobbing rapidly up, down, and sideways.

"When you blow those rubber boats up," Ben Carson said, "it is kind of like a hog racing around in a mud puddle. First of all they are greased, and they fill up and they flop around. Just like when you're putting air in your tires, the tip of the air hose had to be held tight on the filler valve. One Raider did not make a tight connection, and the escaping air sounded like he stepped on a banshee. I thought we woke up every Jap in the Central Pacific."

Once the rafts were inflated, the old outboard motors were hauled up the ladders and attached to the sterns of the boats. The next job was to pour two-and-a-half quarts of fuel into the tiny gas tanks from heavy five-gallon cans. "It was pitching," Carson recalled, "and there is no fence on the subs. I mean if you stumble and slide, you're gone.

We are gripping the two-by-fours on the deck with our toes through our shoes trying to hang on. And we are pouring gas and oil into the outboard motor. It took about three gallons to get two-and-a-half quarts into the thing. Got it all over the deck. I lost the cap. . . . I lost it over the side. I told Lieutenant Griffith that there was salt water in the gas and it wasn't going to run."

Everyone holding a gas can had the same problem. Gas spilled out all over the men, their gear, the rubber boats, and the decks, and some ran down into the open hatches. Many of the men lost the gas can caps, which meant that more fuel would inevitably leak out on the way to the beach. And they would need even more gas for the trip back to the subs when the battle was over.

The rubber boats were lowered over the side and immediately tossed about by the wind and waves. Once they settled in the water, it was sometimes hard to see them because they filled up quickly with water and were indistinguishable from the sea. Two of the boats broke loose and floated away, in the direction of the beach. One of these carried medical supplies, and the other had been loaded with ammunition; new supplies of these crucial items had to be brought up from the subs and distributed among the remaining boats.

While some Raiders held on to the ropes, straining to keep the boats up close against the hulls of the submarines, others prepared to jump down into the boats with their sixty-five pounds of gear. Even when they timed the jump perfectly, catching the boat at the top of a wave, it was dangerous, and a number of men were injured. Some fell on the men already in the boats, where some were so busy bailing sea water with their helmets that they didn't have a chance to dodge.

Lieutenant Joseph Griffith remembered being soaked as the men lined up on the slippery decks waiting their turns. He thought, "If I miss the jump into the boat, I'm gone. Barber's Point was nothing compared to this." Dean Voight remembered feeling the same: "If I miss the boat, I'm going straight down." Although there were some injuries, it was surprising, and fortunate, that no one drowned, given how much gear they were carrying and the rough sea.

Another man recalled that "Corporal Ben Midulla . . . got his foot stuck between the ladder rung and the body of the submarine. He did all he could not to scream out in pain. By the time he reached the shore, the ankle had swollen to the size of his knee and he could barely walk."

Ben Carson was fourth in line. "I had this miserable can of gas with no cover on it. . . . I hit the bottom of the boat and it was full of water. The gas can spewed gas up into my face. They told us we couldn't talk. But nobody said we couldn't swear."

When each boat held its full eleven-man crew, it was time to start the motors. The man in charge yanked a rope curled around a pulley. In Ben Carson's boat, no matter how hard or how often Lieutenant Griffith pulled, the motor would not catch. Each time he tried, the rope recoiled and struck him in the face. Only a few motors started, and a couple of those quickly died. "They were useless hunks of dead weight. The men swore at the motors and kicked at the 40-pound hunks of iron. . . . Nothing seemed to work." The men detached the motors, letting them sink, and grabbed paddles. All the while, the boats were drifting away from the submarines, pushed toward the island by the strong winds and the current.

But it was too early for them to be heading for the beach. The plan, so thoroughly rehearsed and drilled, called for assembling near the *Nautilus* in proper formation before moving out to the beach. Now, however, some boats were drifting out of sight. It was only about four o'clock, an hour before sunrise, and Colonel Carlson was still aboard the sub. The boat that was supposed to transport him was nowhere in sight.

Commander Haines was worried. He paced the deck wondering what had happened to Carlson's boat. He did not want the subs to still be on the surface after sunrise, when they would be easy targets. After some twenty minutes, he spotted Lieutenant Peatross's boat and shouted for him to come close and pick up Carlson.

Peatross, whose boat was one of the few with a working motor, pulled alongside the *Nautilus*. It was 4:20 a.m. Carlson and his runner, Corporal Adrian Scofield, came to the edge. Scofield jumped first, but when Carlson jumped, he "banged his right cheekbone against a

Raiders paddling an LCR-L inflatable rubber boat during a training excercise. The raid on Makin was the first use of these boats in World War II. The raider at the bow is holding a Browning Automatic Rifle (BAR), a light machine gun. (*National Archives*)

Raider's rifle butt with such force that his face immediately swelled. Though the injury bothered him the next two days, no one heard him complain about it."

Peatross's boat was now overloaded with fifteen men, but he took Carlson and Scofield to their assigned rendezvous point. The colonel transferred to the other boat without incident, and Peatross returned to the submarine expecting to meet other Raider boats and lead them to the beach. But there were no other boats. The violent weather and lack of motor power had left them scattered. He moved off in the direction where he thought he might find someone but soon realized that he was heading toward Pearl Harbor. Returning to the *Nautilus*, he found Commander Brockman still on the deck. He yelled to him, requesting directions, and Brockman gave him the precise compass heading.

"Captain," Peatross shouted back, "don't give me an azimuth. Just point." Nobody knew it then, but following Brockman's directions would lead Peatross's group away from the rest of the Raiders.

Carlson was forced to modify his plans. The rubber boats had not been able to gather and form an organized landing party. Time was passing, and they were scattered all about. The beach was a half-mile away, and the men were supposed to land before dawn. In his after-action report, Carlson wrote that he had to alter the plans because he could not communicate with all the boats. He could not even see them all and did not know how many were still afloat.

Four days later, on the return voyage to Pearl Harbor, he wrote, "The resulting confusion in the darkness of the night made a quick change of plan for the landing imperative if we were to get in before daylight and have a semblance of control when we landed. I decided to take both companies to the same beach and passed the word as best I could for all boats to follow me."

Carlson tried shouting over the raging winds and waving his arms about to signal the other boats. Some men saw him and maneuvered into position but many did not. They knew, however, that it was vital to be ashore before daylight, so they headed toward the island, some alone and others in small groups.

"It was raining like hell," Private First Class Ray Bauml said, "and the sea was rough. Unlike Barber's Point, these were short and choppy waves, worse than Barber's Point to get off. We couldn't see our hand in front of our face. . . . A lot of training kind of goes out the window. You never know when you'll get a machine gun burst or a boat will tip."

Dean Voight wrote, "We didn't get tipped over until we got close to shore. I shucked all my stuff, and when I landed I had nothing but my clothes on. The water was quite deep where we tipped over. I was just about to gulp in water when I came up and the next wave took me in."

As Roosevelt's boat neared the beach, he judged that the water was shallow enough for the men to jump out. He told Private First Class Harold Ryan, who was acting as scout, to get in the water and take up his station in front of the boat. But Roosevelt had misjudged the depth. They were still fifty yards out, and Ryan disappeared under the waves. He threw off his helmet and weapons and rose to the surface, only to be knocked under again by another wave. The men grabbed him by the hair and pulled him aboard.

Private Milt Horton was swept overboard. He cut off his gear and sliced through his bootlaces to get rid of his heavy boots. "I came up then and hit the bottom of the boat," he said. Someone clutched his shirt collar and yanked him onboard, right into the same seat from which he had been tossed out.

Ben Carson was having other problems as his boat headed for the beach, with ten men paddling and Lieutenant Griffith trying to steer. The boat rode up on a wave, bent in the middle, and snapped back. "And on that snap," Carson said, "I went out. I didn't have the gas can, but I had everything else. And I hit the water and I took a gulp of air and I went down and I found out I could jump and get another gulp and about three of those and I was ashore. And this gunnery sergeant got ahold of me and dragged me up there. I was coughing. He went 'Shh, we're in enemy territory. You can't suffer anymore out loud.'"

Lieutenant Peatross reached the island without difficulty. At first he thought he and his team were where they were supposed to land; after dragging their boat over the beach into some bushes and camouflaging it, they looked around to get their bearings. He spotted what looked like another rubber boat, but everywhere else there was nothing but palm trees and sand. They raced toward the empty boat and saw that it was loaded with medical supplies. There was no one around and no footprints. They moved on, and after three hundred yards they found a boat filled with ammunition. Apparently these were the boats that had gone missing during the launch from the submarines.

Peatross was worried; no Raiders, no Japanese, no locals were in sight, nor none of the landmarks they expected. They could not use their radio to try to make contact because Carlson had ordered that only his own radio could be used until after firing started. They even thought they might have ended up on the wrong island.

"Have we missed [Makin] altogether and landed on another island," Peatross wrote after the war, "or did we just land too far to the left or right? I considered it highly unlikely that we had missed the island and landed on another, but it was becoming more and more apparent that we had landed in the wrong place"

It turned out to be a good place, however. Without knowing for certain where he was, Peatross and his team would find themselves behind the Japanese force. Unfortunately, Carlson was unaware of this and so was unable to take advantage of their position.

A mile away, the main landing force was also in a confused state, although Carlson was certain he was in the right place. Some fifteen of the eighteen boats had landed together. The men dragged the boats across the sand about twenty yards into the underbrush and covered them with palm fronds to hide them from the Japanese. The boats were the Raiders' only transport back to the subs once the mission was completed.

But the men were stretched out over several hundred yards along the beach. Brian Quirk remembered that "the landing was all mixed up. Everything was in total disarray. . . . Guys were running around in the dark making things even more confused. We decided to wait until dawn to get organized, so we just stayed where we were." When it began to get light, Carlson and Roosevelt worked to restore the organization by getting small units and individuals where they belonged.

Overall, they were lucky. There were no Japanese guards on that side of the island. Because the seas there were always so rough, they assumed that no one would try to make a landing there. The Japanese concentrated on the opposite side of the island, the lagoon side, where the sea was almost always calm and smooth.

The submarines pulled away from the beach after their passengers had disembarked and took up position four miles off the coast to wait for word from Carlson. In his after-action report, written a week later, on August 24, Commander Haines wrote, "Communications by voice radio was established at 0513 with the Raider Unit."

Carlson had sent a message, perhaps a bit exaggerated, that all the Raiders were ashore. He did not know where Peatross's crew was, but he wanted to assure Haines that the mission was proceeding according to plan, even if it wasn't. "Things were pretty fucked up," Quirk recalled. "If you had any intelligence at all, you knew that everybody was going the wrong way. . . . The second thing you knew was that the sun was going to come up in about forty-five minutes, and if you weren't on the beach and moving out, you were in tough straits."

It was the "shot heard 'round the world" as far as Carlson's men were concerned. It changed everything, and it had been an accident, committed by one of the Raiders' best-trained men. No order had been given to fire. No one had an enemy soldier in his sight, but the shot destroyed any attempt to take the enemy by surprise.

Ben Carson saw it happen. "Vern Mitchell was trying to chamber a round in a BAR. The bolt goes back and forth and that is what feeds the gun and fires it. Old Mitch had his hand on his trigger and his hand on the slide and he let it go and away she went. He had it on full auto. And that woke the Japs up."

Every Raider heard the shots and knew what it meant. No matter how it happened, the enemy had been alerted; they knew the Raiders were there. "Jesus, they can hear that in Tokyo," Quirk said. "So they're up waiting for us, and we aren't even ready to move off the beach yet." Private Julius Cotten thought, "They might as well just blow the bugle that says we're here, come find us." Quirk remembered lying on the beach at that moment, staring at his feet in the water. He thought, "I wonder if I am ever going to get the hell off this island."

Peatross also heard the shots. Years later he wrote, "I would bet that there's not one of us who can't recall exactly what he was doing at that moment and who doesn't relate many of his subsequent actions to that burst of fire."

Carlson was so furious that he cussed out the man who did it. It was the only time that those around him could ever recall seeing him so angry.

At 5:43 a.m., Carlson sent a second radio message to Haines: "Everything lousy."

Eight

Let 'em Have It!

"It was a shootout at the OK corral." That was how Sergeant Howard E. "Buck" Stidham described the raid on Makin Island that morning of August 17, 1942.

"Everybody was on his own," Ben Carson remembered. "There was no organization. I was fighting with A Company. I just ran up to the front. I ran past what turned out to be later an old buddy from Michigan. He had been mixed up in one hell of a fight someplace and he did not have a single round of ammunition left in his Tommy gun belt. He was laying there. His entire chest was blown out. He got caught in a burst of machine gun fire. That is when I realized this game is for sure.

"On the way up to where the shooting started, after Mitchell got his round, I was dashing from coconut tree to coconut tree and I came upon a pig pen that was made from cut-off coconut logs. I ducked down behind that pig pen and I looked through the holes in the logs and the pig was dead. And I thought that this was no place to be."

It was around six in the morning as Carlson's main force moved off the beach and began making its way through the coconut palms. His units were pretty much intact, except for Lieutenant Peatross and his eleven men who were a mile away, their location still unknown to Carlson. But he had confidence in his outfit. The Raiders had been trained to take the initiative, both individually and in small groups. Only minutes before, at 5:47, Carlson had sent another message to Commander Haines. This was just four minutes after his previous message stating that everything was "lousy." Now Carlson could afford to take a more optimistic, even hopeful, tone.

"Situation expected to be well in hand shortly." And he was right. His men were off the beach and taking the battle to the enemy, wherever they were.

"At first, we didn't see anything," Brian Quirk said. "After all we had been through getting ashore, it looked so easy. I remember asking myself, 'What the Marine Corps won't go through for a dummy run.' I wanted very much to believe that."

It was only minutes after Private Mitchell had fired his BAR, inadvertently announcing the Raiders' presence. While the marines had been organizing themselves to do battle, Carlson was not yet certain of their location. Were they where they had been trained to be, or someplace else? Carlson sent out a patrol to reconnoiter.

"I immediately directed Lieutenant Plumley, commanding Company A, to move his company across this island, seize the road on the lagoon side, and report our location with relation to the wharves." Plumley sent several men ahead of his outfit, with Sergeant Clyde A. Thomason in charge.

About fifteen minutes later, Plumley received good news from the patrol, and he sent Lieutenant Wilfred LeFrancois to Carlson's headquarters with word that the troops were where they were supposed to be.

"You hit the nail on the head, Colonel," LeFrancois told him. "Where you are now is right opposite Government Wharf, and we've taken Government House without opposition. Haven't seen a Jap yet."

Sergeant Thomason's patrol had come close to disaster, but not because of the Japanese. As they approached Government House, they drew shotgun fire. Thomason shouted the password "Gung," and to their surprise, they heard one of their own respond with the countersign "Ho." They had been shot at by three Raiders who believed the men creeping up on them were Japanese. Those were the first shots fired on purpose that day.

The three Raiders joined Thomason's group and they cautiously explored Government House, finding it empty. By then the sun was higher and they could see their surroundings more clearly. They came upon a straight road; they knew from their briefings that it ran the length of the island. Suddenly, they spotted people on the road walking toward them.

LeFrancois wrote, "A group of tall, well-built native men, women and children was coming down it, laughing and chattering. Apparently, they had taken our firing for Japanese practice maneuvers. When they came upon us, they were startled, but quickly became friendly. A few of them spoke broken but intelligible English. They disliked the Japs and told us that eighty of them were living at the On Cheong Pier."

Back at headquarters, three native men approached Carlson and Roosevelt. They shook hands while the Raiders nearby kept watch, their fingers on the triggers of their weapons. But the men seemed friendly and happy to see Americans.

"We knew you come," one said.

"How many Japs on the island?" Carlson asked.

"Two hundred, three hundred mebbe." That was a lot more than the Raiders expected. The men said that many of the Japanese soldiers were at On Cheong's Wharf and Ukiangong Point. Carlson immediately radioed the submarines and gave them those locations as targets. Shortly after, they heard shells and explosions as the sailors opened fire with their deck guns.

Throughout the battle, the natives assisted the Raiders, providing information on Japanese troop movements. "The native police chief was handed a Garand to hold by a Marine, and he used it to kill two snipers. Some natives opened coconuts to relieve the men's thirst, while others carried ammunition for the machine gunners." Suddenly Carlson heard a flurry of shots, both rifles and shotguns. Some of his men had obviously run into the enemy. At the same time, he received an urgent message on his walkie-talkie.

"Two small Jap transports entering the lagoon."

The *Nautilus* opened fire almost immediately, at 7:16 a.m., putting twenty-four rounds into the lagoon, covering an area a mile wide. The sub's gunners could not see the enemy transport ships, nor did they have spotters in the air or on the ground to give correction, to report where their shells were landing. So the sailors blanketed the lagoon, and in the end the lack of spotters did not matter. The Japanese ships—a thirty-five-hundred-ton troop transport carrying as many as fifty soldiers, and a smaller patrol boat—were hit and sunk as they tried to sail out of the way.

Carlson heard the explosions but could not see the lagoon, but Lieutenant Plumley radioed in a description of the action. "Direct hits," he announced. "The ships are on fire. Lots of Japs drowning."

Carlson asked, "Isn't Peatross with you?"

"No, sir."

"What happened to him? He had eleven men."

"The last we saw of Pete and his boat was just after he left the sub."

Plumley's outfit was coming under increasingly heavy fire. As Lieutenant LeFrancois led a small unit forward, he worried that they were walking into an ambush. They moved slowly along a dirt road through dense vegetation, around bogs, and past some fifteen shacks beside a long building with a high, pointed roof. He considered the open ground on both sides of the road; it was a perfect place to be ambushed.

LeFrancois was also concerned that his men did not appear to be taking things seriously enough. Some were joking around, as though they were still in training. Two of them had a minor scuffle over which one would keep a Japanese flag, and they ended up tearing it in pieces. He wrote later that "none of these fellows seemed to worry about anything and took it for granted that the story was bound to have a happy ending.

"Orders came to move up the road and establish contact with the enemy. . . . With his men, [Corporal Howard] Young went scurrying all over the place, determined to rout any hidden Japs. [Private First Class Frederick] Metcalf and I followed. I was bareheaded. My helmet was slung over my back so I could see anything and hear any sound. I carried my gun on full automatic with the safety catch off. Back of us came Thomason with the guard. I could only see our men here and there in the bush, but I knew that our Raiders, in staggered groups, were following me, ready for the fight."

Suddenly a truck came to a screeching stop some three hundred yards down the road. More than a dozen Japanese soldiers jumped out. Others appeared out of the jungle and joined them. One stuck a large Japanese flag into the ground while the rest scurried into the brush along the roadside and began edging toward the Raiders.

LeFrancois quickly deployed his men onto higher ground and brought up reinforcements. He signaled to Sergeant Thomason to move his men double time up the road. "Without regard for his own safety, Thomason ran up and down the line, picking out good positions for the men."

As LeFrancois scanned the positions his men were now in, he judged the situation too good to be true. "I could see the Japs creeping toward us in bunches along the narrow 100-yard strip of trees and light brush between the road and the lagoon. They were perfect targets and were walking into a trap. Surely, I told myself, things like this didn't happen. No leader could be as lucky as I. . . . It was a perfect setup." Even better, the morning sun was behind the Raiders, shining into the enemy's eyes.

Sergeant Thomason laughed aloud and shouted, "Let 'em have it," and the Raiders opened fire. "There was about four minutes of inferno," LeFrancois wrote for the *Saturday Evening Post* magazine, "in which everybody in the area was blasting at somebody or something. Anything out in the open was riddled. Then we realized we were the only ones making any noise and let up. Later, I found our fire had been so deadly that this Jap combat group in its entirety had seen its last battle."

But the Raiders suffered a grievous loss as well: Sergeant Thomason was dead. The six-foot-four, perfect recruiting poster marine, top student in his high school, varsity football player, boxing champion on the USS *Augusta*, was shot while firing at the enemy and guiding his men to their places on the line. They shouted for him to take cover, but he wouldn't stay down. They were his men, and it was his duty to look after them. LeFrancois heard a sound he described as a "Thut," and then another man yelled that Thomason had been hit.

"I worked my way over to him and felt his pulse. There was no heartbeat," LeFrancois wrote.

Thomason became the first marine in World War II to be awarded the Medal of Honor, "for conspicuous heroism and intrepidity above and beyond the call of duty. . . . Continuously displaying a relentless fighting spirit throughout the action and while leading an assault on an enemy position, he gallantly gave his life in the service of his country. His great courage and loyal devotion to duty in the face of great peril were in keeping with the finest traditions of the United States Naval Service."

One mile away, Lieutenant Peatross and his eleven men heard the gunfire and knew that at least some of the Raiders had met the enemy. Until then, Peatross had no idea how many other marines were ashore. He ordered his radioman to contact Carlson, only to discover that the radio was soaked with seawater. "It didn't work! Not a sound! Not even static. Now, for all practical purposes, we were worse off than we were before. Although we now knew the approximate location of at least some of the Raiders, we still could not communicate with them."

Peatross was certain that the Japanese must be positioned between his outfit and the main force. He decided to follow the original plan and lead his men forward toward the church, one of the few distinctive landmarks on the island. But first they had to pass the Japanese barracks. Just as they reached that building there was another burst of gunfire, and a surprised Japanese soldier ran out of the barracks carrying his rifle.

"Without command and almost as one, three of our group fired, and the luckless Japanese fell dead." Peatross recalled. "These were the first shots that any of us had fired in the war; this was our first face-to-face encounter with the enemy."

Peatross and his outfit explored the barracks but found no one else there, only clothing, rifles, and ammunition. They moved on to the church and found a padlock on the door. They assumed there would be no enemy soldiers inside, with the door locked from the outside, so they moved on toward the sounds of battle. Peatross spread his men out in a skirmish line near the road and settled down to wait for an enemy attack. Some distance along, a Japanese soldier walked out of the bushes and picked up a bicycle that had been left on the road. The Raiders held their weapons at the ready as the man mounted the bike and began to pedal toward them, his rifle slung casually over his shoulder.

Peatross passed the word for the men to hold their fire until the luckless guy came closer to their position, but Private Ernest July opened fire too soon and from too great a distance. Every shot missed the target. Peatross wrote that July's "burst of fire completely surrounded the bicyclist—over him, under him, and on both sides. But that notwithstanding, the man ever so slowly and carefully laid down his bicycle, as if fearful of damaging the Emperor's property, unslung his rifle, calmly and almost deliberately walked to the far side of the road, as if to select a position from which to return our fire."

He did not survive the next burst of fire from the Raiders. A second Japanese soldier emerged from the bushes, got on his bike, and pedaled toward the Raiders. He did not survive either. And then a third did the same, but apparently thinking that speed would save him, he pedaled furiously down the road. He was not fast enough to save his life.

Peatross waited a few minutes to see if any more targets would appear, but when no more Japanese came out of the bushes, he gathered his men and led them toward the headquarters of Sergeant Major Kanemitsu, commander of the Japanese garrison. No one was there. Kanemitsu had already dispatched what he apparently realized would be his last message from Makin: "We are all now dying in battle."

The marines found a radio inside the building along with a safe, exactly as the fisherman had described to Lieutenant Holtom weeks before. Peatross put his radioman, Private First Class Kenneth Montgomery, to work repairing the radio. Private Sam Brown broke open the safe and found a pile of Japanese paper money and coins, which he passed out "as if it were payday, and stuck the bag with the rest in his pack." Brown kept most of the loot.

The Raiders then headed on down the road, hoping to meet up with Carlson and his main force. They saw a man come out of the house next to the headquarters building. He was not in uniform, but rather wore a white shirt, khaki shorts, and a sun helmet. He did not notice the marines; he looked in the direction from which the soldiers on bicycles had come, and it appeared that he might be waving to someone. The marines did not wait to find out.

Sam Brown opened fire, killing the man instantly. It was not until many years later that Peatross learned that the victim was the Japanese commander, Kanemitsu. "Through sheer good fortune," Peatross wrote, "we had decapitated the garrison and cut off its communications with the outside. In retrospect, this goes far to explain the overall lack of control and coordination in the Japanese defense."

But that understanding came later. At the moment Kanemitsu was killed, a machine gun opened fire on the Raiders' position; bullets struck the ground all around them. Peatross led a retreat to the headquarters building. He had no radio contact with Carlson, was cut off from the main force, and a machine gunner was trying to kill them all.

"For Carlson," his biographer wrote, "the hours between 0700 and 1130 were a series of movements and events which crossed and recrossed each other like an intricate maze." A maze that was difficult for him to find his way out of, particularly in the absence of precise reports from his front.

Some natives had described the size of the Japanese force on the island as 250 or more, but Holtom's fisherman had said there were only fifty of the enemy. Who was right? And where was Peatross? Were the Japanese sending in reinforcements or aircraft? Were LeFrancois's men in danger of being overrun?

In his after-action report, Carlson only hinted at the confusion and uncertainty that had plagued him. "Snipers and machine gun fire had taken a heavy toll on our right flank [LeFrancois's position] and little progress was being made there. I then directed that one platoon from Company B enter the line on the left of A Company. The maneuver was skillfully executed by Lieutenant Griffith."

But Griffith did not agree with Carlson's order to join with Company A in its stalled advance. Griffith was concerned that his men would become intermingled with Company A and lose their cohesion. He argued with Carlson that his men should be used to outflank the

Japanese rather than joining a stalled attack against what appeared to be a strong defensive line.

"I'll lose control," he told Carlson.

"I don't give a damn," Carlson said. "Put them in the skirmish line. Did you hear me?"

Griffith knew not to argue further and quickly led his men into the fight, but he recalled, in a 2008 interview, "I never regained control of my platoon. The fighting was pretty much a bunch of individuals."

"Nobody ever told us to look up," Ben Carson said. The Raiders learned a deadly lesson on Makin, one for which they had not been trained. "Here we get ashore," Carson wrote, "and the Japs are up in trees, shooting down on us. It took us quite a while to figure out where they were."

The Raiders had not been trained to deal with snipers in trees because no one expected the enemy to be anywhere other than on the ground. But there they were, tied to the palm trees high up, with the fronds carefully arranged to camouflage them. With their green uniforms, twigs and branches attached to their helmets, and coconuts affixed to their bodies, they were invisible from the ground until they opened fire.

"When they fired that Arisaka rifle," Carson reported, "the palm fronds opened up, and when we saw that we just started hosing down the coconut trees. Some of them were tied up there and they would come down and swing on the ropes and other ones would just fall straight down on the ground. . . . They got a lot of our guys."

LeFrancois found himself pinned down by the snipers. "I felt sure that two of the enemy snipers were out to get me. I was trying to locate them when I heard several bursts of a high-powered weapon on my right. [Corporal Ed] 'Killer' Wygal had located the sharpshooters in their tree nests, had borrowed an automatic rifle to take the place of our low-velocity weapons [shotguns] and had ended my worries."

Most of the Raiders who were wounded had been shot by the snipers in the trees. They had a clear advantage until the marines caught on and destroyed the tops of the palm trees with concentrated rapid fire instead of trying to take out individual snipers with single shots. This was not a time for skilled marksmanship.

The Japanese snipers were on the lookout for the officers and non-coms directing their men by using hand signals instead of trying to be heard over the noise of battle. "We were taught to use arm signals," Ben Carson remembered. "After a couple of guys lost their arms and wrists, they were pretty mute. Then if you had a radio on, the antenna indicated that you were an important target. . . . Quite a few of the gunnies were wounded because they were out there giving arm signals."

Corporal Cotten got close enough to a sniper's tree to try a grenade. Just as he was about to throw it, the sniper fired, detonating a second grenade that was hanging from a strap on Cotten's chest. Instead of exploding, that grenade disintegrated. Cotten pulled the pin on the grenade in his hand, counted to three, and tossed it as high as he could. It exploded at the top of the tree, killing two snipers and a monkey.

Carson also used a grenade to go after a sniper in a tree. A wounded Raider was lying on the ground. "He kept pointing up into this tree," Carson said. "And every time I moved there was a shot. I had two grenades and he told me to throw one of them. . . . If you throw a grenade up in a tree and it comes right back at you, that is not considered very smart, so I wanted it to go all the way. And then it hit and exploded and there was no more fire from the tree."

One unidentified man told Private Bill McCall that he "had to piss real bad." McCall told him "to stay on the ground and pee in a prone position. I don't know if it was instinct or what, but he couldn't resist getting up and going over to a nearby palm tree. He died with his hands in his pants."

Private Howard Craven was crawling through a clearing alongside Corporal Harris Johnson. Suddenly "a Jap sniper in a tree shot Johnson in the head. I asked him, 'How ya doing, Johnny?' He replied, 'OK.' I started to raise up then went limp. The sniper's next shot hit my scalp and helmet. The Raider on my left had a BAR, saw the Jap in the palm tree, opened fire and shot him out of the tree."

Sergeant James Faulkner, one of Carlson's section leaders, had mistakenly been given a shotgun instead of a rifle. He was hit in the hand by a sniper's bullet, then in the stock of his shotgun, and then his head. "He got me good in the side before somebody finally killed him. . . . Marine Gunner Charles Lamb handed me his canteen which was full of scotch. In a short while I was feeling no pain. Someone had emptied his bowels behind the tree where I lay and when the Jap planes [later] came over strafing and bombing, Lieutenant Plumley would drag me from one side of the tree to another to keep the tree between us and the strafing fire. . . . I was 'smashed' on scotch, covered with blood and shit. . . . Plum had his hands full keeping the flies away."

LeFrancois escaped close calls from snipers' bullets when, "Somebody shouted from my right, 'Lieutenant Holtom has been shot and is dying! He needs medical attention!' Then came, slowly, the words, 'Never mind!'" Sergeant Stidham was nearby but pinned down by heavy fire. When it eased for a moment, he made his way to Holtom's body. He stared at it for a moment, "and for the first time I realized how serious this was."

Colonel Carlson was devastated by Holtom's death. He had come to respect and admire the lieutenant, who had gone to the front, to the battle, even though his job as intelligence officer did not require him to do so. He was making his way back to Carlson when he was killed. He had found something written in Japanese posted on a bulletin board outside the island post office.

"He was looking for me," Carlson wrote to Holtom's parents a few weeks later, "when a sniper shot him, the bullet passing through his left chest and emerging behind the right shoulder. He lived only ten seconds. He was buried near where he fell. His face indicated that he died without pain. He was wholly at peace.

"Jerry was respected and loved by all with whom he came in contact. His loss is a terrible blow to me, both because of my personal affection for him and because of the value of his capabilities. Words are futile instruments where human life is concerned. I can only say that my heart goes out to you and his other loved ones at home. He died like a man and a true patriot."

Soon Carlson would have to write many other letters.

Nine

A Free-for-All

"It happened a lot of times," one unidentified Raider said long after the battle was over. "I'd turn around and there was the Colonel, calm as hell, smoking that stinkin' pipe of his. 'Hya, Raider,' the Old Man would say. 'Hya doin?' It helped you feel not so scared, his being right up front with you."

Carlson could not bring himself to stay back in headquarters for long; he had to be out, seeing for himself how things were going, how his boys were doing. He believed he could follow and direct the battle much better in person than if he were waiting behind the lines for scattered reports to come in. That was Roosevelt's job as executive officer, to remain in the tiny, crude shack they used for headquarters (which looked like a pigsty, one man said) and keep track of events.

Once that morning, a Raider was hugging the ground trying to get a bead on a sniper in a tree when he heard someone creeping up close. He looked around and saw Colonel Carlson, who asked how he was doing while the sniper's bullets hit all around them. "Hya Colonel," the Raider said, lining up his rifle on the sniper. More sniper fire erupted. "Get the hell outta here, Colonel," the man added. "Ya gotta get us off this aye-toll."

Many Raiders recalled how Carlson took chances, how he seemed almost unaware, or contemptuous, of the dangers around them. He would walk serenely through the coconut palms, as if out for a stroll, while his men were scurrying to find some sort of concealment. They feared he would be hit, but they also found the sight reassuring. If the Old Man wasn't afraid, maybe they didn't have to be either.

Brian Quirk wrote, "Carlson seemingly had no fear of dying. In combat he was the calmest, like he was delivering an English lecture. He was so calm that he calmed you down. . . . Fear is contagious, and composure is contagious, too."

Major Roosevelt stayed at the headquarters shack, taking care of details and keeping Carlson up to date. Carlson was pleased with the order that Roosevelt was able to impose and maintain at the center of the action, but he was also concerned about the president's son. Nowhere on Makin was safe, and several times snipers got close enough to fire on the shack. Two Japanese soldiers were found and killed nearby.

"I remember a walkie-talkie was shot right out of my hands," Roosevelt wrote in 1976. "I simply asked for another one. I didn't have any sensation of fear until later. I was too busy with the battle at the time to be frightened. The awful noise of the gunfire blotted everything else out."

Sometimes Carson had to be stern with Roosevelt to make sure he remained as safe as anyone on Makin could be. Ten days after the battle, on August 27, Carlson wrote to the president, describing James as "cool as the proverbial cucumber and [he] kept the loose ends tied together, without a hitch. Time and time again, I had to tell him to get into a sump hole, and stay there so that I could be assured that my communications would continue to function, because he insisted on sticking his neck out to see how things were going."

But that expression of Carlson's concern about James Roosevelt came later. Through the morning of the day on Makin, Carlson had more immediate problems. He still had no accurate count of the number of Japanese troops on the island. There could be only fifty, or as many as three hundred.

He also had to consider whether the enemy planned to reinforce the garrison on Makin. Ships or planes carrying troops could be on their way. And the progress of his main fighting force, under LeFrancois and Griffith, was still unknown. Apparently they were holding their own, but with more Japanese soldiers to contend with, they could be outnumbered and overrun.

And where were Peatross and his men? There had been no contact; no radio messages, no word from a runner. Carlson had been out scouting but still did not have a clear picture of how the plans, which the Raiders had rehearsed and drilled so diligently, were working.

Peatross and his men were in a concrete pillbox a few yards from the empty Japanese headquarters building on the far side of the island. They were taking fire from a Japanese machine gun and trying to get their radio to work. Private First Class Montgomery, the radioman, had disassembled the walkie-talkie and put it back together without success.

"We had been issued this model [walkie-talkie] early in our training—the first unit in the Corps to get it," Peatross said, "and besides having received special schooling in it, Montgomery had worked with it for several months. Thus, when he proclaimed our set to be a hopeless case, there was no arguing with his diagnosis." So there was no way to communicate with Carlson or the submarines. Peatross and his group were trapped in the pillbox.

While the machine-gun fire continued, Peatross ordered Corporal Mason Yarbrough to lead an assault team consisting of Private First Class Floyd Bigelow and Field Music First Class Vernon Castle, the bugler. Peatross and the rest of his men followed a few yards behind. Castle, carrying a Tommy gun, crawled within thirty yards of the machine-gun emplacement when the Japanese saw him and opened fire. Although he was hit several times, he kept dragging himself forward, firing his weapon. With the rest providing supporting fire, Peatross wrote, Castle "struggled close enough to the enemy to throw a grenade, killing the gunner and two of the crewmen. The rest of us shot two riflemen near the gun. By the time Bigelow got to Castle, he was dead . . . in the bravest act that I witnessed in all of World War II."

Suddenly Peatross and his men began taking heavier, closer fire. Peatross led them to an area behind the headquarters building. There were two more casualties: Corporal Yarbrough was killed, on his twentieth birthday, and Private First Class Montgomery died as the men withdrew. Three other men were wounded.

The costly attack left Peatross with "holes in my shirt, trousers, and in my field glasses; my knees were skinned and oozing blood, and I was exhausted." His unit was still cut off from the main force. He sent three men, including Private Raymond Jansen and Private First Class Alexander Donovan, to reconnoiter the ground between their position and the lagoon to see if they could outflank the Japanese soldiers who had them pinned down.

But before the patrol could move out, they heard the sound of an engine and then saw a small Japanese car speeding toward them, "like a rabbit flushed from cover. It roared past at full throttle," Peatross wrote. "We all fired. The car bore straight on down the road in a cloud of dust. About 500 yards beyond, the road curved and there, as we watched, refusing to believe we had missed, the car continued straight and, never slowing, ran off the road."

The car and its two occupants were riddled with bullets. Peatross did not say whether they were Japanese or natives, although it is likely that only the Japanese would have had access to a car.

The patrol Peatross sent out to reconnoiter came back with word that there were no enemy troops southwest of their position. This news meant that the entire Japanese force, however large it was, had to be to the northeast, between Peatross and Carlson's main force. Thus, the enemy was between the two groups of Raiders. Peatross's force was too small to launch an attack, but now he understood that it was even more urgent that he get word to Carlson about his location.

He again chose Jansen and Donovan, who had just returned from the patrol, to try to get through to Carlson. Peatross told them to return immediately if they came under fire. However, in a surprise move, Peatross's outfit was suddenly confronted by a group of about seventy-five native men, women, and children who came from the direction of the gunfire. They were led by a short elderly man armed with a machete.

Peatross and an aide, both well-armed, walked up to greet him. "When we were about 50 yards from him," Peatross said, "he bowed to me and I bowed to him, much relieved, but still keeping an eye on his machete. Then he bowed to me again, and I to him, and he to me, and so on; back and forth, until we were almost close enough to bump heads."

The leader spoke enough English to confirm to Peatross that the main body of Japanese troops lay between him and Carlson's force. Then the natives moved on down the road. Peatross again dispatched Jansen and Donovan to get word to Carlson. They had gone no more than three hundred yards when Japanese soldiers opened fire. Jansen turned and headed back to the outfit, as Peatross had ordered. They heard nothing from Donovan. If he did not get through with his message, Peatross and his men would remain trapped.

At the position of the main force, LeFrancois heard a bugle from up ahead. It sounded only two notes, but that was all it took to unleash the repeated cries of "Banzai" as the Japanese charged. They held their rifles, with bayonets fixed, above their heads and fired at the Americans as they raced forward.

"It seemed like there was no end to them," LeFrancois wrote. "It was an amazing and fantastic piece of showmanship, and we were so fascinated by this attempt to scare us into panicky flight that we waited until they were uncomfortably close before we mowed them down with a withering fire."

Ben Carson said they had never seen anything like it. The Japanese kept coming, no matter how many were cut down. "They would yell and holler," Carson wrote, "and make a lot of noise. I guess they were half drunk or something. . . . It was pretty easy with all our automatic firing. It must have taken 500 bullets to wound one Jap."

Sergeant Victor "Transport" Maghakian, an ever-present cigar in his mouth, waved his right arm over this head to give directions to his men. A sniper's bullet struck him. "My arm went dead almost immediately," he said, "but I still had full use of my left as I dropped to the 'deck' and played dead for fifteen minutes until another shot by [the sniper] revealed his location. When he showed himself I silenced him with my automatic rifle."

Maghakian wrapped a tourniquet around his bleeding right arm, shifted his weapon to his left shoulder, and kept firing. When asked in a 1977 interview how he had been able to stay so calm in the face of imminent death, he said, "It seems to get you mad. Good and mad. Furious. You make up your mind you're going to get that so-and-so if it costs you a slug in the belly."

Maghakian was awarded the Navy Cross for wiping out a Japanese machine-gun nest that came close to killing Lieutenant Stephen Stigler, who was a navy doctor, and his corpsman, Pharmacist Mate Walter Elterman, who were out looking for wounded Raiders. They found Maghakian, patched him up and advised him to go to the aid station, but he refused and went back to the line. Stigler wrote in 2000, "There is no doubt in my mind that had Victor not wiped out that machine gun nest, Elterman and I would have been killed or badly wounded. He saved our lives."

Lieutenant LeFrancois saw two Japanese soldiers in the bushes about twenty feet away. "I poured almost twenty precious slugs into their bodies before I could control myself. The noise of our firing exceeded any noise I have ever heard." The attacking Japanese infantry in the "Banzai" charge were followed by four machine-gun crews who set up positions within thirty yards of the Raiders, while the treetop snipers kept up their fire. Private First Class Fred Kemp took a hit in his cartridge belt; when it exploded one of his tracer bullets, it left him looking like smoke was pouring out of his body. He survived without any burns.

Corporal I. B. Earles was hit in the mouth by a sniper's bullet. He jumped up and shouted, "I'll get those heathen by myself! Show me where they are!" His buddies yelled at him to stay down. But Earles tore through the brush firing off rounds at the enemy he saw, or thought he saw. He took out a machine-gun nest and kept running and shooting until he fell dead. When his body was examined later, it was found that he had been shot eleven times.

A Japanese machine-gun bullet hit Private Joe Woodford a glancing blow, setting his grenade jacket on fire. If a grenade in one of the pouches went off, they could all explode and Woodford would be gone. He tore off the jacket, "like a madman" someone said, and ran away as fast as he could. "The fellows told me afterward that the bullets of Jap snipers could be seen kicking up the sand right behind me as I ran," Woodford said later.

Corporal Howard Young silenced one of the machine guns, killing five Japanese troops. "We had Japs in front of us," Young said, "above us, alongside of us, to our left and behind us also to our left. [Corporal Ladislaw] Piskor and I, in the prone position, calmly squeezed [the bullets] off as if we were on the 200-yard range at Camp Elliott."

To Sergeant Mel Spotts, the battle was a "free-for-all. Every man was trying to move up to the front to get his score of Japs before they ran out." He said later that he could not see anything clearly, which was why he made his way forward in order to find more targets. But instead he found that "the Japanese were near perfect at concealment and camouflage," so he just advanced and blasted away at anything that moved.

LeFrancois was caught in the crossfire of four enemy machine guns. He tried to move forward but did not get far before bullets tore into his right arm and shoulder. "One of the boys crept up to me, took his belt off and tied my arm to my body. I tried to recognize this lad, but my mind was foggy. I knew that I was of no use anymore, that I was bleeding to death and would soon be unconscious."

He rolled over into a swampy patch of ground and tried to inch back from the firing line. A Japanese soldier stood up and took aim at him and was shot down by some of the Raiders. LeFrancois made it to the aid station, one step at a time, with pain radiating through his arm. When he regained consciousness he was lying on a straw mat being examined by Dr. MacCracken. "Frenchie," the doctor said, "this isn't so bad as it looked at first. You just lie here and relax until we go back to the subs. Everything is going to be all right." And it was; Le Francois was among the survivors.

The fighting slacked off briefly after the "Banzai" charge, but it did not stay quiet for long. The Japanese launched a second charge, led by the shrill notes of a bugle. But there were fewer of the enemy this time, and the Raiders beat them back fairly quickly.

Carlson's men had held their own, but the main force was still much in its initial position, having advanced little. One historian argued that Carlson "could have ordered a rapid advance by both companies, but lacking clear intelligence about the size of the defending force, he opted to place his Raiders in a set line, thereby stalling their advance across Makin and handing the initiative to the enemy. He could have ordered a flanking attack . . . but he declined. In the early hours, the Raiders' commander had substituted caution for aggression, timidity for audacity."

In Carlson's defense it should be noted that without knowing how many troops he was facing, or where they were located, caution may have been the wisest approach to take.

Beginning at 11:30 a.m., Carlson faced a new threat from the air. Two Japanese biplanes flew over the island at a leisurely pace, as if sightseeing, with no thought that an adversary might be training guns on them. The planes were Nakajima ESN, Type 95 reconnaissance planes, designed to be catapulted off ships. Immediately upon sighting the planes, both US submarines submerged.

Carlson ordered his men to hold their positions and not to fire at the planes, so as not to reveal their locations. They watched in silence as the aircraft circled overheard, but just the sight brought home to the Raiders just how isolated they were.

"They were on an island, a tiny island 1000 yards wide and 10 miles long, in the middle of the Jap Empire. Only two slim subs, easily vulnerable from air and sea attack, were their lifeline home, eight days away, while Jap help was only an hour's flying time distant. From Makin there was no place to go, no terrain into which they could disappear, retreat, withdraw, get new weapons and forces."

The Japanese reconnaissance planes crisscrossed the island for about fifteen minutes, released two bombs, and flew off. Two hours later, at 1:30 p.m., twelve planes appeared, a mixed lot including two four-engine Kawanishi H6K flying boats capable of carrying up to sixty-four troops. The other aircraft were four Zero fighters, four Type 94 reconnaissance bomber biplanes, and two Type 95 seaplanes. They proceeded to bomb and strafe the island for an hour and fifteen minutes, while the Raiders dug in and stayed motionless. Not a single marine was hurt in the attack.

The Japanese lost two planes and some thirty-five to fifty troops who were being brought to the island as reinforcements, according to reports from the natives. The downed planes (one of the four-engine flying boats and one of the smaller Type 95 single-engine seaplanes) landed in the lagoon. The Raiders were more than ready to open fire on them as soon as Carlson gave the order. So many men were shooting at the enemy planes that nobody has ever been quite certain since just who was responsible for what happened next.

Some of the Raiders were armed with 55-caliber "Boys" (named after British captain and small-arms designer H. C. Boys); these were British anti-tank rifles also known as "elephant guns." Others opened up with machine guns. Dean Winters recalled that he fired twenty rounds at the larger plane and more at the smaller one. "They were both knocked out. Everybody was firing at it so I couldn't take any credit for dropping it down, but I know I hit it twenty times."

The small seaplane burst into flames. The big flying boat tried to take off across the lagoon while under fire. It rose about twenty feet above the surface of the water, then dropped nose first and sank. In 2001, Ben Carson said, "That old ship is still there today in the harbor. . . . I have a picture of it taken last year. Parts of it. Tourists are dragging it away now."

Buck Stidham, operating one of the machine guns, recalled in a 1988 interview: "There is no doubt in my mind that it was those guns that set the plane on fire. I fired on the large four-motored plane. 'Transport' Maghakian was standing directly behind me with his binocs and he told me my first shot was low and skipped the water. I aimed at the center of the fuselage. I raised my sight and he said I was in the black. I kept firing until the plane was on the step and about to be airborne."

Calvin Inman was also on a machine gun. "Our light machine guns opened up along with the Boys gun on the four-motor job. It was far away, but we could see our tracers going into the plane. . . . The four-motor job took off and got about twenty feet in the air, then just nose-dived into the ocean. Everyone took credit for the kill." The men agreed that it was one of the best moments of the day for the Raiders.

About three hours later, at 4:30 p.m., an uncounted number of Japanese planes flew over Makin, bombing and strafing the areas where the marines had been earlier but had since vacated. Under orders, the Raiders did not fire back, and no one was hit. "They strafed and bombed us," LeFrancois wrote, "and did everything they could to make us disclose our positions. We were too wary, too sick, or too sleepy to fall for their game."

Around two that afternoon, while the second set of Japanese planes was bombing the island, Private First Class Alexander Donovan, whom Peatross had sent out to find the main body of the Raiders, finally made it to Carlson's command post. He ran toward the post, dodging between the buildings, not wanting to be mistaken for an enemy soldier and shot. He shouted the password "Gung" over and over, as loud as he could. When a Raider finally shouted "Ho" in return, Donovan came out in the open and reported to Carlson.

"I was with Lieutenant Peatross," Donovan said.

"Pete landed!" Carlson said, surprised and pleased to hear that Peatross was safe.

"Yes sir."

"Where is he?"

Donovan pointed south.

"About a mile or so. The current took us. We been ashore since seven o'clock, cutting up Japs no end. We knocked over a small radio station near the trading post. . . . We lost three men. Three good men! We killed over twenty, though, burned the houses, burned a Chevy truck. We heard you firing up here but we couldn't get through. The Japs is between us."

Carlson thanked Donovan for his report and told him to take a rest. Later, while they were on the submarine returning to Pearl Harbor, Carlson told Peatross that hearing the news that he and at least some of his men were still alive had been the high point of his day.

Carlson updated Roosevelt on their situation. It was now eight-and-a-half hours since they had landed on Makin. "We've got another two hours before it's time to get back to the submarines," Carlson said. He noted how high the waves were then and hoped they would calm down before the Raiders had to climb into the flimsy rubber boats. It had been dangerous enough getting to the beach, but returning would be tougher, because they would have to battle the waves instead of riding them in.

"Jimmy," Carlson said. "Let's go up front and take a look"

When they reached the front line, Carlson and Roosevelt decided that the Raiders were in a bad location, surrounded by too much thick underbrush that reduced their field of fire. Roosevelt suggested that at least some of the men be moved to a more open area. Carlson agreed, and he ordered the right end of the line to shift to a more open spot, leaving the left flank in place.

When the Japanese planes came over again at 4:30 p.m., they bombed and strafed where the Raiders had been earlier, an area in which the Japanese on the ground had moved into and occupied. They paid a heavy price for being in the wrong place at the wrong time.

When Peatross found out that Donovan had gotten through the Japanese line and reached Carlson with the news of his unit's location, Peatross hoped Carlson would try to link up their two forces and go on the offensive. Over the years to come, however, Peatross became increasingly critical of Carlson's actions.

"It seemed to us," Peatross wrote in a 2008 article in a popular Marine Corps magazine, "that the main body had an excellent chance to link up with us, and we couldn't understand why they didn't. . . . [W]hy weren't they making some effort to establish contact with us?"

Other postwar critics also faulted Carlson for not displaying more aggressiveness in attacking the Japanese rather than holding the defensive position with his main force, and for failing to make use of Peatross's small unit behind the Japanese line.

One military historian suggested, "It appeared that Carlson, who had proved his courage in Nicaragua, in China, and even on the first day with his complete disdain for enemy bullets, at Makin had become indecisive."

At about three that afternoon, Peatross decided there was little else his outfit could do, since it did not appear it would be joining forces with the main unit. The men set out to destroy everything that might be of use to the Japanese, beginning with a Chevrolet truck with Marine Corps insignia, which the Japanese had captured when they took Wake Island back in December. The truck was loaded with ammunition and supplies, and the men shot the gas tank full of holes, threw a couple of grenades into it, and ran like hell.

They sat through the bombing raid at 4:30 and then moved out to the lagoon. Peatross and Corporal Sam Brown walked out to the end of Stone Pier and saw some Raiders from the main force firing at the wreckage of the patrol boat and the seaplane that had been downed earlier. Peatross and Brown "waved, shouted, whistled, and fired our weapons in the air to attract their attention, which we surely did, but not as we wanted." The Raiders across the lagoon opened fire on them. They missed, but only because the men dashed for cover.

"We were running out of steam," Peatross wrote. "Time was running out, and we still had before us the hike across the island to our boat and the trip back through the surf to the submarines."

There were no more "Banzai" charges on Makin. The battle had settled into a stalemate, with no advances on either side. The fight was carried on by the Japanese primarily by snipers in the trees and moving about in the dense undergrowth.

Peatross wrote later that he believed there were no more than a dozen Japanese soldiers left alive on Makin by midafternoon. Carlson, on the other hand, believed there could still be 80 to 150 Japanese troops still alive. Carlson also believed the story he heard from some natives that thirty-five Japanese troops had landed from the big seaplane before it was destroyed. He was concerned that more reinforcements would arrive by air as long as daylight held. So in the face of a potentially large enemy force, Carlson erred on the side of caution by not ordering his main force to advance.

It turned out that Peatross's estimate was far more accurate, but that small number was concealed and camouflaged so effectively that they kept the main Raider force busy operating in pockets of lone marines or small teams. Each focused on single or a few enemy soldiers who kept them under fire from one concealed spot before quickly and silently moving to another to fire again, thus giving the impression of a larger force.

Private Neal Milligan noted, "In that bush, we didn't know where everybody was at, who was getting hit, or who was hitting who. Everybody was alone at their spot." Ben Carson said in a 2007 interview that each man was "on an individual mission there. It was like that for most of the guys. There was very little integrity of organization. Whatever you could see to shoot at, you shot, as long as it wasn't a Marine. I shot about three clips, sixty rounds. I'm not sure if I hit anything, but we hosed down a lot of trees."

But even without any massed charges, even with so few of the enemy left, Raiders were still getting wounded. "There were quite a few guys that were shot," Dean Winters said, "and I saw several men dead on the ground. It's always hard to see a buddy get killed, but you don't have time to think about it. You have to do your job. But it's something you'll never forget."

At 5:00 p.m., Carlson gave the order to withdraw to the shoreline, leaving a small group of Raiders to provide cover for the men trying to reach the rafts to return to the submarines. "All of a sudden," Ben Carson said, "the word came to withdraw to the beach. I got back near the government house and the sergeant from A Company said, 'OK, you guys that were in Gallagher's squad, you wait here.' To form a protective line. We were going to be the last off the beach. We would be the final protective line."

The original plan had called for the return to the subs to commence from the shore at 7:30 p.m. It would be dark and the tide would be high enough for the rubber boats to clear the reef. The boats were brought out of hiding and carried to the beach. The wounded, who would be the first to leave, were made ready. Everything was proceeding according to plan.

"No one was apprehensive of difficulty in getting through the surf," Carlson wrote in his after-action report. "However, I had failed to take into account the speed of the waves and the rapid succession in which they followed each other. The following hours provided a struggle so intense and so futile that it will forever remain a ghastly nightmare to those who participated."

Ten

Getting Off the Island

B y seven that night, all the surviving Raiders, except for Ben Carson and the others serving as rear guard, were back on the beach. By 7:15, all eighteen rubber boats were arrayed neatly side by side in a line along the shore. The men loaded the wounded into three of the boats and climbed aboard in the dark. At 7:30, they started toward the waiting submarines.

"We walked the boat out to deep water," Colonel Carlson wrote, "and commenced paddling. The motor refused to work. The first three or four rollers were easy to pass. Then came the battle. Paddling rhythmically and furiously for all we were worth, we would get over one roller only to be hit and thrown back by the next before we could gain momentum. The boat filled to the gunwales. We bailed. We got out and swam while pulling the boat, to no avail. We jettisoned the motor. The boat turned over. Our weapons, compass, radio, ammunition were lost."

It was the same up and down the ragged line of rubber boats. Dean Winter's boat capsized "and we lost all of our weapons into the ocean, and I took off all my clothes, that's how I got naked. And there was a line, some guy had a line, so I helped him take a line out into the ocean, through the waves; I was a pretty good swimmer. We went through the waves and out where the water was calm and was trying to tie it to a piece of coral. The man that I was with, he hollered 'shark' and then he screamed and I got back to the beach as quick as possible."

Winters never saw that man again or heard what might have happened to him. But Winters had problems of his own, believing he was the only man who had not made it to the submarines. "I figured I was on the island three thousand miles away from a friendly joint. I had no weapons; I was naked." He walked a few miles up the beach, heard someone firing—at him, he thought. He crawled into some bushes and went to sleep, convinced it was all over for him.

Winters was not the only one sure he was about to be killed or captured. Colonel Carlson and the men in his boat were still trying to break through the pounding surf to reach the submarines. They, too, thought they were alone; that everyone else had reached safety. One man, trying to swim to the *Argonaut* by himself, simply disappeared. Another Raider was swept away by huge waves. "God in heaven!" he was heard to cry out. "What am I doing here!"

Carlson kept his crew working for an hour after they left the beach, until men from other boats swam by and yelled that their boats had turned back. He then gave the order to turn around and head for shore. When he got there, he was surprised to find more than half of the rubber boats on the beach, and the men nearly lifeless from exhaustion. Most of the weapons and supplies were gone.

The wounded Raiders had the worst time. Lieutenant LeFrancois, who had been hit five times and was too weak to paddle, had been tied to a stretcher and placed in a boat, attended by Dr. MacCracken. "Some of the men paddled," LeFrancois wrote later. "Others waded, cutting themselves on coral ridges and often sinking into deep holes in the rocks. They managed to keep the craft pointed out to deep water. Once there, all hands climbed aboard and the oarsmen worked to take the waves head-on. Those waves were anywhere from four to ten feet high."

LeFrancois's boat was washed back to the beach five times. After the last time, he and another wounded man, Gunnery Sergeant

Lawrence Lang, decided they were "dead weights," keeping the rest of the guys from reaching the relative safety of the subs. The two wounded men disembarked and made their way into the undergrowth "to try to get a good night's rest in spite of rain, pain, and worry."

Gunnery Sergeant Norman Lenz had been grazed in the head by a bullet. He was tied to a litter across the stern of one of the boats. The nine-man crew paddled frantically but made little progress. A wave "flipped the boat over and dumped everybody out. Quickly grabbing for their weapons and paddles, some of which were lost, they dragged the boat back to the beach and counted noses.

"Everybody okay? Where's Lenz?"

"'There he is,' someone replied. 'See the poles sticking out of the water?'"

Lenz, bobbing up and down in the water, clinging to one of the poles of his litter, gave a "thumbs up" sign to show he was all right. The others dragged him to the beach, put him in the boat, and launched it again, only to overturn a second time. On the third try they were able to clear the raging surf. They had only four paddles left, but two of the men used the stocks of their rifles to help row the boat toward the dim red light of one of the submarines.

Private Ray Bauml recalled:

> We were so exhausted paddling, yet we kept on. You can't believe when there is danger how you respond to it. The current kept pulling us back, but somehow we made it to the sub.
>
> There were about four of us holding to the side of the sub while the rest of them got Lenz up to the conning tower and down the hatch. I was straining to hold the rubber boat, the sub was going and you were trying to hold the rubber boat close to the sub, all of the sudden, the sub started going uuur-rrrhhhhgggggaaaa. It's diving! And here I'm still out there in the boat. I looked up, and I'm the only guy holding the rubber boat. I heard a guy in the conning tower yell, 'Get your ass up here, we're going down!' I said, 'Holy shit!' I never swore

before I got in the Corps, and I haven't stopped since. I dove
down the hatch, and somebody caught me.

Brian Quirk was also among the lucky ones. The motor on his boat
started right away and kept running. Nevertheless, the crew was struggling because the boat was pushed sideways by every new wave, which
often flipped it over. The men had to climb back aboard each time,
restart the engine, and even then they had to paddle to keep from
being swept back to the beach.

"We got overturned, overturned, overturned," Quirk reported in
2007. "It was frustrating. You started to get a hopeless feeling about
getting off the island; and we knew if we didn't get off, the Japs would
be coming back the next day or the day after. We had no ammunition
now. I had thrown over my gear."

Lieutenant Griffith's boat also made it, but it, too, was tossed several times, dumping men and equipment into the sea. They took off their
wet clothing and slogged through the surf, dragging the boat alongside, until they got past the worst of the waves. One man had been able
to keep hold of his flashlight, and he flashed the universal SOS signal
in the direction of the submarines, but there was no answer. The crew
of the *Nautilus* had seen the signal but was under orders not to
respond lest they give away their position to the enemy.

Private Cletus Smith swam out to sea alone, heading for the subs.
He passed the reef into the open water but was never seen again.
Almost every boat was overturned at least once by the churning waves.
Gear and weapons sank, and some men had shoes and clothes ripped
off by the jagged coral reef, leaving their bodies bloodied.

"Getting off the island the first night was a bitch of the first order,"
Private Bill McCall said. "The outboard motor from our boat was useless, so everyone grabbed a paddle and got out to where the surf was
building up. A huge wave hit us broadside and picked up our boat and
hurled it back to the shore.

"Most of the men were down to their skivvies. I took off my boon-
dockers [Raider boots] and ammo belt and helmet to lighten myself.
. . . [T]ime and time again we tried to get past to where the surf would

build up and to where the sea was somewhat calmer. We knew the two subs were patrolling out there waiting to pick us up. But every time we'd hit the area where the surf was building up, the rollercoaster waves would wash us back to the shore. At about the fifth time we were hit by the surf, I was washed overboard and separated from the boat and crew. I swam back to shore and dug a hole in the sand to keep warm."

Ben Carson and his small rear guard could do nothing to help the floundering men in the rubber boats. Their orders were to stay put until the rest of the Raiders reached the submarines. Carson described the experience as "harrowing." It was heartbreaking to watch his friends' ordeal.

"It got dark," Carson recalled, "and we could see the guys down there trying to get the wounded off. They would put two wounded men across the gunwales of the boat and with four on each side paddling. They would get the boat to [the] surf line and they would come right out and dump everything, including their weapons and the wounded and everything else in the surf. We watched that for about four hours. Finally, we were the only armed people left on the island from the USA with armament that still worked."

Carson watched the boats being overturned and smashed by the huge waves. "Raiders would stick with the wounded and drag them out of the surf back up on the beach. Nowhere could we see a boat drilling its way through that surf, and time after time the boats would wash up on the shore only to be righted by the dumped out crews and the struggle through the surf would begin again. We rearguard Raiders were wondering just how long this thing could go on."

To Private Milligan, the waves appeared to be about eighteen feet high. "It was kind of like being in a football game. You don't know when or who's going to hit you, but you know you're going to get hit." Sergeant Kenneth McCullough said that trying to get off Makin was "the toughest thing I've ever done." And Private Bauml recalled that his muscles ached so much from the paddling, "You could see them about popping out because they were so strained."

The men in the rear guard grew anxious, wondering how they would defend themselves since so many weapons had been lost. What would happen when the sun came up and the Japanese on the island— who knew how many there were—decided to attack? And how would they survive air attacks or attempts to land reinforcements? Would the submarines be able to wait if the men did not get off Makin that night? Their prospects looked increasingly dim.

One group of Raiders reached the submarine with few difficulties. Lieutenant Peatross led his men back across the island to where they had landed that morning. Their rubber boat was where they had stowed it. They pushed aside the palm fronds they had used to camouflage it and poured the remaining gas from the can into the fuel tank.

Peatross looked out to sea, hoping the *Argonaut* was waiting for them. The plan had called for the *Argonaut* to show a small red light and the *Nautilus* a green one. Peatross stood quietly on the beach for about fifteen minutes, observing the timing of the waves. They were coming in much faster than they had trained for back at Barber's Point. Every fifth wave, he noted, was smaller and lower than the others.

He timed it well. As the third wave of the next cycle came rolling in, he told his men to put the boat into the sea. It was 7:30, the time the plan called for them to leave Makin and get aboard the subs. "Wading and pushing until we reached the surf," Peatross wrote in 1995, "we piled in one at a time, grabbed our paddles, and dug in for all we were worth." The engine caught right away, and they sailed out smoothly toward the calmer seas.

"In all of our training," Peatross wrote, "I was the only member of our boat team who had never been thrown out. This time, however, as we were going over the last breaker, my turn came, and I went flying into the foam. Assisted by several pairs of willing hands, and motivated by not a few smirks in the faces behind them, I quickly climbed back into the boat."

Corporal Sam Brown, who was steering the boat, glanced at Peatross, silently questioning him about their direction. "That way,

Sam," Peatross replied, "but if you can't find a submarine, just get me as close as possible to North Carolina." *

Fifteen minutes after they shoved off from the beach, they saw the green light of the *Nautilus* right where it was supposed to be. Peatross and his men climbed aboard and hauled up their rubber boat, weapons, and gear. It was just like their training drill at Barber's Point, except that Peatross was soaking wet.

Commander Haines told Peatross that his crew was the first to reach the sub. Haines also said he had lost radio contact with Colonel Carlson at 10:30 that morning and had heard nothing from him since. Peatross was surprised, but he made his report to Haines. Sipping what he called a "medicinal brandy," however, Peatross relaxed so much that he fell asleep with his head down on the wardroom table.

He awoke some time later when several small boats were seen approaching the *Nautilus*. He went on deck to meet the Raiders and was dismayed at their exhausted condition. "They all looked to be pale shadows of the men I had last seen early that morning, and I knew they had been through a terrible ordeal. This impression was reinforced over the next several minutes as other boats came alongside. If the occupants of the first boat seemed pale shadows of their former selves, these later arrivals looked like nothing less than zombies."

The later arrivals had lost everything—weapons, gear, clothing. Peatross wrote:

> Some had their eyes fixed in a thousand-yard stare and seemed almost catatonic, paddling like automatons. Not a paddle, however, was to be seen; instead, the boat was being propelled by palm fronds and hands. I barely recognized my fellow platoon commander, Lieutenant Joe Griffith. The last time I had seen Joe was the day we embarked [from Pearl Harbor], and in the intervening ten days, he looked like he had aged twenty years.

---

*Peatross was born and raised in Raleigh, North Carolina, and attended North Carolina State College before joining the Marine Corps.

The two submarines continued their watch throughout the night, the crews hoping to sight more boats, but only five more were picked up by the *Nautilus*. Eighty of the Raiders returned safely to the submarines, leaving over 140 missing and unaccounted for. Carlson described it as the "operational low point of the expedition."

By about 11:30 p.m., all further attempts to reach the submarines had ceased. The men were too exhausted from continuously struggling against the surf. "The situation at this point was extremely grave," Carlson wrote four days later in his after-action report. "The battle with the surf had disorganized us and stripped us of our fighting powers. Planes would undoubtedly return at daylight, and it was probable that a landing force would arrive. My plan was to await daylight, move to the north end of the island and attempt to find sufficient outrigger canoes to take us to the submarines. A check showed that 120 men were still on the beach, and there was no assurance that others had not landed at points farther away. Rain and the fact that most of the men had even stripped themselves of their clothes in the surf added to the general misery."

But first they had to survive the night. When the rains came, some of the Raiders clawed out shallow holes along the beach. Others went inland and found shelter in the native villages, where they were often given dry clothing, food, and drink. Private Kenneth Seaton recalled that he was armed with only a knife and one hand grenade, all he had if the Japanese attacked. Others were not much better off. "Someone else had a rifle and another a Tommy gun but most were cold, wet, exhausted, and weaponless," Seaton said. "We were miserable and scared. There were no personal heroics, just an effort to hang on until the next day. We wondered if we would be captured or killed by the expected Jap reinforcements." Sergeant Stidham wrote that the men "bottomed out in the absolute depths of despair on the beach."

Some Raiders, like the wounded Lieutenant LeFrancois and two other injured men, were convinced they were the only marines left on Makin. They spent the night hiding in a grove of trees, planning to search for a boat or canoe in the morning to ferry them to the subs—if the subs were still there.

Colonel Carlson got very little sleep. He was concerned about his continued inability to contact the submarines by radio, and about how long the navy would allow the subs to remain off the coast. If enemy planes flew over in the morning, which seemed likely, the subs would have to submerge. Also, if Commander Haines believed there were no more survivors on the island, he would have no reason to wait and would set out for Pearl Harbor. But Carlson's biggest worry was the fate of his executive officer, James Roosevelt. Carlson was relieved to find him alive, but he, too, was still on the island and not safely aboard a submarine.

Captain Ralph Coyte, one of those left on Makin, later told Peatross that "Carlson was extremely upset by their failure to get away and was particularly concerned that Roosevelt was still on the island. [Carlson] implied that he felt personally responsible for the safety and well-being of the President's son and indicated that he felt that the death of Jimmy Roosevelt might seriously hamper the war effort and was ready to go to any extreme to save him."

But Carlson had other men to look out for as well, and so he paced the beach that night, trying to be positive about their chances of getting out alive. Above all, he had to appear confident.

"Don't say I didn't warn you, boys," he told one group. "I told you it would be tough in the Raiders."

"Gung Ho!" they said in return, trying to sound more chipper than they felt.

"Gung Ho," he replied, "and don't worry. We'll be in Pearl next week this time."

He stopped to talk privately with Coyte, the only company commander remaining. Together they agreed that their highest priority was Roosevelt's safety. They had to somehow make contact with the submarines and get him off the island.

On board the *Nautilus*, Peatross remained concerned about the deplorable condition of the men who had made it off the beach. As late as 10:30 p.m., Commander Haines ordered both subs to stay as close to the beach as possible, in case any more of the Raiders tried to reach them during the night.

Peatross hoped to do more than just wait, so he asked Haines's permission to take ten men back to the island to assist those who might be stranded. Haines refused, arguing that since Japanese reinforcements were unlikely to come during the night, the Raiders on the island were in no danger. They should all wait for sunrise before deciding on a course of action. Agreeing reluctantly but unable to sleep, Peatross went back to see Haines before daybreak to ask permission to go ashore.

"Peat," Haines said, glancing at this watch, "it is now 0450; within the next few hours, the situation will clear itself up. . . . The results are going to be good, too. Before these two submarines leave these waters, we're going to have Carlson and the rest of his Raiders on board."

Ben Carson and the rest of the rear guard heard noise from in front of their position. It was about 11 p.m. "It was darker than the inside of a black cow," Carson said. "We could hear this rustling out in front of us. Finally, over on our right, Jesse Hawkins started shooting and the Japs started shooting back."

Hawkins, a mere ten feet from Carson, had seen eight figures approaching through the brush and trees. He fired at the center of the group, at the same time the Japanese opened up on him. Hawkins was hit twice in the chest; three of the enemy went down, and the rest fled. Carson and some others went after them, but they got away.

Dr. MacCracken examined Hawkins's wounds and saw quickly that he had little chance of surviving. He administered morphine and told him he would be okay. Hawkins said he would be okay once he got to the sub, and then he went to sleep. He turned out to be correct. His buddies were able to take him to the submarine where he could be operated on.

The sudden appearance of the eight Japanese soldiers intensified Carlson's worries about the Raiders' fate. The attack showed that the Japanese on the island were still a significant threat. There might even be sufficient Japanese troops to launch a major assault in such strength as to overpower the weakened, exhausted Raiders.

It was impossible for the men to reach the submarines that night. It would also be risky to attempt to evacuate the island in the morning. They would be vulnerable to Japanese air attack, which would also force the submarines to submerge. The thought of holding out through another day without enough weapons and ammunition, and with enemy reinforcements likely, was daunting. Carlson wondered if there could be any satisfactory way out.

Eleven

Surrender

To the Commanding Officer, Japanese Forces, Makin Island.

Dear Sir:

    I am a member of the American forces now in Makin.

    We have suffered severe casualties and wish to make an end to the bloodshed and bombings.

    We wish to surrender according to the rules of military law and be treated as prisoners of war. We would also like to bury our own dead and care for our wounded.

    There are approximately 60 of us left. We have all voted to surrender.

    I would like to see you personally as soon as possible to prevent future bloodshed and bombing.

That letter was written sometime between midnight and 3:30 a.m., August 18, 1942. According to some accounts, the signature on the letter is illegible, but Lieutenant Peatross contended that it was written at the instigation of Colonel Carlson and signed by the officer he designated to deliver it to the Japanese, twenty-eight-year-old Captain Coyte.

The letter, as well as any other mention of surrender, was kept secret for fifty years. It was finally made public in the United States in 1992 by

Peatross, then a retired major general, in an article in *Leatherneck: Magazine of the Marines*. Peatross discussed the issue in greater detail in his 1995 book, *Bless 'em All: The Raider Marines of World War II*.

Carlson did not mention surrender in his after-action report, and it was forbidden to be discussed by Admiral Nimitz. Private William McCall, who was to play a role in the attempt to deliver the surrender note to the Japanese, told Peatross that Carlson had ordered him not to divulge it to anyone.

Coyte, whose signature was on the note, according to some sources, wrote that Carlson had told him and other officers that Admiral Nimitz "had told him that we should re-write our report [on the Makin raid] deleting all reference to the offer to surrender."

Carlson's biographer, Michael Blankfort, who wrote a detailed account of the colonel's life, made no mention of the surrender note or the meeting at which surrender was agreed upon. Instead, he described a situation in which an unnamed Raider said, hysterically, "Let's surrender! Goddamit. What are we waiting for? Let's find the Japs and surrender!" Blankfort then added that Sergeant Maghakian told the man to shut up and slapped him when he continued to sob and carry on about surrendering. In this version of events, Carlson made no comment and walked away.

Not long after the raid, Samuel Stavisky, a former *Washington Post* reporter turned Marine Corps combat correspondent, interviewed a half dozen wounded Raiders in a San Francisco hospital. In separate interviews they told Stavisky about being present at the meeting at which the decision to surrender was made.

Stavisky knew that after all the praise and glory written about the Makin raid, his story about surrender would never be approved. He realized, so he wrote in 1999, that he "had to accept the unpleasant fact that none of the armed services' censors would or could, let this disturbing account leak out into public knowledge. I didn't give the censors a chance to kill this incredible story. I killed the story myself."

Ben Carson told Peatross about a conversation he overheard between Carlson and Coyte in the submarine on the way back to Pearl Harbor. Carlson told Coyte to "forget about the surrender note. . . . If you want to be a hero you can't talk surrender." Private McCall, who was with Coyte when the surrender note was delivered, told Peatross that "Carlson told me not to say anything about it." In 1999, McCall told Peatross, "There was a tacit agreement between Carlson, Coyte, and I that nothing more be said between us about the surrender note. What's done and said is over with."

Some Raiders continued to believe, and to argue publicly, that Carlson would never have suggested or agreed to a surrender of his men, no matter how desperate their situation. Dean Voight stated in 2007 that "Carlson would never think of [surrender]. Some of the guys thought of it, but I wouldn't surrender. I don't think he would, either. As far as I was concerned, he said he was going to stay and for us to get off. . . . I don't think Carlson would ever have surrendered."

When Sergeant McCullough, in 2007, was asked about the surrender, he said: "I heard about the note about fifty years after the raid. There was no way in hell Carlson would have surrendered with the President's son with us. Carlson would have died defending us."

Private Milligan claimed in 2008 that he never heard that surrender was being considered. "I didn't learn about it until I came back. We didn't know what the officers were planning." Private Bill Nugent said, in 2008, "As far as I know, talking about surrendering never happened. I don't know where that came from. . . . The group I was in, we never heard about it until a lot later."

Reflecting on the offer to surrender some thirty years later, Brian Quirk, who retired as a lieutenant colonel, said he could "see Carlson's side too. It's easy to second-guess him. He didn't know if another 250 Japs had landed on the island. . . . Half of his weapons were lost in the surf, they had no ammunition, and nothing to defend themselves with. I can see why this was an option for him, a course of action. Carlson was certainly not a coward. Believe me, he was one courageous guy."

The origins of the surrender letter are lost in a haze of contradictory testimony, claims and counterclaims, denials, and assertions. Which version of what actually happened has not been resolved in the more than seventy years since the incident. There is not even general agreement about who was present at the midnight meeting that may have led to the writing of the letter. Major Roosevelt insisted that he was at the meeting but denied there was a plan to surrender. In 1976, he wrote, "That night we voted on survival, whether to surrender or try to survive the night and escape when the tide went out in the morning. We voted to stay and try to escape."

Lieutenant Peatross, based on his questioning of Raiders who claimed to be at the meeting, said Roosevelt was not there. "As far as I have been able to determine," Peatross wrote, "and based on my personal impression of his character and what I have heard and read about his relationship with his father, he probably would have objected strongly to being a pretext for surrender, had he been present."

According to Corporal Julius Cotten, some of the Raiders wanted to continue the fight, while others wanted to try for the submarines at first light. A third group, Cotten said, were in favor of surrender. In Cotten's version, Carlson listened to each viewpoint in the democratic spirit that characterized all the Gung Ho meetings. Typically, he did not openly express his personal opinion.

Captain Coyte, who was present and apparently remained in close contact with Carlson that night, recalled that Carlson seemed upset that so many of the Raiders had not been able to get off the island. Cotten remarked that Carlson was "shaken by the recent firefight with the Japanese [when Hawkins was wounded]. He regarded the enemy patrol as proof that the Japanese had landed reinforcements on the island." In addition, Carlson remained concerned about Roosevelt's fate if they were not able to reach the subs in the morning. The remaining Raiders could easily be overrun if the Japanese attacked in force. Carlson could plainly see that his men were exhausted and many no longer were armed. Did he consider the situation to be hopeless, leaving him with only one option? Around three that morning, Carlson told Coyte to make contact with the Japanese commander on the island, "to arrange for the surrender of American troops, providing they would be treated as prisoners of war."

He also told Coyte to take along Private McCall. Ben Carson later wrote that McCall "was a really savvy guy. He said that he was selected as a part of the surrender party because Carlson thought he could speak

Japanese because he lived in the Philippines. He said all he knew was 'Sayonara' [goodbye] and said that was not used in the negotiation."

The two unarmed men went off looking for Japanese soldiers, hoping to avoid being shot on sight. To prove that they carried no weapons, they took off their shirts. They had lost their shoes so were dressed only in pants. It was about three in the morning when they headed inland.

After a short walk, they saw a hut up ahead with a light inside and found a native man, woman, and small child. While McCall asked where they could find the Japanese commander, Coyte lit a cigarette the man had given him. Suddenly a Japanese soldier barged into the hut brandishing a rifle. He seemed angry, but it was not because he found the marines; it was because one of the marines was enjoying a cigarette. Only moments before, the natives had told the Japanese soldier that they did not have any cigarettes.

"He was most unhappy," Coyte recalled. "He kept threatening to shoot me and was sticking the end of the rifle in my stomach. I was so tired and exhausted that it really didn't make much difference. I would push the rifle aside and . . . demand that he take me to his commanding officer."

Finally, with help from the natives, Coyte and McCall calmed down the soldier and got him to agree, albeit reluctantly, to take the surrender note to his commander. The soldier did not say anything more and walked out of the hut. A few minutes later, several shots rang out, and Coyte went outside and saw two Raiders who told him they had just shot a Japanese soldier going the other way.

Coyte assumed that was the messenger and went back to the beach and told Carlson he had been unable to get the message to the Japanese commander.

After the war, however, McCall told Ben Carson quite a different story of what happened that morning.

In his version, the Japanese soldier was a corpsman, or medic, and when he left the hut to take the note to someone of higher authority, Coyte waited about twenty minutes and then headed back to the beach to report to Carlson. McCall, left to himself, decided to try to find a weapon, which he did: a rifle and an ammunition belt he took from several dead Japanese troops.

McCall continued walking around, apparently to see what else he could find. He came across a pit used by the natives to raise taro, a tropical vegetable. In the bottom of the large pit, McCall spotted two Japanese soldiers. He shot both of them with his new rifle, then picked up a pistol from one of them and shot a third soldier who was running away. That turned out to be the corpsman carrying the surrender note. "Bill [McCall] said that was the biggest mistake of his life, not taking that note. When the Japanese came back to Makin and found a non-combatant soldier with a shot in the back and a surrender note, they figured something was funny."

When Japanese reinforcements arrived on the island several days later, they found the note. According to Peatross and other sources, it was read a number of times on the radio broadcasts of Japanese propagandist Tokyo Rose, which were beamed to American forces throughout the Pacific. It was also reputed to be published in "a popular Japanese history," which was never identified.

Meanwhile, on the beach, word of the surrender note was spreading among the marines, and they were not happy about it. "The word started around here that we would surrender in the morning," Mel Spotts said. "This didn't set very good with everyone, but there appeared no choice." Private John Inman said "not many of us accepted the surrender policy," and Ben Carson called it, "The most terrible message I have ever been given."

It was a tough night for those still on Makin and worse for the wounded, left to wonder whether they would reach the subs in time to get medical treatment or would die of their wounds first. Lieutenant LeFrancois was among them; he wrote that the men with him that night were "the most disheartened, forlorn, bloody, ragged, disarmed group of men it has ever been my experience to look upon. Their heads hung low, and despair had frayed their spirits. Only one man, Olan C. Mitchell, of Houston, Texas, had a rifle." The only thing that helped was a bottle of whiskey passed around by Sergeant Maghakian. But it was soon empty.

"Few men enjoyed any sleep back at the beach. They gathered in clusters and huddled near brush one hundred feet from the water and hoped that daylight, should they last until then, would somehow bring newfound optimism."

When Dean Winters awoke before sunrise, alone and naked in his hiding place among the bushes, the first sound he heard was women's laughter. He looked up and saw that "a bunch of native women were standing around where I was at, giggling. I guess they hadn't seen a naked white man. When I got free of the bushes so the women weren't watching me, I knelt and prayed to the Lord. If I ever prayed in my life that was one of them." He believed his prayer was answered. He looked up and saw a native man in a tree motioning for him to get down, apparently to keep from being spotted by Japanese troops. A few minutes later, he approached Winters, "and he gave me three hand grenades, American hand grenades, a pair of Jap skivvies shorts. And he had a coconut shell full of juice of some kind, so I drank that and it had quite a lot of alcohol in it so I was looped a little bit. Then he made me understand that the submarines were still here."

Ben Carson and his rear guard saw the submarines that morning. He had heard during the night that it was every man for himself, news that left him disheartened. But the sight of the subs off the beach gave him hope, even though he knew the fate of so many Raiders who had tried to leave the island the night before. Still, if there was any chance of getting back to Pearl Harbor, Carson thought they should take it.

He knew that the rear guard could not leave its post without Carlson's permission, and so he sent Private Sylvester Kuzniewski to find the colonel and ask him if they could try for the subs. Carlson was amazed to learn that there were still Raiders on Makin who had dry uniforms and weapons. He had thought the rear guard had gotten away the previous night. He also believed, incorrectly, that he was in the last boat to attempt to leave the island.

Carlson quickly gave permission for the rear guard to try to get through the surf. The dozen men with Carson gave their guns and ammunition to those who had lost theirs. Carlson also spread the word that any man who wanted to head for the subs had his permission to go. About fifty Raiders decided to take the chance. Among them was one who had no choice: Carlson ordered Roosevelt to leave. Carlson intended to stay with the wounded. His plan was to move them to the lagoon side of the island, accompanied by the men who chose not to try their luck in the surf. They planned to wait until dark.

James "Jimmy" Roosevelt, President Roosevelt's oldest son and second-in-command during the raid on Makin. (*National Archives*)

Ben Carson and his team of six quickly found out why so many had not been able to reach the submarines. After walking a boat out as far they could into the water, they clung to the rope that encircled it and propelled themselves through the heavy waves using their feet and their free hand. Once they passed the surf, they climbed aboard and started paddling.

The swells were so high that the men could not see the submarines. Some men thought they were lost or that the subs had submerged or moved out. Carson said later that it felt like they were paddling all the way to Southeast Asia. But then they heard the sound of diesel engines and a moment later saw the *Nautilus*. They were able to board at 7:39 a.m. They were welcomed with a shot of brandy and soon fell asleep.

Frank Lawson, Peatross's platoon sergeant, was in another boat leaving the beach. His crew reached the *Nautilus* even earlier than Carson's, at 7:19. Peatross was on deck to greet him.

"What's going on back there?" Peatross asked.

"Lieutenant, everybody's been having a helluva time getting off the beach, and when we left, the Colonel was getting ready to surrender."

"What?" Peatross said, not believing what he just heard. "What are you talking about? Surrender?"

"Yes, sir. The Colonel decided to surrender to the Japs."

Lawson briefed Peatross on the situation and explained why Carlson was talking of surrender. He had the wounded to consider, as well as Roosevelt. Lawson told Peatross that the rear guard had been attacked, and that many Raiders had no weapons or clothing. Peatross went immediately to inform Commander Haines. He asked again that a relief party be sent ashore to rescue those still there.

"Peat," Haines said, "that crusty old boss of yours isn't going to surrender; he's just too tough for that. But I do believe he could use some help, so here's what I want you to do."

Peatross listened to Haines's plan, and then found five Raiders to volunteer to take a boat to the beach. They rounded up all the equipment they would need, including medical supplies, arms, ammunition, and gas cans, and loaded it into the rubber boat Carson had arrived in. The preparations took more than half an hour, and it was not until eight o'clock that they were ready to shove off. Peatross told them to pass on a message, a promise from Haines. "We are going to stay here until we get every living Raider off that island and if we have to, we'll send every able-bodied man ashore, sailors included."

On the beach, Raiders were still trying to find a way off. Among them was Roosevelt, obeying Carlson's order to leave. "I had to lay the law down," Carlson later wrote to the president, "in order to get him to go back to the sub so as to assure that at least one of us would be in position to carry on with the battalion."

But more marines wanted to leave with Roosevelt than the rubber boat had room for, and so several had to cling to the rope that encircled the boat. The waves were strong and high, and the boat tipped over, tossing everyone into the water. Lieutenant Charles Lamb almost drowned, but he was able to help right the boat again. When it was secure, he stayed to assist in pulling the boat away from the shore, then bid goodbye to Roosevelt and made his way back to shore, hoping that Carlson's boat might be less crowded and offer a better chance of reaching one of the subs.

With Roosevelt's boat under way once more, Sergeant Stidham was paddling furiously when he spotted a giant manta ray—"big as a barn door," he said—leaping out of the water about twenty yards away. Others saw it, too. Stidham wrote, "I don't recall anyone uttering a single word but I couldn't help but notice that the rhythm of the paddles picked up a beat or two."

One man, still unidentified, was unable to board Roosevelt's boat after it capsized, so he decided to swim toward the submarines. He had almost reached one safely when the subs had to dive, so he swam all the way back to the beach. Private Herb Oliver also started out swimming. He was also too late to make it to the submerging submarines, and swam all the way back.

Roosevelt's boat reached the *Argonaut* at about eight o'clock, before it submerged. His would be the last group to escape from Makin that morning. Melvin Spotts said, "Getting back aboard the submarine seemed to me as the happiest moment of my life. I was completely worn out. Immediately upon going below the doctor gave me a glass of half alcohol and half water. I went to bed and slept for eight hours."

The rescue boat full of supplies, manned by the five Raider volunteers, headed toward the beach. The men on the shore spotted it immediately and greeted it with waves and shouts. One man in the boat fired a long line toward the beach; another jumped into the water and winched his way to shore using the line. He delivered Commander Haines's message, then hauled himself back to the boat.

And that was the moment when everyone looked up: 8:21 a.m. Japanese planes roared low and fast over the lagoon and across the island toward the submarines, catching the rescue team out in the open. The rubber boat was about two hundred yards away from the *Argonaut*. Roosevelt was on deck, watching its progress, when, over the noise of the diesels, he heard the planes' engines and the subs' klaxons, indicating the ships were preparing to dive. Roosevelt wrote years later, "I pleaded that [the skipper] wait for the last raft, but he said he couldn't. We went under. And we never saw the men from that raft again."

Dean Winters was also caught out in the open. The native who had given him the Japanese shorts, three hand grenades, and some strong alcohol that left him woozy, was rowing him out to the subs in an outrigger canoe. The planes came over, strafing them. Winters dove down into the water as deep as he could to escape the flurry of bullets. When he surfaced, he found that the canoe had been shot to pieces and the man was nowhere in sight. He made it back to shore and realized that escape was now impossible. He vowed to kill as many Japanese as he could with two of the grenades and use the third on himself.

Lieutenant LeFrancois and others watched from shore as the Japanese planes attacked:

> The planes concentrated on the subs. They flew low, hedge-hopping from the lagoon side of the island. The boatload of men in the water away from the sub was strafed and bombed. The submarine was bombed while in its crash dive. A huge geyser of water shot up into the air at the stern of the ship. Someone near me said softly, 'There goes our transportation too.'

Twelve

We Never Saw Them Again

P eatross jumped into the hatch when the klaxon on the *Nautilus* sounded the signal to dive. By 8:25 a.m., four minutes after the planes were spotted, the sub was on its way down. Peatross made his way carefully to the wardroom, trying to keep his balance while the angle of dive increased. When he got there, he saw the sub's diving officer, Lieutenant Tom Hogan, calmly drinking a cup of coffee.

Suddenly, they were plunged into darkness as every light on the boat went out. Hogan ran toward the fuse box, fiddled with something, and the lights came back on. When Hogan returned to the wardroom to pick up his coffee, Peatross asked what would have happened if the lights had not come back on.

"She would have gone straight on down, and down, and down, until CRUNCH," Hogan said, squeezing his hands together tighter and tighter until there was no space left between them."

They stayed submerged for a half hour and resurfaced at 9:01, but were prepared to dive again thirteen minutes later when the sub's radar picked up another flight of aircraft, eleven miles away and approaching fast. Captain Brockman, skipper of the *Nautilus*, waited until the planes were only five miles away before giving the order to dive, taking the boat down to a depth of eighty feet. A few minutes later, the sub was violently shaken by a series of explosions.

An hour after that, while the sub was still submerged, Brockman entered the wardroom, seeming quite casual and calm. Peatross said it felt like they had experienced a close call. Brockman shook his head and said it had not been a problem because the planes had used bombs designed to explode on impact. "Had they been depth charges," he said, "it would have been another story." Peatross did not feel reassured.

Back on Makin, Colonel Carlson and the seventy Raiders still left took stock of their situation. "My duty," he wrote three days later in his after-action report, "was to remain until the last man could be evacuated." Many of the Raiders were speechless after seeing the Japanese planes attack the submarines. "They were all wondering the same thing, but nobody was brave enough to say it aloud. Had the Japanese planes sunk the submarines? If so, they were certainly doomed."

Carlson sent out patrols to discover how many Japanese soldiers were still alive on Makin. Neither Carlson nor anyone else knew the size of the force they might be facing. Until they had that information, they could not plan anything. Carlson told the patrols to gather weapons and food to last them through the day. He also planned to destroy the Japanese radio station, find and bury the American dead, and arrange for evacuation after sunset, assuming the subs had not been sunk.

Word came back quickly from the patrols that they found only three enemy soldiers alive, and the Raiders had quickly disposed of them. The battle for Makin was over; the marines had won. Now all they had to do was get out. Carlson gathered them together for a "Gung Ho" meeting, though he did most of the talking.

He wanted to reassure the men that they were going to be safe and that he had a plan for getting them all to the submarines. Since there were no more Japanese troops on the island, the Raiders could move to the lagoon side, where they would not have to battle the surf and high winds to reach the subs. It would be smooth sailing, he insisted.

Not long after, the Raiders made their way to Government House overlooking the quiet lagoon. The area provided ample water and was a better defensive position in case Japanese reinforcements were sent to Makin during the day. The men dug in as best they could and waited for the long day to end.

While searching for Japanese installations and equipment to destroy, the Raiders set fire to the radio station and up to one thousand barrels of aviation gasoline. "This was fired by shooting into the barrels and using TNT for ignition," Carlson wrote, "On this trip the office of the Japanese Commandant, who had been killed in the battle, was searched and all available papers plus a chart were secured." A count of enemy dead yielded eighty-three bodies, Carlson reported.

They also counted eighteen American dead, not including the five Raider volunteers presumed killed in the morning air attack. And Carlson did not know that seven other marines had been lost while trying to get through the surf to reach the submarines the night before.

The eighteen bodies were laid out together. Carlson turned each man on his back and recited a prayer, one at a time. He had wanted to bury them, but the coral was so tough under the sand that it would have taken an ax to break through it, and they did not have one. Nor did they have a lot of time. Carlson located the native police chief, Joe Miller, and his brother Bill, and asked them to bury the marines inland where proper graves could be dug. He requested that each man be given a Christian burial. Carlson handed Joe Miller fifty dollars, all the money he had.*

Throughout the morning and into the afternoon, more flights of enemy aircraft attacked Makin, bombing and strafing. There were four such attacks all told, the second at 11:00 a.m. In addition to bombing Makin, they also hit some of the other tiny islands nearby. LeFrancois remembered the eleven o'clock raid in particular:

---

*On November, 21, 1943, James Roosevelt returned to Makin with an American occupation outfit. "He sought out [Joe] Miller, who showed him the graves. They had been well cared for. They had little headstones and palm fronds and a few flowers over them. 'It be done,' Miller said."

I was sitting cross-legged in the middle of the floor [of a shack] with several of the boys . . . . One stick of five bombs fell right in line with our shack, and the flimsy structure began to shake as one explosion tore the air in shreds. If there had been a sixth bomb we would have been torn to pieces. The whole terrain around us looked as if it had been blasted clear and swept by a giant broom of concussion. I looked around the shack. We were all scared, and some of the men had folded up into balls.

The Raiders' spirits grew stronger by the afternoon when no Japanese reinforcements had appeared. They grew so relaxed that they started looking for souvenirs to take back with them to remind them of the time they had spent on Makin Island. "In years, if not in experience, they were boys, and like all boys, wanted souvenirs," LeFrancois wrote.

Still weak from his wounds, which had not yet been fully treated, LeFrancois was given more morphine, and he lay down in a hut overlooking the lagoon. Suddenly, Private McCall burst in wearing a blue silk undershirt, which was decidedly not Marine Corps standard issue, along with a Japanese helmet.

"Lieutenant," McCall asked, "how would you like a nice cool quart bottle of Japanese beer?"

"Get out of here, McCall. This is not the time for kidding."

"I ain't kidding and here's the beer."

LeFrancois took a sip, then more, and concluded, "The Nips make a good beer."

Other Raiders looked for souvenirs, particularly weapons and clothes to make up for what they had lost in the surf trying to reach the submarines. Carlson picked up a couple of souvenirs as well, including a Japanese flag he hoped to give to President Roosevelt and a sword intended for Admiral Nimitz.

Before he had escaped from the island the previous night, Mel Spotts had tried to take another kind of remembrance of Makin: pictures. "I had brought a small camera and ten rolls of film with me," he wrote in 1980, "but up until now I had been unable to take any pictures. . . . I shot a few of the [Government] House, shacks, trees, the front lines, wounded men and Jap planes. I had some good ones of the Jap planes but all were lost in the surf when leaving the island."

The most prized souvenirs of all for some Raiders were taken from a pile of sky blue and baby pink Japanese silk underwear. "Soon our raiders were wearing this stuff," LeFrancois wrote, "and they looked like a child's-picture-book-version of a gang of pirates."

Carlson set the departure time for 7:30 that evening, well after sunset. This time they would try a different way of reaching the submarines— not only leaving through the quiet lagoon, but also in a different manner. There were not enough rubber boats left to take all seventy Raiders, including the four stretcher cases. But out in the harbor sat a forty-foot sloop with an auxiliary diesel engine. It looked perfect for getting out to the subs.

Three men, led by Lieutenant Lamb, who had come close to drowning in his attempt to escape the previous night, got into a rowboat and headed out to the sloop. It was 5:00 p.m. When they pulled up alongside, a pistol suddenly appeared in an open porthole and fired. It missed all three marines, and Lamb quickly threw a hand grenade through the porthole. When they climbed aboard a moment later, they found a dead Japanese soldier who had apparently been hiding out aboard the vessel. The grenade had killed him, but it also damaged the sloop, leaving it half full of water.

They would have to use their four remaining boats after all, tied together with two native outrigger canoes to form a makeshift contraption big enough to hold all the marines. Carlson sent a team back across the island to carry and drag their four usable rubber boats over to the lagoon. He then put Lamb in charge of putting together the strange craft, which was dubbed, inevitably, "Lamb's Ark." Captain Coyte was part of Lamb's construction team, along with Corporals Julius Cotten and Howard Gurman.

Lamb's Ark was an ungainly looking affair, with the rubber boats tied together from side to side and the canoes attached at the ends. There was just enough room in it for all seventy Raiders. The four wounded would be placed between the center seats of the rubber boats, lying down. Two outboard motors would be used, but enough paddles were collected so every man could have one. They would need them in such an awkward vessel even if the motors worked for a change.

The *Nautilus* surfaced at 6:10, just after dark. Fifteen minutes later, the *Argonaut* rose to the surface five miles away. Both subs then headed toward their designated positions about a half mile off the reef, the same location to which the Raiders had headed the night before. It was 7:30 by the time they reached their positions, when a lookout on the bridge of the *Nautilus* spotted a blinking light onshore. Commander Haines was relieved to see the light, but he was also wary that it might be a Japanese trick to lure them into a more vulnerable position. He had to be certain it was a Raider flashing that light.

Sergeant McCullough was the only communications man left alive on Makin, and Carlson had told him earlier in the day to stay close to him. Carlson knew that if something happened to the sergeant, they would be out of luck, because no one else knew how to quickly send and receive messages in Morse code.

Carlson had led McCullough and a small patrol back to the ocean side of the island, where they had landed and from which some had made it back to the subs. Carlson glanced at McCullough and pointed to a palm tree, which the sergeant dutifully climbed to get high enough for his signal to be visible out at sea.

"I was in this coconut tree," McCullough said. "I was scared stiff, because I could feel about a dozen Jap rifles aimed right at me. Although we thought we had the place secure, I had been through a lot in the past two days, and was not quite a believer. I also thought the batteries in the light would go dead before I could get the message off."

McCullough's message from Carlson was for the submarines to move to a precise location on the lagoon side of the island and to wait for the Raiders at eleven that night. He flashed it several times, before getting a brief reply that read, "Who?" Haines was still concerned about a possible Japanese trick to lure them to a location where they could be an easy target. He even thought that perhaps Carlson might have been captured and was being tortured to get him to pass along a place where the subs should go so the Japanese could sink them. Haines wanted to ask a question that only Carlson would be able to answer.

Haines wrote that McCullough "requested by blinker the acknowledgment of his request, which I refused to give him until I was satisfied that it was actually Colonel Carlson. . . . The night before we had disembarked the raiders, at supper the Colonel and I had been talking over the fact that my father was a marine officer and had been head of the Adjustment and Inspectors' Department of the Marine Corps. In the course of that conversation we had discussed who had relieved him [Haines's father], and I knew that he would remember this and that if he gave me a prompt reply, I could accept as a fact that it was in effect, he."

Haines kept sending the message asking who had succeeded his father, but McCullough kept repeating the message he had been sending as soon as he read the word "Who?" not getting beyond that. At one point McCullough flashed, "This is Evans." This went on back and forth for several minutes, until McCullough finally stopped sending long enough to receive Haines's full question. Carlson laughed when he heard it and told McCullough to reply, "Squeegie Long." That was the right answer, the nickname of General Long, the man who had replaced his father. The evacuation of Makin was on.

The wounded were carried to Lamb's Ark and placed between the middle seats of the rubber boats. All the other Raiders then took their places and piled their souvenirs at their feet. The strongest paddlers, like Dean Winters, took the front positions in the hope that they would set the pace for the others. They let go the lines holding their makeshift craft to the shore and drifted into the lagoon. It was 8:30.

"Start the motors," Lamb ordered. As LeFrancois described it, "The motors sputtered and stopped and the coxswains cussed under their breaths. We kept our fingers rigidly crossed. Again the motors went 'sput-sput-sput' and 'blup.' We were tense and hardly breathing. All at once there came a steady purr from one motor and then from the other one. It was a sweet sound." But it did not last long.

One of the motors stopped and had to be refueled from the few remaining five-gallon cans. Even in calm water, it was a difficult and time-consuming job. The motor restarted, but neither engine was running at full power, and the heavy raft took a lot of hard paddling to make as much as two knots of speed, even in the lagoon's quiet waters. It took two exhausting hours just to get across the lagoon, and it was past ten by then. They were already a half hour behind schedule in order to make the rendezvous with the submarines. As they headed out into the open sea, the wind and tide and currents slowed them even more.

"Can you imagine," Cotten said in 2008, "being in a rubber boat, with five-to-six-foot seas, in the black of night, and you're two miles away and all you've got to signal was a flashlight? The chances of locating the submarines weren't good. The conning tower rose only fifteen to twenty feet up, and then trying to locate a pinprick light was small." The men at the paddles were getting worn out.

McCullough recalled, "I could see that Carlson was concerned about our slow progress. He was also worried that the Japs had time to get a sub or surface vessel to where we were. Because we were strafed a lot the second day, they knew we were still on the island."

Both submarines had reached their assigned positions by 9:30. Haines ordered signals to be flashed in the direction where the Raiders were supposed to be. There was no response—no return signals, no shouting, no sounds at all beyond the waves and wind. Haines began to wonder if the marines were heading off in the wrong direction, but he did not dare to turn on the subs' powerful searchlights for fear the enemy might still be around looking for them.

Aboard Lamb's Ark, the eight to ten men (no one remembered exactly how many there were) in one of the rubber boats were running out of patience with their tediously slow progress, which was even slower the farther they got out into the open sea. The men in that one boat started asking Carlson to let them cut loose from the raft and try to make it on their own. Carlson refused, arguing that they had a better chance if they stayed together, which meant more hands at the paddles.

The men persisted, however, and finally Carlson gave in and said they could go. "So, they cut loose," McCullough said, "and moved out at a much faster pace. . . . We never saw them again. When we got to the *Nautilus*, we figured they had reached the *Argonaut*. We never knew that we had lost them until we were back in Honolulu." At the end of an interview published in 2006 McCullough said, "I realize that sixty-four years is a long time to remember all of the small details but some things are as vivid as if they had happened yesterday."

The waves got higher and the wind stronger, tossing Lamb's Ark about, breaking some of the lines holding the remaining boats together, and slowing their progress even more. McCullough tried flashing his light in the direction where he thought the subs were supposed to be, but it kept getting dimmer as the battery weakened.

"We hung on to one another and to the raft," LeFrancois wrote. "It pitched and tossed, and the rubber boats groaned as they beat and tore against one another. Lines snapped and were replaced. The current twisted us in the wrong direction, and the oarsmen strained and pulled us back on the right course again. The two big outboard native boats transformed the waves from avalanches into great showers of spray."

At 10:13, observers on the *Nautilus* spotted a tiny brief flash of light. It was McCullough, signaling with his weakening flashlight. The signalman in the conning tower of the *Nautilus* replied, and the Raiders aboard Lamb's Ark cheered and yelled. A few cried. They were going to be saved. They put more power into their rowing, but even with the extra effort, they did not reach the *Nautilus* until 11:08 p.m., almost an hour later, and three hours after they had left the island. Haines took a big chance that there were no enemy ships around and ordered the powerful searchlights to shine on Lamb's Ark.

"Never before or since," Peatross wrote, "have I seen such a motley looking group of humans or such an outlandish looking craft as that which came alongside the *Nautilus* that night. . . . As I watched Carlson come aboard, I was astounded at the change in his appearance. He had always been somewhat lanky, but now he was gaunt—a walking skeleton. In the 43 hours that had passed since I put him aboard the company 'A' boat for the trip to the beach, he seems to have aged at least ten years."

The wounded Raiders were divided between the two submarines, with the most serious cases taken aboard the *Nautilus*, where Dr. MacCracken would treat them. The less serious cases went to the *Argonaut* under the care of Dr. Stigler. LeFrancois was one of those chosen for the *Nautilus*. He remembered sitting in the rubber boat and being blinded by the white light of the searchlights, feeling "utterly dazed; then somebody leaned heavily on my wounded shoulder and I was ready to fight again, this time either friend or foe. I climbed aboard into the hands of [sailors] who got me down the hatch into a clean soft white bunk."

The officers on both submarines moved out of their cabins to make quarters for the wounded, and they emptied out the wardrooms so they could be used as operating rooms; mess tables became operating tables. The sailors and officers took their meals in the crowded passageways, eating their food standing up. Dr. MacCracken spent the next twenty hours performing surgery.

There was no way to get an accurate head count since radio silence was being maintained and so many of the men were not aboard the same submarine they had sailed to Makin on. In addition, no one, not even Carlson, knew how many Raiders were missing in action. But there was no reason to suspect that any men had been left behind on the island.

Most of the Raiders found it hard to calm down once they were back in the subs. Corporal Cotten felt so shaky that he had to hold a cup of coffee in both hands to keep it from spilling. "I think I just let down after I got into the security of the submarine and felt the security of people, the weapons. You're living on adrenalin for so long, it took both hands to get that cup to my mouth. We had only eaten rations, so we were hungry. I found a secluded corner, put my head between my knees, said a prayer. One of my favorites—the 23rd Psalm. By the time I got to the last part, I probably dozed off or something. I had good intentions, anyway."

After a couple of days of peace and quiet aboard the submarines, as well as plenty of good food, the Raiders began to calm down, compare

Evans Carlson, left, and Corporal Edward R. Wygal and First Sergeant C. L. Golasewski, right, aboard the U.S.S. *Nautilus* following the Makin raid. The two marines are holding a captured Japanese pistol and rifle. (*National Archives*)

experiences with one another, and start to wonder what might come next for them. There was even some tension-relieving humor, at the expense of the skipper of the *Nautilus*, Captain Brockman. As Peatross observed, the captain "finally lost his cool—with himself. While flushing the toilet he inadvertently closed the wrong pressure valve and received the full blowback from the toilet bowl all over the fresh, white uniform that he had recently donned. He, of course, was a mess and in a high dither but got no sympathy from his fellow officers."

One Raider, Dean Winters, was delighted to be back to his job as Crapper Copper. "I was sure glad to get back with my toilet," he happily announced in a 2001 interview.

As the submarines got farther away from Makin, some of the Raiders began to rehash elements of the mission, what went right and what went wrong. They knew they had fought well, but they also knew that the raid had come close to being a disaster, and that many of the men now going back to Pearl Harbor could have been killed, or worse, become prisoners of the Japanese.

In 1993, Buck Stidham wrote in the US Marine Raiders Association newsletter, *Raider Patch*, that their "prideful feeling . . . was tempered by the fact the we got ourselves into that predicament in the first place, suffered many more casualties than expected, and ended up losing a large share of our weapons and equipment. In other words, we were not exactly like a whipped dog coming home with his tail between his legs, but we were not at all boastful of how we executed our carefully laid and rehearsed plans."

There were also those, in a minority to be sure, who were less than pleased with Colonel Carlson's performance. No one questioned his personal courage or bravery under fire, but some officers expressed among themselves a degree of disappointment with regard to his over-all leadership on Makin. They were particularly critical of his decision to surrender, especially when there were so few Japanese troops left on the island, suggesting that he had lost his fighting spirit. Such criticisms of Carlson and of the unit's effectiveness in its first battle were expressed quietly among a small portion of the Raiders, and the situation never reached the point of open debate, especially not after the glorious welcome they received at Pearl Harbor. They were all celebrated heroes. Admiral Nimitz himself told them so. And the bands played, and the reporters and photographers crowded around them and would not let them alone on that day of victorious homecoming, or the days to follow. It was hard to hold onto doubts about themselves while being hailed with such praise; the cameras kept clicking and the reporters kept asking them questions about how it felt to be such heroes.

On Wednesday, August 26, 1942, back at Camp Catlin, Carlson delivered a eulogy to those who did not come back from Makin. He stood on the porch of his quarters, with a large American flag on the wall behind him. Admiral Nimitz was there, along with most of his staff and large numbers of reporters and photographers. Carlson's Raiders were still in the headlines. The Pacific Fleet Band played patriotic music as well as hymns, with Carlson and everyone else in the audience singing along. When the music ended, Carlson stood behind a microphone and spoke in a clear, ringing voice, glancing occasionally at the speech he had composed and written down with great care:

"We are gathered here today to honor the memory of our comrades who remain at Makin. Each had his special place among us, and that place is imperishably his. Being human we mourn the loss of each. But I believe that these gallant men who so eagerly, so willingly went forth to meet the enemy would not have us weep and bemoan their passing. They loved life, these comrades of ours. They were vital, eager, thoughtful, realistic. They had convictions even to the point of sacrificing their lives. They believed that if this country of ours is to be saved, the job of saving it belongs to those who enjoy the benefits of our institutions. They didn't ask someone else to perform the task for them. They went out to do it themselves. By their example of self-sacrifice, they have lifted themselves to the supreme heights of human achievement. Rather than having us weep over this achievement, I believe they would have us rejoice with them at the example of courage, of fortitude and nobility of character they have set for us.

"Moreover, they are still with us in spirit. . . . Allard, with his boyish smile, Johnson, with his strange scowl, Jerry Holtom, with his lumbering stride and eager, half embarrassed manner, the others you know the characteristics of each as well as I. Who will say that the spirit of all these men does not remain with us? . . .

"We salute you as comrades. We salute you as Raiders, as Marines, as Americans, as men. . . . God bless you!"

When he finished speaking, he stood straight and still for a moment, saluted the men of his battalion, and quietly left the porch.

Thirteen

To Honor the Souls

The wooden cell was the size of a narrow closet, about six feet long and two feet wide. The prisoner was dazed and beaten when he was thrown into it. "Over his head, was a thatched roof about seven feet up. The only window was a hole, about a foot square in the door. The floor was strewn with gravel, dirt, and wriggling maggots, and the room buzzed with flies and mosquitoes, already beginning to swarm onto him."

There was just enough light to see that someone had meticulously scratched some words in English in the wall above his head. It was July 16, 1943, eleven months after the Makin raid. The prisoner was a young, skinny US Army Air Corps navigator whose B-24 had crashed into the Pacific Ocean in the middle of nowhere. He had drifted for forty-seven days in a life raft with one other survivor of the crash, the pilot of the plane. They had buried the third survivor at sea. The man in the cell was Louis Zamperini, well known for his running at the 1936 Olympics in Berlin. He was a prisoner on the Japanese-held island of Kwajalein, wondering if he was going to live through the day.

Whoever had scratched those words over his head in the cell wanted someone to know who he and the others were and what had happened to them. The message read:

"Nine Marines Marooned on Makin Island, August 18, 1942."

Nine names were listed below it. They were given in alphabetical order, but with no ranks. The list, as Lieutenant Zamperini remembered it, included "Robert Allard, Dallas Cook, Richard Davis, Joseph Gifford, John Kerns, Alden Mattison, Richard Olbert, and Donald Robertson." They were all Carlson's Raiders.

The next day, a Japanese guard looked in the cell and drew his finger across his throat, pointed at the words on the wall, and then at the prisoner. Zamperini knew what the gesture meant. He would be killed in the same way they had been: by beheading. The guard turned out to be only partly right. Zamperini would survive the war. The nine Raiders did not.

"Allard, with his boyish smile," Carlson had said in his eulogy at Camp Catlin. He was certain, as were all the Raiders, that they had left no one behind. Carlson had sent out patrols to check. They had looked all over the small island and found no other marines alive. Carlson would not have left if had he so much as suspected there were still Raiders alive on Makin.

Sergeant McCullough, among other Raiders, strongly agreed. He noted that everyone on the island was told that they would be leaving Makin that second night from the lagoon side. "They weren't left behind," McCullough said in an interview in 2008. "I'll tell you. We were close together, and how could they not know? That's one of the things that really burn me, where they blame Carlson. . . . [T]here is no way one living Marine Raider was left behind on Makin because of negligence, indifference, or incompetence."

Sergeant Allard had been one of the lucky ones who got back to the *Nautilus* on the first night. When Lieutenant Peatross called for volunteers the next day to go back to Makin to help those still there, Allard stepped forward. As the ranking man of the five rescuers, he was in charge when the raft headed toward the island. The last time anyone on land or aboard the submarine ever saw them was when the Japanese planes came over and strafed the raft. Neither Allard nor any of the others aboard it were seen again by the Raiders, and so it was assumed they had all been killed.

The other group no one saw again were those in the rubber boat that broke off from Lamb's Ark in order to head for the submarines on their own. There is no record of their names, no list of who was on which rubber boat. McCullough, among others, suggested that if one or more men pulling the oars on one side of that boat was in better shape or stronger than those on the other side, then their boat could have headed off to the right or the left and missed both submarines that night in the darkness. They could have ended up on the island called Little Makin, only a few miles away. They could also just as easily have rowed out into deep water and been totally lost. It was dark and they had no lights for others to see where they were, and more important, in what direction they were heading.

Brian Quirk remembered that all five of those in the volunteers' boat had been well rested and fed in the previous twenty-four hours. They were also in fine physical shape and excelled at swimming, Quirk said. Not all marines were good swimmers, but these men were, and they could have drifted with the current and the tide and come ashore on Makin at the farthest point from the lagoon side. They would not have known that was where the rest of the Raiders were gathering to try again to reach the submarines that night.

It had been impossible to conduct a head count aboard the submarines, since radio silence was maintained and so many men were returning on a different sub than the one they had sailed to Makin on. Once back at Pearl Harbor, a roll call revealed that eighteen men had been killed, but that twelve Raiders were unaccounted for. It was assumed they had drowned.

The first Japanese reinforcements came to Makin, according to some accounts, on August 20, two days after the main body of Raiders had left. Thirty-three of them landed in the lagoon in a large seaplane. More troops arrived by ship the following day.

Stories differ about how the nine missing Raiders were captured, but they all agree it happened on August 24, six days after the last Raiders left and one day before they were welcomed home as heroes at Pearl Harbor. They had been prisoners for two days when Carlson gave his eulogy. One version of how they were captured was told by Raider Ben Carson in 2001. It was based on what he had heard from other Raiders:

> There was an Italian priest on Little Makin and on the evening of the 18th, these guys [the nine Raiders] wandered up to him and asked him for help. He said there were three Irishmen and a Pollock and the rest of them were Protestants. So he offered supreme unction to the Catholic members and he knew they were all in trouble. He got them a big war canoe. They had nothing to navigate with except the stars, but they were getting away from Makin. The priest stood on the shore and watched the Japanese destroyer intercept them and capture them.

Historian Tripp Wiles conducted extensive research on the missing Raiders and published his results in a book in 2007. Wiles tracked down and quoted from the diary of an island native whose name was George Noran. In his diary, Noran described what he saw on the day the Japanese returned to the island, two days after Carlson and the others got away.

According to Noran's account, "We were surprised when we saw four men in one of the native huts, and when we looked at them they pointed at the plane [the large seaplane that brought Japanese troops to Makin] and made signs with their hands to tell us to come to them. And when we came near to them we saw that they were American soldiers. I wondered how didn't the Japanese soldiers see them; and the Japanese soldiers passed them, about half an hour before us."

Years after the war, Noran and other natives gave different descriptions of how and where the marines were captured. Some told of seeing Japanese soldiers capturing all nine together on Makin, which they said was also witnessed by a French priest. In some versions, the priest arranged for their surrender to the Japanese. Other descriptions support Ben Carson's account of events in which they were captured offshore in a native outrigger as they tried to escape. The elderly priest, who had been in the Gilbert Islands for decades, was Father Pierre Clivaz. Even accounts of the priest's nationality differ, with some remembering him as French and others as Italian. While we will probably never know the true story of how the marines were captured, their fates after that are well documented. On August 30, they were taken by ship to Kwajalein, arriving there on September 2. They were then put in those tiny cells where Louis Zamperini later saw their names.

At first, the Raiders were apparently well treated by the Japanese, who gave them sweets and candies and even medical treatment for some of the men who had severe diarrhea. Some guards joked with the marines about all the wonderful sights they were going to see when they got to Tokyo, which is where the marines had thought they were going to be sent. At least one Japanese officer later claimed (at his war-crimes trial) that he had been "good friends" with the Raiders.

The marines were held for six weeks on Kwajalein, waiting, as far as they knew, for a ship to take them to Japan, where they would be interned. But it was not to be. In early October, the Japanese admiral in command of the Marshall Islands, Vice Admiral Koso Abe, was getting impatient with the continuing delays in shipping the Raiders out. He ordered them to be executed because they had become "an administrative nuisance."

The man Abe ordered to carry out the executions, Captain Yoshio Obara, claimed during his war-crimes trial that he had obeyed his order with reluctance, having protested against it without success. Obara said he had two brothers living in the United States and nephews serving in the American army. Obara chose October 16 as the day for the executions, in honor, he said, of the Yasukuni Shrine Festival, dedicated to all those who had lost their lives fighting for Japan. He later testified that he chose that day "to honor the souls of those executed."

Lejana Lekot was a forty-six-year-old native worker on Kwajalein in 1943. On October 16, he was told by the Japanese to take a table to an isolated spot on the island. He was told he was then free to leave that location, but instead he hid behind some nearby bushes, curious to see what was going to happen there. At 10:00 a.m., he saw a truck arrive with nine Americans and a number of Japanese soldiers. In his testimony at a war-crimes trial in 1946, he referred to the Americans as fliers, because the only Americans he had ever seen in uniform were shot-down fliers. They were actually the Marine Raiders from Makin.

"The Japanese dug holes," Lekot said at the trial, "and placed lumber over the holes. The American fliers were blindfolded and hands were tied. They were ordered to kneel down on the lumber. The Japanese then talked with the fliers and chopped off their heads with a sword. About forty Japanese were present. One Japanese swung the sword. The fliers were then buried. I witnessed the execution and burial of the fliers."

Only one man carried out the executions, and Obara testified that it took about a half hour before the killings came to an end. He also said that some Japanese sailors stood nearby with orders to shoot the Americans in case the beheading was not done skillfully, "in order to prevent the Americans from suffering needlessly."

Apparently, none of the marines had to be shot. Captain Obara went on to say that after the beheadings, he felt as if he had been released from a heavy burden and that he returned to his quarters and drank some whiskey.

Commander Hisakichi Naiki, who was accused of being the executioner, denied any role in the killings, claiming he could never obey such an order. He arrived at the execution site, he said, only after the beheadings were completed, and he saw the nine bodies laid out together in a common grave. Once there, he testified, "I ordered a thin woven straw mat . . . placed over the bodies. . . . They were then covered . . . with dirt and we found some flowers and placed them around the edges of the hole. We prayed for them and . . . made out final farewells and departed."

Admiral Abe, who ordered the beheadings and who claimed he was only following orders, was hanged following his trial. Captain Obara was sentenced to ten years in prison but was given a parole after serving four. Commander Naiki was sentenced to five years but released after three.

The nine Raiders have never been officially identified. Lieutenant Zamperini, who spent so much time in that cell thinking about the names and wondering what the lives of the men had been like, remains uncertain of the exact names. Long years of research have narrowed the list of those missing to the nine believed to have been executed on Kwajalein.

In 2002, Zamperini went along with a National Geographic expedition to Kwajalein to look for artifacts and remains from those days. "I stayed a week," he said, "but had to leave before they discovered anything more than an array of munitions, military artifacts, and bones of Japanese and Marshallese. No Marines." The highly detailed, long-lasting research conducted by historian Tripp Wiles was unable to locate the execution site. He concluded in 2007 that "the whereabouts of the raiders' remains may never be known." No American bodies have ever been recovered.

On Memorial Day 2002, sixty years after the Makin raid, a plaque in honor of the nine Raiders was put in place on Kwajalein. In his book *Forgotten Raiders of '42*, Wiles wrote that a few members of the US Marine Raiders Association "were so outraged that the memorial read, 'The marines were mistakenly left behind,' that they demanded the wording be changed. In response, a new memorial was dedicated on Memorial Day, 2003. It reads, 'The marines were captured following their participation in the 17–18 August 1942 raid on Makin Island.'"

Even six decades later, the Raiders know in their hearts that they would never have knowingly left some of their own behind.

While the nine lost Raiders were on their way to Kwajalein on a Japanese ship, those who made it back from Makin were having the time of their lives at one of the most popular and glamorous hotels in the world. The Royal Hawaiian Hotel overlooking Diamond Head and Waikiki Beach was called "The Pink Palace of the Pacific." It was turned over to the US Navy after Pearl Harbor and used primarily by submarine crews when they returned from their long and dangerous missions in the Pacific.

No Marine or US Army outfit had ever been asked in by the navy until after the Makin raid, when the crews of the *Argonaut* and the *Nautilus* invited the Raiders to come and party with them. And party they did, day and night. Buck Stidham remembered it well. "I was billeted in the same room as Charles Kilgore," he wrote in 1993, "and the pre-war prices were still posted in the room. We were living for free in a room that would have cost the exorbitant sum of $13.50 a day.

"Daily liberty in Waikiki was super, and evenings in the hotel rooms were one continuous party. Those sub sailors seemed to have an inexhaustible supply of torpedo alcohol and the expertise and know-how to refine it." The sailors set up stills all over the hotel, producing a steady supply of booze for a young and thirsty lot. Some men were "happy" the whole time they were there, while others who were not used to drinking so much got sick or passed out completely. Private Bill McCall said in the colorful language of the day, "The party at the Royal Hawaiian Hotel was a humdinger and a peedoodler."

They also played practical jokes and pranks on one another—and on anyone who got close enough. "We changed clothes," Dean Voight, said in 1995. "I went out as a Navy man and he went out as a Marine and my buddy was about 5'7" and I was 6'2" so we looked like a couple of raggedy-assed people. But we got caught, but they didn't do anything to us because they were so proud of us for beating the Japs on Makin Island. It was a lot of fun."

Carlson and the other officers did not spend as much time at the hotel as the enlisted men did. They knew that the Raiders needed to let off steam, and that their presence could prevent them from relaxing completely. The officers did take some of their meals there, however, and Lieutenant Griffith remembered one evening when he, Commander Brockman, Commander Haines, and some others were having a few drinks in the hotel lounge.

Someone asked Haines why he decided to stay close by Makin on the second day, even though he had lost contact with Carlson and so many Raiders had been unable to get to the subs the first night. The submarines would be at greater risk if they stayed a second day, when more Japanese planes, as well as ships, could arrive. The answer, Haines said, was simple.

"I didn't want to go back to the United States, be taken directly to the president, and tell him why I left his son on the island. So we stayed." James Roosevelt's presence not only assured a high level of publicity for the raid, but it saved lives as well.

The publicity continued while the enlisted men were celebrating at the Royal Hawaiian Hotel, and so did the presenting of a large number of medals and awards. Admiral Nimitz's staff was overwhelmed by a mountain of forms to fill out and papers to process for all the awards.

There was one Medal of Honor, awarded posthumously to Sergeant Clyde Thomason, and a staggering twenty-three Navy Crosses, given for extraordinary heroism in combat. The Navy Cross was considered second in importance to the Medal of Honor. Almost all the officers on the Makin raid received Navy Crosses, which led to a degree of quiet resentment on the part of the enlisted men, who did not get nearly as many awards. Before a "Gung Ho" meeting held after getting back to Pearl Harbor, when the enlisted men had assembled but the officers had not yet arrived, Private First Class Clarence Healey walked back and forth in front of the men, yelling like a hawker at a baseball game selling his wares, "Peanuts, popcorn, Navy Crosses."

A few days after getting back to Pearl Harbor, Peatross, newly promoted to captain, was in the middle of a spirited volleyball game when First Sergeant Chester "Ski" Golaszewski came out and stopped the game. Whenever this had happened in the past—when an NCO stopped officers playing—it had meant something really important was about to happen.

"The Colonel wants to see the captain right away," Golaszewski said to Peatross.

Peatross was dressed in scruffy clothes and smelled even worse than the goats back in San Clemente Island. But he decided that it must be something urgent and so he went to battalion headquarters right away. Carlson told him that Nimitz wanted to see Peatross at eleven the next morning, and that a member of the admiral's staff would pick him up an hour before the meeting.

Carlson said he had no idea what it was about, which left Peatross worried, tossing and turning in his sleep that night. He kept wondering if he had committed some error so damning that Nimitz wanted to chew him out. He woke up exhausted and still worried. He was picked up by a lieutenant commander and taken to navy headquarters, where several staff members asked him a series of questions. By now Peatross was worried that Nimitz wanted to question him about the surrender note. And if that was what this meeting was about, why ask him? All he knew was what he had been told by others. He was not even on the island then. What could he possibly tell Nimitz?

As it turned out, all his worry and concern were for nothing. The surrender note was never mentioned. Over coffee served elegantly by a steward, Nimitz talked about the raid and how he thought it had accomplished its purpose. Peatross stayed for twenty minutes and left thinking, "I had never before in my life spent a more pleasant 20 minutes. . . . [T]he meeting with Admiral Chester Nimitz was now the highlight of my young life."

There was one thing Nimitz said to Peatross that morning that did not register at the moment as being very important. At one point, the admiral told the young marine captain about the navy's current operations in the Pacific. He pointed to a small island in the Solomons chain on a huge wall map and said the marines were having some "difficult times" there.

The island was Guadalcanal. In less than a week, Carlson's Raiders would begin a two-month journey there. They would never forget it.

Fourteen

Another One of Those Zero Hours

The party was over. The men had been promised a week in the
Pink Palace of the Pacific, but it was not to be. Sergeant
Golaszewski showed up at the hotel on the afternoon of the third day
and did his best to spread the word that the Raiders' leave had been
canceled. Buses would be outside the front entrance at nine the next
morning to take them all back to Camp Catlin—and the men had better be there.

Not all the Raiders wanted to go back. Who knew when they would
have another chance to have so much fun in such glorious surroundings? And not all of them were in condition to go back. Some were no
longer even at the hotel. They were in jail.

Those who made it out to the buses—most of them under their own
steam, while some had to be helped aboard—were given that day and
the next at Camp Catlin to become marines again. The roll call was
held a little before nine the next morning. The Raiders had pretty
much dried out by then, and every man was accounted for, though not
all of them were present. Several officers, including Captain Peatross,
headed back to Honolulu to get them released from police custody.

Being drunk and disorderly was the usual charge for servicemen on
leave who had had too much to drink, but two of Peatross's men had

the distinction of being charged with stealing a city trolley bus and going joy riding in it. They had been waiting for a bus to take them into town, and when one appeared, they were ready to go, but the driver had other ideas. He stopped, got out of the bus, walked across the street, and went into a grocery store. The two waiting Raiders did not think that was right.

"Apparently," Peatross wrote, "reasoning that, as long as the driver was in the store and the bus was not in use, it would be unpatriotic for two of our nation's finest to be without transportation, so they took the trolley bus for their own personal use. After going about seven miles without mishaps, they were stopped by the police and hauled off to jail. An hour or so after our muster, we managed to get them released, and finally all of Company 'B' was present."

Four days later, on September 6, only eleven days after Carlson delivered his Makin eulogy, the men of the 2nd Marine Raider Battalion boarded the twenty-year-old troop transport USS *Wharton*. It would be their home for the next two weeks. Life aboard a packed troopship in wartime is far from that on a luxury cruise. The quarters are crowded and cramped, and there is little room for training and exercise and trying to keep in shape. The men played cards much of the time, along with checkers and chess; leafed through old, out-of-date magazines; and lined up for the small number of books in the ship's library. For some reason, the book in greatest demand was *Call House Madam*.

It was a boring two weeks at sea after all the excitement of Honolulu, with constant interruptions. "Once again," Peatross said, "there were the familiar shipboard drills: general quarters, abandon ship, man overboard, debarkation, and the routine musters. Also there were 'calls' without number: sick calls, chow calls, church calls, and the ubiquitous 'now hear this' announcements . . . the smoking lamp is out, the smoking lamp is lit . . . sweepers man your brooms, all interrupted with a generous amount of 'be-nos' . . . there will be no movie tonight . . . there will be no skylarking on the quarterdeck . . . there will be no sunbathing on the fantail."

It was a noisy, crowded, foul-smelling, seasick-inducing experience, with one dreary day pretty much the same as the last. Officers seemed to be always nosily coming through the men's quarters day and night with their constant inspections—of the men, their bunks, and their equipment. One of the few breaks in the routine—and it quickly became routine, too—was the daily issue of the two-page newsletter called *Poop Sheet*, their only source of news from the outside world. Or at least what the government thought it was OK for them to read about.

There were stories about what was happening all over the world, but the Raiders quickly came to realize that the major focus day after day was about the fighting on an island called Guadalcanal. It did not take a genius, or an expert navigator, to figure out that the *Wharton* was heading toward that part of the world.

The men already knew that their raid on Makin had been linked to the invasion of Guadalcanal. That had been the reason given for the Makin mission—to serve as a diversion, a feint, to convince the Japanese that American forces might be planning to attack more of their possessions in the hope that this would keep them from sending reinforcements to Guadalcanal.

When the Makin mission was over and the raid became front-page news, Commander Haines told reporters that a huge Japanese force had been on its way to Guadalcanal but had been diverted because of the Makin raid. There was no truth to such a claim, however. In fact, though it was not known for another year, the Makin raid actually led the Japanese to further strengthen parts of the Gilberts, especially an island called Tarawa, ninety miles from Makin. Marines would pay a terrible price to take it, as would be seen first-hand by an officer sent along to observe the invasion: Evans Carlson.

In early September 1942, Carlson and his men were needed right away on Guadalcanal, or so they were told. Marines had landed there on August 7, ten days before the Makin raid. They had gone to that obscure, inhospitable place because of intelligence reports that the Japanese were building an airfield there, from which they could easily threaten, even cut off, the major shipping lanes from the United States to Australia and New Zealand.

Guadalcanal was the first large scale American amphibious assault in the Pacific theater. The invasion was carried out by the 1st Marine Division, with the support of Carlson's biggest rival, Merritt Edson's 1st Marine Raider Battalion. It went well, and within five days, the marines had captured the airfield, which they called Henderson Field in honor of a Marine pilot killed at Midway.

Before long, however, the marines became the ones under siege—by large numbers of determined Japanese reinforcements, almost constant bombardment by Japanese ships, and bombing raids by Japanese planes. In addition, jungle diseases and hunger took their toll on the Americans, who seemed to be barely holding onto a defensive perimeter not far from Henderson Field

The newly reinforced Japanese troops attacked day and night, and by October, two months after the landings, the situation seemed very much in doubt. One of the heroes of the defense was Edson, whose outfit of 880 Raiders held off massive Japanese attacks for two days and one night. Some historians argue that Edson saved the entire Guadalcanal campaign. In the process, he became the newest American hero and was awarded the Medal of Honor for his heroic stand on what came to be called Bloody Ridge and was often referred to as Edson's Ridge. Guadalcanal was getting more press coverage and greater publicity, replacing the raid on Makin, which had quickly become old news. But the situation remained critical, and the marines could still lose the fight.

Reinforcements were needed to save Guadalcanal, and that was why the nearly one thousand men of Carlson's Raiders were steaming southwest from Hawaii at sixteen knots, and learning all they could about how to fight in a jungle.

Carlson's men had never trained in jungle warfare, primarily because they never had a jungle in which to train, at least not the dense tropical kind they would find on Guadalcanal. Neither Carlson nor the other officers had any experience in jungle fighting either. Despite that lack of experience and being on a ship in the middle of the ocean,

Carlson ordered them to get a start in learning about the kind of terrain they were heading for.

The doctors onboard gave lectures on the diseases they could get in jungles, particularly malaria, jaundice, beriberi, and dysentery. They told the Raiders how vital it would be to take those new foul-smelling Atabrine pills every day, even though they would turn their skin yellow. It was their only defense against malaria, which could send a man to a hospital as surely as if he had been shot. Unfortunately, at about that same time, Tokyo Rose was broadcasting to the marines in the Pacific that taking Atabrine would render them sterile. As a result, some men throughout the Pacific refused to take the pills, and they got malaria.

The doctors also warned them not to drink water that had not been purified. Each man had water purification tablets in his kit. They made the water taste awful, but at least they would not get sick from drinking it. The Raiders would also be given lots of immunizations before going into the jungle, against smallpox, yellow fever, typhoid fever, and tetanus.

As to the jungle itself, the Raider officers scoured the ship's library and found two books on jungles in the Philippines and Borneo, along with a couple of issues of *National Geographic* that contained graphic pictures. Based on those skimpy sources, Captain Peatross wrote that "we were able to assemble a few facts, on what we could expect, heavily biased toward the more gruesome aspects of tropical jungles: poisonous snakes and plants, crocodiles and horrible weather—heat, humidity, typhoons, monsoons, and heavy rains that caused flash floods. Even information on the natives was depressing, couched in terms such as 'barbaric,' 'head-hunters,' 'primitive,' and the like."

Not everything the men were told about jungles may have been strictly relevant to Guadalcanal, but the stories certainly got their attention. They did not provide any reason for optimism about the conditions under which they were going to fight.

There was also little reason for optimism about the nature of the enemy, based on what the majority of Raiders who had not gone on the Makin raid were told. They already knew from news reports that their fellow marines on Guadalcanal were having a hard time and were just hanging onto the area around Henderson Field. They also knew that Japanese ships and planes were still pounding the island day and night.

What Captain Peatross and the other officers who had fought on Makin told the men in their shipboard training gave them nothing to cheer about, beyond their motto of "Gung Ho." Nor did a War Department training pamphlet each man was given. Titled *Lessons Learned in the Philippines*, it was based on an analysis of the American defeat and surrender to the Japanese.

According to Peatross, it described the Japanese soldier in fanciful terms as being "the ultimate development of man-the-warrior, signaling his attacks with bird calls and by rapping on lengths of bamboo, demonstrating in one area and attacking in another, speaking flawless English to lure the Americans into the open to provide easy targets for his superior marksmen, and other such rot. The Japanese themselves could not have produced a document better designed to further their cause." Or to lower the morale of the majority of the Raiders who had not yet met the enemy.

The officers and men from the Makin raid tried to dispel the pamphlet's frightening depiction of the power and fighting ability of the Japanese soldier by telling them their own stories of fighting the enemy on Makin. They also tried to be optimistic and upbeat in their presentation, stressing how superior their firepower had been on Makin and pointing out that the Raiders had automatic weapons while the Japanese had fought with only single-bolt-action rifles, firing one shot at a time.

On September 20, after nearly two weeks at sea, the *Wharton* reached the island of Espiritu Santo, meaning "Holy Spirit." It was part of the New Hebrides chain and was the closest American base, just five hundred miles from Guadalcanal. It was from there that reinforcements and supplies were shipped south to join the fighting, but when the Raiders arrived, their new home was still pretty primitive and not exactly a Garden of Eden.

"The flies were terrible, terrible," Lieutenant Robert Burnette wrote about life on Espiritu Santo. "There were dropped coconuts all over the place and that drew the flies. At chow you had to wait to get the flies out of the way to take a bite." Occasionally, a lone Japanese plane would fly over and drop a bomb or two, and some Japanese submarines surfaced offshore and lobbed a few shells onto the island from time to time. It kept the Raiders on their toes, and the officers reported that the men always put more vigor and concentration into their training after each incident.

Colonel Carlson had marched his Raiders off the *Wharton* to their new camp overlooking the harbor, which he called—what else?—Camp Gung Ho. The mess hall was dubbed Coconut Grove because it was built in the middle of an abandoned grove of coconut trees. The official government name for that part of the island was Base Button, and it was being turned into one of the largest military bases in the Pacific theater.

Eventually, a half million troops would be processed there before being dispatched to other islands. The base was also a vast storage facility in which whole "jungles were cleared to make way for miles of stacked munitions." At the end of the war, huge amounts of equipment, mountains of uniforms, tons of rations, and hundreds of cases of Coca-Cola would be disposed of in a vast underwater dump at one end of the island called "the Million Dollar Point."

"The Seabees built a ramp running into the sea and every day Americans drove trucks, jeeps, ambulances, bulldozers, and tractors into the channel locking the wheels and jumping free at the last second. Engine blocks cracked and hissed. Some Seabees wept." It was easier and cheaper to destroy the equipment than to try to take it home. And, besides, the war was over by then, so nobody needed it anymore.

When Carlson's outfit got to Espiritu Santo, the buildup was in its early stages, and conditions were still quite primitive. "Consequently," Peatross wrote, "we lived in pup tents for several days, while literally building Camp Gung Ho from the ground up: clearing brush, pitching tents, and digging ditches. Only when the troops were under canvas did we begin a rigorous training schedule designed to prepare us to operate in the jungle." But even before their new home started to grow, they began losing men, and not to the enemy.

The first cut to Carlson's Raiders came by way of a radio message received aboard the *Wharton* while on its way to Espiritu Santo. It was addressed to Carlson and Edson, and ordered them to detach two officers and twenty-three men from each of their battalions and send them to Samoa, where they would form the nucleus of a new Raider battalion, the 3rd. In a way, it was a compliment to both leaders, for it showed that the Marine Corps seemed to be impressed enough by what Carlson and Edson had accomplished in developing the raider concept to want to start another unit.

Then, on September 29, nine days after they arrived on Espiritu Santo, came the news that a 4th Marine Raider Battalion was to be formed in California. This good news was countered by the devastating announcement that James Roosevelt had been chosen to organize the new outfit. From Carlson on down to the lowest ranks, every man was sorry to see him leave. He had more than proven himself as a leader and a fighter. He had truly become a part of them. In addition, everyone knew how much added luster and recognition his presence brought to the unit.

His loss was also deeply felt on a more personal level: every man in the outfit was losing a good friend and a loyal and helpful companion. "I miss you keenly," Carlson wrote to Roosevelt shortly after he left. "So does the outfit." Platoon Sergeant Rhel Cook said in an interview in 2008 that Roosevelt "was a good man. He was just one of us. The last time I saw him he had tears running down his face because he wanted to go to Guadalcanal so bad."*

All the Raiders were itching to end the seemingly endless days of training and get to Guadalcanal. But one dreary week followed another with only an occasional shell from a Japanese submarine to break the

---

*James Roosevelt served the rest of the war in staff jobs and left active duty in 1945. He remained in the reserves until his retirement in 1959 as a brigadier general. He returned to California and was elected to Congress for six terms, serving from 1955 to 1965. He married four times and had seven children; he died in 1991.

routine and monotony. "We thought we'd never see action again," one unidentified Raider said. "Even the Old Man despaired. He'd come to the Friday night Gung Ho meetings and tell us he had seen Nimitz or [Admiral Richard Kelly] Turner [commanding officer of US naval forces in the Solomons], and that things might cook for us soon. But he'd say it week after week, and still we were doing nothing but train."

Meanwhile, the situation on Guadalcanal did not appear to be much better. On October 16, a reporter in Washington asked Secretary of the Navy Frank Knox if he thought American forces could continue to hold on there. "I certainly hope so and expect so," he replied. "I will not make any predictions. . . . There is a good stiff fight going on. Everybody hopes we can hold on." It was not a very encouraging statement.

Carlson was getting more and more frustrated and feeling that he and his Raiders were being sidelined on Espiritu Santo. His men were more than ready, and he knew that if they just kept training while a major battle continued to be fought five hundred miles away, their morale would sink even lower than it had. In October, Carlson made two trips to Guadalcanal looking for a way to get his men back into the war. He saw General Alexander Vandegrift, who was in command of the marines there, and assured him that his Raiders were trained, eager, and ready for action. But no new orders came.

On October 24, with the situation on Guadalcanal as precarious as it had been, President Roosevelt took action by telling the Joint Chiefs of Staff to send more troops to the island as soon as possible. The president knew the country could not afford another major defeat in the Pacific. There had been too many of those as it was.

Carlson had been on Guadalcanal that week, urging everyone who would talk to him to put his Raiders to use. They were of no help to the war just sitting at Camp Gung Ho on Espiritu Santo. Finally, he got his chance, though it was far from what he wanted. When he returned to Gung Ho, he called a meeting with all of his officers.

He told them that soon, two companies of Raiders, along with Carlson and his staff, would leave for Guadalcanal. The other four companies would remain but should be ready to head out within six hours of receiving notification. The initial group would embark on two

APDs, which were old destroyers dating back to World War I that had been converted to troop transports. The men would land at Aola Bay, about forty miles from the defensive perimeter the 1st Division was still holding around Henderson Field. After landing, their mission was to provide security for a naval construction outfit while it brought ashore the equipment it needed to build another airfield.

There was a sense of disappointment in the air when Carlson made his announcement. The good news was that finally, at least some of them were going to go to Guadalcanal. The bad news, some of which he had not told them yet, was they were not going to make another commando-type raid, as some of them had done at Makin. All they were being asked to do was essentially be bodyguards to a bunch of Seabees.

The other bad news was that only two companies of Raiders, out of the six eager for action, would be going to Guadalcanal. Worse, the plan called for them to stay on Guadalcanal for only one or two days, at which point they would be relieved by an army unit and sail back to Espiritu Santo. It was not much of a mission, but at least it might somehow lead to other opportunities for the entire battalion to get back into the war.

"If Carlson was disappointed at this rather lame assignment," one historian wrote, "he didn't let on. He had gotten his foot in the door at Guadalcanal and for now, that was all that mattered to him."

The two companies of Raiders, 133 men in each, plus Carlson and the more than two dozen men of his headquarters staff, left Espiritu Santo on the last day of October aboard the USS *Manley* and the USS *McKean*. Both ships seemed barely seaworthy to the marines who came on board, and to most of their own crews as well. It was bad enough on the first day in a calm sea, but a big storm hit them on the second day, tossing the ships around like tiny corks, as Private Lowell Bulger described it in 1981. He was aboard the *Manley*:

> The bow plunged under 25 foot waves and doused the entire ship with sea water. . . . Nearly every Marine aboard suffered from mal du mer, that sickness of death called seasickness.

The tiny jam-packed holds were filled solid with deathly ill men who lay in their bunks and vomited in their helmets. . . . The stench was almost overpowering and infected even the 'old salts' of the ship's crew.

Both ships rolled from side to side and were tossed up and down from bow to stern. This was supposed to be the tropics, the men thought, but with the heavy rains and strong winds, it was cold up on the decks where a few of the Raiders went to get away from the stench below. Bulger took off his web belt when he got topside and strapped himself to a locker and stayed there, despite the continuing strong rain and the waves breaking over him. As bad as it was, it was better than being belowdecks.

They were due off the Guadalcanal coast at Aola Bay on November 3, but the storm was still so strong that the landing had to be postponed until the following day. The Raiders were eager to get back on solid ground, but many were also apprehensive about what they might find when they hit the beaches. Were Japanese troops waiting for them, dug in along the jungle line? Could Japanese artillery blow their landing boats out of the water before they even reached the beach? "We had no idea what to expect coming in," Lieutenant Burnette said. "We didn't know if we would get opposition. I thought we might." He was not the only one who thought the Japanese would be meeting them at the beach. Those two companies of Raiders had not been on the Makin raid, so this was their first time landing on enemy territory.

In the wardroom of the *Manley*, Carlson was writing a letter home to his father and sister. "Another one of those zero hours. First Makin. Now somewhere else. Always there is the same suspense—the wondering about the shape events will take when the landing occurs. From the standpoint of pure adventure there is nothing to equal it. . . . Well, the morrow will tell the tale."

The plan for the landing had called for a friendly reception committee composed of Martin Clemens, a British coast watcher; Major John Mather and Sergeant Robert Howard of the Australian Army; and a group of native scouts. They had been waiting since the day before and had lit three bonfires twelve feet high out of logs to indicate to the Raiders where they were supposed to land.

At four o'clock in the pale, predawn light, the marines climbed down cargo nets on the two destroyer transports and jumped into bobbing, thirty-six-foot plywood Higgins landing craft that held thirty-six men each. When each boat was full, the navy coxswain gunned the 225-horsepower diesel engine and headed for shore. As the boats got closer to Aola, the men could clearly see the three large, roaring bonfires, but the sight did not ease their concerns that they might be heading into a trap.

Because of the one-day delay in landing, the Japanese could have spotted the fires, captured or killed the waiting team, and be lining the Raiders up in their sights as the Higgins boats got closer to shore. "We thought we would have to fight our way onto the beach," Private Darrell Loveland said. "Definitely. Sure, we were nervous going in. Sort of like going into a football game, only you're 130 pounds and the guy across the line from you was 230! That kind of fear. We really didn't know what to expect. Some guys said prayers. You could see crosses going, saying 'Hail Marys.'"

As the Higgins boats got closer, the Raiders saw the thick line of jungle just beyond the beach, so thick it looked like a whole army could be hiding in there. No one was waiting for them, as they had been told there would be. The boats came to rest in shallow water, the bow doors opened, and the marines waded onto the shore with fixed bayonets, then ran as fast as they could toward the jungle.

Just then, a husky young man with a fair complexion wearing a tropical shirt and shorts walked out from the tree line to greet them, followed by his feisty little dog, Suinao. It was Clemens, the coast watcher and a former star athlete at Cambridge University.

"I say, what kept you chaps?"

A dapper man wearing an Australian Army uniform walked out of the jungle behind Clemens. This was Major Mather. Behind him was Sergeant Howard. Mather was calmly smoking a pipe and looking amused at the intensity of Carlson's Raiders as they stormed ashore and ran by him heading toward the jungle. As one Raider went by,

Mather asked him what he was looking for. "Nips, of course," the Raider replied. Clemens wrote, "Howard laughed and told him there weren't any for miles around."

While this was going on, Private Loren Foster, known as "Kudge," got a bug in his ear and became the only known casualty of the landing. Private Ervin Kaplan saw him cussing and holding his head while jumping up and down. When he asked Kudge what was wrong, he pointed to his ear and pleaded with Kaplan to help him.

"I made the decision to suffer a great sacrifice," Kaplan wrote in 2000. "We had each prior to the landing been issued a two ounce bottle of medicinal Hennessy brandy. I uncapped the bottle, instructed Kudge to tilt his head and I instilled two drops of the brandy into his ear. The insect exited with great dispatch, and was last seen heading for Mount Mambulo fifty miles away." Perhaps inspired by this experience, Private Kaplan later became Dr. Kaplan.

Carlson met with Clemens and Mather and directed his men to move inland for a mile until they reached the Aola River. The Raiders dug in as best they could and began to get acquainted with a real tropical jungle, which was not at all like what they had seen in popular movies of the day. Ben Carson remembered it as "a crocodile ranch. It was a swamp and there were crocodiles on the island." The swamp was at least two feet deep, smelled putrid, and was full of swarming insects and ugly crawling beasts large and small.

Private Bulger remembered during that first day and night, "drenching rains, eerie jungle noises, huge crawling land crabs, two feet long, tree lizards, crocodiles swimming in the hundreds of rivers, creeks and slews. . . . And millions of insects and voracious mosquitos."

Bulger's outfit was camped along the banks of the river when the men spotted a huge crocodile swimming toward them. Two of the men threw grenades at it and watched them explode beneath the murky water. "We saw no more of that crocodile." They were very happy they were going to stay for only a day.

They were even happier to see the sun come up the next morning. Nobody had shot at them during the night. They had expected the US Army troops to replace them that morning, but the day dragged on, and it was not until one that afternoon when they were finally relieved. Now they would get back on the destroyer transports and have another miserable cruise back to Espiritu Santo, and more monotonous training day after day.

But suddenly everything changed with a note dropped from a small plane. It happened some time during a heavy rain on November 5. No one agrees on the exact time, but they all remember seeing a single-engine US Navy scout plane, perhaps an OS2U Kingfisher, flying back and forth over the beach at Aola Bay as if making sure it was at the right place.

Finally, a signal light blinked from the cockpit of the plane, indicating that it was going to drop a message, which it did. It was from General Vandegrift, announcing that Japanese reinforcements had come ashore between Aola Bay and Henderson Field. He ordered Carlson to head west into the jungle and go behind Japanese lines to scout out the strength of the reinforcements, and to find and destroy another force of Japanese, 150 strong, who had escaped from a trap set for them, and to keep them away from Henderson Field. The two destroyer transports were ordered to get under way immediately and return to Espiritu Santo to bring back three more companies of Raiders.

The Long Patrol was about to begin.

Fifteen

The Long Patrol

"This is a very unusual set of circumstances," Carlson told his Raiders, according to an interview with Frank Duesler, who was a private back then. Carlson was describing the dangers of the coming mission on Guadalcanal, one of them being care for the wounded. Duesler recalled that Carlson said, "We don't have any facilities to take care of you if you get hurt. If you get hurt or sick or wounded, or whatever to the point where you can't stay with us, you have to go on your own. We have to abandon you. There's nothing we can do. We don't have any doctors with us."

Carlson paused for a moment, letting the impact of what he had just said sink in before he continued.

"Now, I'm going to tell you this right now. If you don't want to go in, under the circumstances, you're free to back out and go back to the ship with no penalty, no punishment, no nothing."

Duesler, a radio operator back then, told the man interviewing him in 2002, "And not a single guy switched. We all stayed right there."

That was how one Raider remembered it sixty years later. It would turn out not to be as bad as Carlson had thought. This time no one still alive would be left behind.

The two companies of Raiders were ready to head west into the jungle on the morning of November 6. Going with them were 150 native scouts and bearers under the command of the Australian, Major Mather. Carlson was impressed by the scouts and in his after-action report wrote about the value he placed on them. "Great reliance was placed on these scouts to provide information concerning trails and the location of enemy groups. Their service in this respect was invaluable." Not even the Raiders, with their high level of training and readiness, could have made it through such a large, hostile, unknown jungle without the help of those who lived there.

Private William Douglas Lansford remembered what the long patrol was like from that first morning to the last when he wrote about it in 2007. "Next morning, we started by rolling our horseshoe packs for the march. The night rain had soaked our fires, so there'd be no warm chow. By the time we'd gulped down the cold leftovers, here came Sergeant Major Rudy Teerela, our skinny top kick [first sergeant], followed by Gunnery Sergeant Edgar McMurray, yelling 'E Company! Off your asses and on your feet! We're moving out!'"

Carlson planned for the men to take four days' worth of food in their packs. More would be supplied every four days by a Higgins boat that would make its deliveries at preset points along the coast. Patrols would make their way to those spots every fourth day, accompanied by native bearers who would then carry the food back to the main body. If all went as planned, the Raiders would be supplied enough food to keep them going. If not—if the Japanese intercepted a delivery—then they would have to live off the jungle the way Carlson had taught them.

The single file of Raiders, scouts, and bearers stretched for a mile through the thick tropical growth. The marines quickly learned that the jungle was to be as unforgiving and determined an enemy as the Japanese. They managed to go no more than five miles that first day, not much of a distance for Carlson's men, who were used to going five miles in less than two hours in open country, like the kind they trained in back in California. There, fifty-mile hikes in one day were common, but not on Guadalcanal. At times they could not see more than a few yards ahead of them, and in some places the jungle was so thick that each Raider had to take hold of the man in front of him to avoid getting lost. And often the men at the tail end of the column had a hard time keeping up with the men at the front.

It was tough going. "I was in a machine gun squad," Private Lathrop Gay said in 2008, "and we carried eighty pounds of ammunition. . . . I'll tell you, walking through those rivers and jungles with eighty pounds of that on you, plus your personal gear was a job. The first time we stopped for a break, I sat down. When we had to go again, I couldn't get up. Every time we stopped for a break after that, I'd lean against a tree instead of sitting down."

When the men stopped that first night, during a torrential rain, they fell asleep almost the instant they lay down. Even random shots fired during the night by nervous sentries shooting at noises and random shapes in the darkness failed to awaken them. The jungle was even more formidable than they had expected. And it would get worse in the days to come.

"We who lived through Guadalcanal remember it as a kind of wild fantasy which lasted thirty-one days." So wrote Carlson's biographer after talking with some of the survivors. "First there was the jungle, the Siamese-joined trees, the thickness, the damp, rotting smell, skeins of rootless branches, spider webs of brush tying us up like flies as we passed, the grasping vines. . . . And the jungle noise; the crazy, nameless birds, the cracked grunts of rotting wood breaking and falling, the sharp senseless breaking of a branch in the night when the same sound meant an enemy sniper.

"Day after day, we marched warily among the broken trails, walking as if every piece of earth beneath us had been mined. Five paces ahead was a Raider, five paces behind was another Raider—and all else, everywhere, on top of your head in the trees, underfoot, down at the sides in the screen of brush, in your thighs and back and on your neck that suddenly grew as large as a horse—was the enemy. You held your breath until your chest ached."

Everything the men saw, touched, and walked on was wet, slimy, and slippery, particularly to a man with eighty pounds or more of dead weight hanging on him. Some tripped and went down on the millions of slippery leaves that carpeted the entire floor of the jungle. And those who reached out to grab something for support often took hold of

Elements of the 2nd Marine Raider Battalion along with Solomon Islander guides begin the "Long Patrol" behind Japanese lines on Guadalcanal in November 1942. (*National Archives*)

sharp, razor-like vines and branches that cut deep into their hands and tore away layers of skin. It was like grabbing hold of a piece of barbed wire.

Those lucky enough not to slip on the wet jungle floor and fall were just as likely to trip when their boots came up against the thick, twisted maze of roots sticking up all around the banyan trees. They reached high enough above the ground to hide a Japanese sniper, and in the dark of the jungle they tripped many a Raider.

Some men got caught up in tangles of stiff liana vines that were shaped like fishhooks and were just as sharp. Private Bulger wrote that a Raider who fell or slipped into those kinds of vines was trapped. He "simply could not move and it would require several minutes to free himself and continue. Those vines would rip and tear your face and hands or arm right through our dungarees. These lacerations quickly festered and became a running sore which remained during our stay on Guadalcanal."

Captain Richard Washburn, "Jungle Jim" to his men, remembered a rare bit of humor in a line thrown back at Carlson in the jungle in response to something he once told the Raiders. Carlson "had been giving us one of his lectures—I can't remember where—when someone gave him the so-called perfect squelch. The colonel had just pointed out how we would have to travel from one end of a very thick jungle to the other end.

"'But gentlemen,' he had said, 'it's only twenty-two miles as the crow flies.'

"'Yeah, colonel,' came from the audience, 'but we ain't crows.'

"This broke up the unit; even Carlson laughed. It became somewhat of a catchword in the 2nd Raiders from then on."

They were not laughing, however, on that first day on Guadalcanal. There were too many days and miles yet to cover. It had only just begun.

Conditions were far worse at night. The men's clothes were soaked through with sweat. Canteens were running low. Itches and rashes were starting to spread and torment the marines. The five miles they had covered left even the well-trained Raiders exhausted, and no one knew for certain how many more days and nights they would have to keep going. As they made camp that first night, the sounds of the jungle got even louder, with many strange noises, any of which could be the enemy sneaking up on them in the darkness.

"When you first go out into the jungle," Ben Carson said in 2001, "the first night is just a horror. Because if you have untested people they see stumps that become a whole army and they want to shoot it. The worst thing you can do if you are out behind the enemy line is let them know where you are. We were constantly beating on people who were having hallucinations."

Carson and Private First Class Cyril Matelski dug a foxhole together in the dark, and Carson said he was going to stop digging after having gotten no more than a foot down. "I put my pouch down and the way you survive in the jungle under conditions like that is to get yourself just as miserable as you can and then everything gets better from that point on. I was soaking wet, I hadn't eaten anything for dinner. I lay down in the foxhole. Matelski was going to have the first watch and I was going to have the second. . . . Anyway, I was laying there and the next morning I said that I was going to get rid of that damn rock that had been in the middle of my back all night. I took my pouch and pulled it off and it wasn't a rock, it was a Japanese hand. They had buried people in the taro patch and we had dug and slept right on top of them."

Colonel Carlson made it clear that morning that he was disappointed that they had covered only five miles the previous day. He was determined to do better, and to show them by example that they could cover more distance. He headed out first, with the point platoon, which included two native scouts and which always stayed several hundred yards in advance of the main column. The platoon's job was to locate any signs of enemy activity and, if necessary, take the hit from the Japanese soldiers lying in wait to ambush them. They would then hopefully be able to hold out until the main force rushed forward to outflank the enemy.

Private Bulger was in that twenty-seven-man platoon, and he remembered going through an almost impenetrable rain forest, sending men out to search every trail that led off to either side for a distance of two hundred yards. They found no sign of Japanese activity. Carefully, they made their way through one village in which no sign of any life— not even dogs—could be found. The stillness and quiet were eerie.

By noon, they reached a second empty native village, which their scouts called Reko. The men searched through every grass hut and a large communal building but found no one alive or dead. Suddenly, around noon, Bulger wrote:

> A strange stillness of an ominous and eerie nature raised the hairs on the back on my neck. Even the macaws and myna birds were strangely silent as we conducted the search. The Japanese had shredded English bibles and bibles printed in the Solomon Island dialect and scattered the pages throughout the huts. . . . [T]he native gardens were stripped clean of yams, corn, melons, etc. Papaya trees were cut down and mango trees were bare. Empty Japanese field ration boxes and cigarette packages indicated that the enemy was well supplied

and equipped. We estimated the force to be of an estimated 20 man patrol size from footprints and various signs.

The Raiders were even more soaked through with sweat in the high noon heat and humidity. Carlson posted sentries all around the abandoned village and settled in to wait for the main body to catch up. Those Raiders not on guard duty had the chance to take a bath in the river and try to get their clothes clean, while keeping alert for any signs of crocodiles. One of the native scouts returned to the village carrying a huge pile of ngali nuts, which contained meat that tasted like avocado. It was a rare treat; something that was delicious and did not make them sick.

All in all, it was not a bad day so far, even if the main body of Raiders had still not shown up by 2:00 p.m. Everyone began to wonder what was keeping them when a rifle shot rang out loud and clear. There was no doubt in anyone's mind that it was not a Raider rifle. It was Japanese, and it came from across the Bokokimbo River.

The men dived for cover in the thick brush, and one of them, Private First Class Warren Alger, landed in the middle of a cluster of fishhook-shaped liana vines. "He stopped like a man trying to slide on barbed wire and remained suspended about 3 or 4 feet above ground in a most precarious position. . . . After being trapped for a full ten minutes and cussing for help, we cut him free amidst our laughter at his plight."

While that was going on, the enemy was still firing but not hitting anyone. Carlson ordered his men to cross the river, which they did with the water up to their necks, holding their weapons over their heads. More shots rang out when they were in the middle of the river, unable to return fire. A few of the men turned back, but most kept going, climbing out of the water and starting to run through jungle toward the firing.

They had not gone far when they stumbled into a clearing and saw about a dozen Japanese soldiers busily skinning a dead pig. Both sides were caught by surprise, but the Raiders fired first, killing several of the enemy and then chasing after those who managed to get away into the jungle. One of the native scouts was hit in both arms in the brief firefight but was apparently taken back for treatment by other scouts.

Private Kenneth "Red" Meland Lowell Bulger found a wounded enemy soldier who had been shot in the gut. They hauled him out of the brush, with his intestines dragging along the ground behind him. When they got him to a small open spot along a trail, Carlson knelt down and looked through an oilskin bagful of money and papers that was sewn inside his uniform. He wanted to question the man and sent back to the main force for Ho, one of the two Korean interpreters, but the man died before Ho could get there. Bulger never forgot that scene. "As I stood guard over the wounded man, he kept talking and begging for water which we were forbidden to give any gut-shot man. He was a Sergeant."

Another Raider, Captain John Aspergis, walked around looking at the Japanese dead. "The image of the young soldiers, even though they belonged to the enemy, bothered him. Those boys were individuals with hopes and dreams for the future, much like him. Their ambitions had suddenly ended with a few bullets. But for fate, one of those bodies might just as easily have been his. . . . Aspergis gazed at the fallen enemy for a few moments, then walked away."

The Raiders had not seen Japanese dead before. There would be many more in the days to come, so that the sight would become commonplace and as much a part of the background as the jungle itself. Just something else to see in passing, but nothing to dwell on.

The rest of the outfit caught up with the advance unit as it was getting dark, around 6:00 p.m. They ate generously for a change from the pig the Japanese had been skinning, then spent a sleepless night wondering how many enemy soldiers might be sneaking up on them in the darkness.

The next morning, Carlson sent his men about seven miles to the west, to the village of Binu, which was between two rivers. It was the only village still inhabited by natives between Aola Bay and Henderson Field, their ultimate destination. From Binu, Carlson planned to send out a number of aggressive patrols over the next few days to root out any Japanese in the area, including a new force of fifteen hundred enemy troops who had escaped the main Marine force on Guadalcanal and were thought to be heading to a point not far from Binu. Carlson was determined to intercept them and wipe them out.

The patrols would head out the next day, November 11. The tenth was the 167th birthday of the Marine Corps, a reason for celebration. Another reason was the arrival of three more companies of Raiders from Espiritu Santo. The one remaining company would follow in a few days. For the first time, all the Raiders would fight together as a unit.

Captain Peatross was with the new arrivals. He wrote: "Now we were miles from nowhere, and all we had was what we wore and carried with us. . . . [O]ne set of dungarees we had on, one day's rations (one C-ration plus six 'food' socks of rice, raisins, tea and fatback for use on the trail), one unit of fire, one spare razor blade, 10 feet of quarter-inch rope, and two packages of cigarettes." All that was stashed in their packs along with a blanket roll made from half a pup tent, a poncho for the rain, and a blanket. Then there were their weapons and ammunition, canteens and canteen cups, and first-aid packets.

The first thing the new men noticed that night was the enticing, enchanting aroma of roasting barbecue in the air. The smell led Peatross and his men to the sight of the other Raiders cooking larger pieces of meat than they had seen in some time over hot coals in a small clearing. Peatross asked one of the men what was going on.

"Oh," the man said, "you haven't heard about the pig? The Japs' pig is what they're cooking—insides and outsides, hide, hair, hooves, and all." Welcome to Guadalcanal.

The next day, November 11, was Armistice Day, but there would be no time for commemoration. The men bolted down their chow and waited for orders, sensing that they were going to meet the enemy soon. They did not know that the immensely popular radio announcer Raymond Gram Swing spent part of his Armistice Day remembrance broadcast telling his listeners about Evans Carlson and his Raiders.

He spoke at length about Carlson and how "he was no great shakes as a speaker. He was rather ungainly. His clothes hung awkwardly on

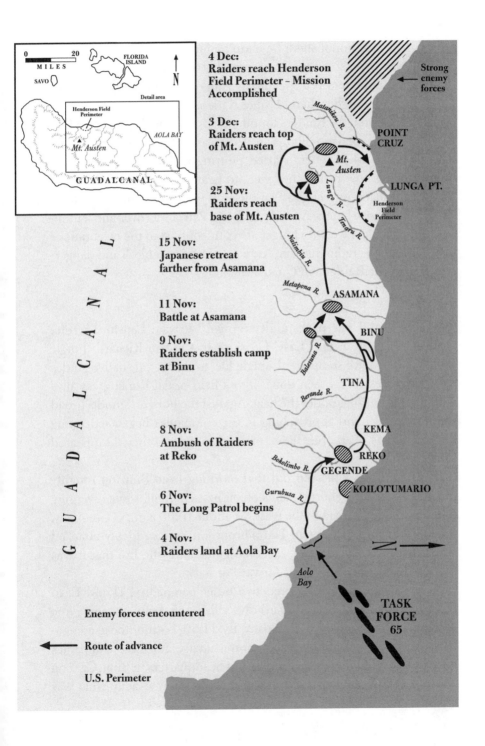

0   20
MILES

FLORIDA ISLAND

SAVO

Detail area

Henderson Field Perimeter

AOLA BAY

Mt. Austen

GUADALCANAL

N

4 Dec:
Raiders reach Henderson
Field Perimeter – Mission
Accomplished

Matanikau R.

Strong
enemy
forces

3 Dec:
Raiders reach top
of Mt. Austen

POINT
CRUZ

Mt.
Austen

Lunga R.

LUNGA PT.

25 Nov:
Raiders reach
base of Mt. Austen

Tenaru R.

Henderson
Field
Perimeter

Nalimbiu R.

15 Nov:
Japanese retreat
farther from Asamana

Metapona R.

ASAMANA

11 Nov:
Battle at Asamana

BINU

9 Nov:
Raiders establish camp
at Binu

Balesuna R.

TINA

Berande R.

8 Nov:
Ambush of Raiders
at Reko

KEMA

Bokolimbo R.

REKO

GEGENDE

6 Nov:
The Long Patrol begins

Gurubusa R.

KOILOTUMARIO

4 Nov:
Raiders land at Aola Bay

Aolo
Bay

N

G U A D A L C A N A L

TASK
FORCE
65

Enemy forces encountered

Route of advance

U.S. Perimeter

him. . . . He was unpolished; he hadn't a mote of histrionic talent, all he had was a personality so sincere that it filled a room." Swing described the Raiders as a "peculiarly American band of commandos. . . . [T]hey are tougher than Marines if there can be such a thing."

Six weeks later, the Raiders found out about Swing's Armistice Day tribute and the praise millions of Americans heard about them that day. That was when letters started pouring in from their folks back home "telling how proud they were to hear Mr. Swing talk about us that way. It made us feel good because we were not being forgotten." By the time those letters arrived, the Long Patrol was over and a number of the Raiders were no longer alive. In contrast to the celebrations broadcast on the radio that day, Armistice Day was a bleak and dangerous one for the Raiders on Guadalcanal.

"We shouldered our packs and weapons," Private Lansford wrote, "and at a sign from our 'Easy' Co skipper, Captain Richard 'Jungle Jim' Washburn, we stepped off, single file, following our native guides up a razorback ridge, then down into a field of tall Kunai grass alive with insects buzzing under the heat. Against the horizon stood a broad stand of jungle, and approaching it, the companies began separating like the fingers of an open hand, moving apart until they disappeared from our sight."

Four companies headed out that morning from Binu on roughly parallel tracks for a short distance, then branched off, some diverging to the north and others to the west. At about 10:00 a.m., C Company, under command of Captain Hal Throneson, was suddenly attacked with such force by mortars, machine guns, and rifle fire that it was pinned down, unable to move forward or back.

Carlson immediately ordered two other companies, D and E, to reverse course and head toward the village of Asamana along the Metapona River to help C Company. By 11:30, both of those companies had also come under heavy mortar attack. All three companies were now just holding their own. Back at headquarters in Binu, Carlson was not getting enough solid information to know exactly what was going on and what he could do about it. But the sounds of heavy fire were clear, and they indicated that the situation was not getting any better for the Raiders and even appeared to have reversed itself.

When the Raiders had left Binu earlier that day, they had been the aggressors, hunting down their prey. The initiative was theirs. Now it looked as if the initiative had shifted to the other side. The Japanese appeared to be doing the hunting, and it sounded as if they were finding their prey.

Carlson was worried. He knew that it would not take long for the Japanese to realize that an organized force of Americans was behind their lines, coming after them with different units moving in different directions. The element of surprise, so vital in any battle, would then be lost, and the Japanese would be even more circumspect in their movements, while no doubt making plans to counterattack. Carlson feared that the day's operation, even the mission as a whole, could be in jeopardy.

As more information came in to headquarters, Carlson learned that one company was falling back, another was too far away to be of any immediate value, and there was no definite news where a third company was. He had to quickly improvise a new plan.

"Hold on," he told his patrols. "Regroup and hold!"

Sixteen

He Knew He Would Die

The Raiders called what happened around Asamana that Armistice Day the "Bloody Plains Battle." It began and ended with Raiders getting hit. C Company was the first to be caught by surprise, and Corporal John D. Bennett was the first man to die. He was leading his squad through a field of kunai grass almost four feet tall when he sensed something ahead and raised his hand, the signal for his men to stop. It also served as a signal for the Japanese to open fire. Machine-gun bullets blew Bennett's chest apart and also killed two other men close by, Larry Spillin and Joe Harrison.

"Man, I never heard so much goddamn firing," Private Pete Arias said. "I couldn't get close enough to the ground. . . . One f-cking machine gun firing didn't sound too f-cking friendly in front of me. Lt. Maitland ordered 'Okay men, let's get up and charge them.'

"Sergeant 'Bull Dog' Evans said, 'Okay, Lieutenant, you get up first and we will follow you.' But that ended any foolish charge talk.

"I was one of those who didn't get the word when everyone withdrew. Happy Sanchez and everybody thought I was killed, but Happy kept saying, 'Nobody can kill that goddamn Mexican.'"

And no one did, that day or any other day through the rest of World War II, and he lived long enough to tell his story on the highly popular Ken Burns PBS series *The War* in 2007.

Others in C Company were not so lucky that day. "The whole platoon got clobbered," said James Van Winkle, who had survived Makin. Six men from his platoon were killed and three wounded, including him. "I got mine after I went back out into that open field to tell Lt. Maitland that our mortars would deliver cover fire. . . . Some snipers lined up on me and I went down just as Sgt. Fye got shot in the cheek of his ass. I was lucky to get out alive."

Private Bulger of C Company was in the 2nd Platoon, which was ordered to move forward and attack the Japanese across a hundred-yard front. "We charged full speed ahead as fast as we could run," he wrote in 1980. They got as far as fifty yards from the end of the field of kunai grass to where the jungle began again, where they were met with mortars and hand grenades and machine-gun fire. "We hit the deck and rolled to the right or left . . . . Bullets whined around us like angry wasps; exploding mortars and grenades showered us with dirt. . . . We knew at once that this was no small enemy patrol. We were in fact facing an enemy force of considerable size."

The order came to fall back. Bulger tried to dodge enemy fire coming at him and the other survivors from no more than 150 feet away. They had to crawl through the sharp grass, making sure they did not leave any wounded behind. Bulger and Corporal John "Sully" Sullivan saw other Raiders getting hit, including Private Woody Greenlee, an ammunition carrier, who got shot in the hip. He was in great pain as he started crawling to the rear. The men of the machine-gun crew to which he had been carrying ammunition were all dead.

Bulger called out to two of his buddies, Private Kenneth Meland and Platoon Sergeant Banks Staley, but got no answer. "The realization that we were alone and that there was no Raider help available to counter the obvious superiority of the enemy position hit John Sullivan and I at the same time. . . . We surmised, in whispers, that the 1st Platoon was badly shot up or wiped out and that my 2nd Platoon was heavily hit and withdrawn from the field."

They and some others stayed in the middle of that field of tall grass for the next three hours, and by 1:00 p.m. decided they had to get out of there. They knew they could not hold out against a new Japanese attack and that their only hope was to try to make it through the field and back to the shelter of a grove of coconut trees. Sullivan fired all the bullets he had left in the general direction of the enemy, and he and Bulger and Private Darrell "Buck" Loveland started "creeping and crawlin'" through the grass a few feet at a time at the hottest part of the day with the boiling sun directly overhead and no shade to shelter them.

"We felt naked as a jaybird and knew that any enemy sniper in a tree could spot our progress through the grass." They kept crawling and eventually caught up to Greenlee, who was nearly delirious from the heat, pain, and loss of blood. They gave him and another wounded Raider, Norman Bauer, some water, but they knew they could not leave Greenlee there. They had to take him along with them. Bauer could still make it on his own.

"'Let's stand up,' Bulger said, 'and carry Greenlee out between us!' We were still within easy range of under 200 yards but by that time we simply didn't give a damn. We simply stood up and walked out . . . as we carried Greenlee between us." The Japanese fired a few mortar rounds, but the one that hit the closest failed to explode, and the others were too far away to do any harm. The Raiders made it to the coconut trees, where medics came out to help them. They had saved Greenlee's life.

At about the same time, Carlson showed up to find out what the problem was. He took a quick look at the situation and called in an air strike against the Japanese position. He told Bulger and Loveland to make a white arrow pointing to the enemy line to direct the planes. They gathered up twenty white T-shirts and put them in a line with an arrow-like tip pointing toward the Japanese front. Ten minutes later, six planes from Henderson Field flew over and bombed and strafed the Japanese.

Bulger then led five other Raiders back over the Bloody Plains battlefield looking for wounded. They would find out the next day to their horror that two men had not been found. They would never forget what had happened to one of them.

Carlson was not happy with the situation, and with the C Company commander, Captain Throneson, who had survived the battle. "I found 'C' Company in a bad state of disorganization," Carlson wrote a month later in his after-action report. "The Company Commander appeared to be in a daze. His CP [Command Post] was nearly a mile behind the fighting line. Moving with him to the front he indicated what had happened."

Carlson concluded that after Company C's forward movement had been stopped by heavy Japanese fire, Throneson had done little more than direct his own mortars to fire back, and that his command of the operation, or lack of command, was responsible for the failure to advance as well as the loss of five killed and three wounded.

While C Company was under attack and forced to pull back, E Company, under the command of Captain Washburn, radioed Carlson at 11:30 a.m. that his outfit had also come under a mortar attack but was holding its own in the jungle along the east bank of the Metapona River. Carlson ordered him to advance toward the village of Asamana and hit the Japanese force that was beating back C Company from the rear.

"Like a Civil War outfit, we rode to the sound of the guns," wrote Lieutenant Cleland Early, one of E Company's platoon leaders. Private Lansford remembered that time in somewhat less romantic terms:

> For us, time had lost all meaning. Endlessly we kept running, sweat-soaked, gasping for air, our senses reeling. Twice the column halted while Sgt. Maj. Jacob Vouza, head of the native constabulary, and his scouts went on ahead. We didn't know what was happening. People kept yelling for us to move faster. As Raiders, we were trained to carry abnormally heavy loads of ammo and to work under pressure, but nothing had prepared us for this nightmare.

Lansford and the others heard Japanese machine guns firing up ahead, along with answering fire from BARs. Mortar shells began exploding in the treetops over their heads, showering them with steel and wood fragments. They ran even faster than they had before, and miraculously no one was hit.

"Like a mile-long snake," Lansford wrote, "Co E wound and twist-ed through the jungle, following the Metapona River. Swollen by three nights of rain, its brown waters engulfed us as we slid in. Every Raider carried a 10-foot rope, so the lead squad tied itself together to steady us against the current." *

The 1st Platoon was the first outfit to get across the Metapona and approach the village of Asamana, which was nothing more than a few huts along the riverbank. The platoon's commander was 1st Lieutenant Evans Carlson Jr., the colonel's son. Two of his enlisted men, Corporal Fred Bobb and Private Robert Wilinski, moved for-ward with great stealth to check out the huts. Inside the first one, they found four Japanese soldiers sound asleep.

At the same time, Lieutenant Carlson's Raiders heard the sound of men laughing and splashing in the river nearby. They were Japanese troops as well, naked and having a good time washing themselves in the brown water. There were a great many of them, and they were unaware of the Americans watching them.

"For the Japanese," an editor of *Leatherneck Magazine* wrote, "bathing is more than a cleansing of the body, it is a social ritual of pleasure and relaxation. It must have been too tempting even for offi-cers and noncommissioned officers who should have known better, but those men, too, were naked in the water, temporarily forgetting about the horrors of war. Even their pickets were too busy watching the bathers to hear [Lieutenant] Carlson's men silently surround them.

"The last sounds they heard were the explosions of grenades, the slap of bullets, and their own screams. The massacre turned the river red in less than a few minutes. No one survived and the 120 bodies, white except for their infantrymen's tans, dotted the shore line or drift-ed pathetically on the water."

At the same instant, Private Wilinski opened fire inside the hut and

*William Lansford survived World War II and served as a captain in the Korean War, after which he became a writer in Hollywood. He wrote movies and episodes of pop-ular TV series, including *Star Trek: The Next Generation*, *Starsky and Hutch*, *Ironside*, and *The Virginian*.

killed the four sleeping Japanese soldiers. It was a smashing victory, but other Japanese troops a short distance from the riverbank opened up with mortars and machine guns and moved forward through the dense jungle to try to outflank the Raiders. Lieutenant Carlson sized up the situation in an instant, just as his father would have done, and ordered his men back to form a tighter defensive line.*

Lieutenant Early's platoon caught the Japanese as they were trying to cross the river upstream, holding their clothes and weapons high over their heads. "They were rightfully surprised when we opened up on them," he said. "We practically annihilated them."

The battle around Asamana lasted about six hours, with each side attacking then falling back and trying to outflank the other again and again. Captain Washburn's headquarters was in a shallow hole covered with branches, vines, and brush. It was no protection against the almost constant stream of mortar rounds the Japanese let loose, but at least they were protected from snipers who could not see them under-cover.

For the last several hours, Washburn's radioman, Ervin Kaplan, had been unable to get through to Colonel Carlson, so Washburn had to keep fighting on his own without any help or advice. By five that after-noon, "they still held Asamana. But our company had paid a toll," William Douglas Lansford wrote. "We were exhausted, our canteens were empty, and we were almost out of ammunition. . . . [A]s the sun set, we could see large groups of Japanese infantrymen closing in around us. In minutes, we'd be trapped against the riverbank in the dark." He continued:

> Then I saw something I'll always remember. It was [Private Art] Monte, between two Raiders, bloody, his helmet askew,

*Evans Carlson Jr. was awarded a Silver Star for his actions at the battle of Asamana. After World War II, he became a pilot and won a second Silver Star for bravery in the air during the Korean War. He retired from the Marine Corps in 1967 as a colonel and died in 2005.

but still defiant with a pistol in his hand. Wounded by a sniper, Monte had pulled the backplate off his jammed machine gun, kicked the gun into the river and crawled under a bush from where he watched hundreds of Japanese moving in. Seeing us withdrawing, he'd jumped up yelling, attracting the Raiders who went back to help him. They were the last Raiders out. By then Asamana was crawling with Japanese. But we were gone.

Washburn, still unable to reach Colonel Carlson by radio, decided to withdraw. Continuing to hold out against far superior numbers while running out of ammunition could have only one outcome, he believed: E Company would be wiped out. Washburn made the right call.

To escape the Japanese, his men had to go single file through a narrow gully and then follow a trail to the north. Washburn knew they had to leave a rear guard behind to keep the Japanese from storming into the gully right behind them. The job went to a twenty-year-old machine gunner, Private Joseph Martin Auman, of Chicago.

"He knew he would die," a friend said later, but he stayed at his post and kept firing his machine gun until he was killed. He was awarded the Navy Cross posthumously, and a US Navy APD, the same kind of modified destroyer/troop transport that had brought them to Guadalcanal, was commissioned in 1945 and named for him.

When Washburn brought E Company back to headquarters, having killed at least 160 Japanese and saved most of his men, Carlson was so pleased with his performance under fire that he promoted him to major. "He used his head," Carlson later told a reporter for *Time* magazine. "I promoted him on the spot and it was good for morale because every man in the company knew that Washburn deserved it."

D Company, under the command of Captain Charles McAuliffe, fared much worse. It was actually only a platoon in numbers, because Colonel Carlson had taken many of its men to replace those in other companies that had lost them when they were sent from Espiritu Santo to form new Raider battalions.

D Company was hit heavily at around 11:30 that morning by mortar and machine-gun fire. McAuliffe had been out in front of the main body, leading the thirteen-man point squad. When the attack began, he and the others with him were cut off from the rest of the unit, which was about one hundred yards behind. McAuliffe and the ones with him held on for about two hours but heard nothing from the rest of the company, and so assumed it had been wiped out. He had lost two men killed and four wounded by then, and decided to retreat to Carlson's headquarters at Binu.

One of McAuliffe's squad leaders, Sergeant Hubert D. Faltyn, wrote, "Finally, the word was passed to 'get the hell out of here' and we did just that." Unfortunately, the men in D Company had already separated into two sections and gone in two different directions. The main body went back to the coconut grove where they had started out that morning; Captain McAuliffe and those with him headed off another way and promptly got lost.

Every way he and his men tried to go, they ran into more Japanese machine-gun fire. It looked like the Japanese were succeeding in encircling them. "Finally, in desperation," Corporal James Davis wrote, "he turned to his native scout and said, 'Take me to your home in the mountains,' and though they were continuously under fire, the scout safely led the balance of the patrol out towards the hills."

Once they were safe from the Japanese, the patrol of D Company was able to find its way back to Binu. Captain Peatross, stationed at an outpost forward of headquarters, saw them coming in. He wrote in 1995 that he was "amazed at how haggard and battle weary they looked. To a man they reminded me of the Raiders we had picked up at the mouth of the lagoon on the second night of the Makin raid."

Peatross walked along with McAuliffe to see Colonel Carlson and stayed while McAuliffe made his report. McAuliffe told Carlson that he and the nine others who made it back with him were the only survivors of D Company, that all the others were dead. "Although Carlson usually did not let his features show, now his face flushed, and I could see that he was angry," Peatross wrote. "However, he calmly asked McAuliffe for the last known location of the company and, turning to me, directed that I take a platoon to that area and search for the survivors."

Peatross assembled one of his platoons, briefed the men on their mission, and headed out, with McAuliffe in tow. They had not gotten far, no more than a few yards from their forward outpost, when they ran into the rest of D Company, very much intact and led by Gunnery Sergeant George Schrier. They had carefully buried their two dead buddies and brought out their wounded with them.

Peatross brought the shaken McAuliffe back to Carlson to tell him what they had found. John Mather, the Australian officer and head of the native scouts, described McAuliffe as looking "quite hysterical and exhausted. . . . I formed the opinion that this particular officer had no idea of what he should have done. . . . He certainly did not appreciate the enormity of his offense in abandoning a portion of his force whilst engaging with the enemy."

Carlson was visibly angry with McAuliffe, as he had been earlier with Captain Throneson of C Company, and both men met the same fate. Carlson wrote in his after-action report that he relieved both men "for incompetency. Both had displayed total ineptitude for leadership in battle, and both were so badly shaken by their experience as to be incapable of commanding my confidence or that of their men."

Captain William Schwerin, known to his men as "Wild Bill," led F Company north out of Binu that morning. By 11:30, they heard the sound of mortar shells exploding and machine guns firing in the distance. Carlson sent orders for F Company to reverse course and return as quickly as possible to Binu. When it got back after an exhausting three-hour run, Carlson told the men to rest and eat while he made plans for them.

"Wild Bill" Schwerin had been given his nickname for a good reason. He "was as impulsive as Washburn was prudent, as reckless as Washburn was careful. He was a brawler, a boozer, and often a pain in the ass. But Washburn and Schwerin shared one undisputable trait: Both were courageous and inspired leaders." Schwerin also wore two ivory-handled revolvers, just like General George Patton.

In early afternoon, just after Captain McAuliffe came back to Binu with only nine of his men, Carlson ordered Schwerin to assemble his Raiders. After hearing McAuliffe's report, Carlson ordered Schwerin and his men on an extended patrol through the area where C Company had been attacked. They quickly discovered that the Japanese had left the area and were no longer an immediate threat. Carlson went to Asamana and told Schwerin to form a defensive line around the village, while he and others combed through the area searching for Raiders who had been killed to give them proper burials.

The search continued the next day, November 12, when they discovered a body, the condition of which shocked and angered them all. They had never seen anything like it. Then they found another Raider, Private First Class James Clusker, wounded but still alive, and he told them what had happened.

Clusker had been hiding in tall kunai grass since being hit the previous day. He spent most of the time unconscious but came to after dark. When he regained consciousness, he involuntarily gave a little cry of pain. Immediately after that, he heard voices calling out to him, "Over here, Yankee, over here."

Even in his dazed condition, he recognized that no Raider would call out like that in the jungle, or anywhere else. He burrowed down deep in the grass and tried not to make a sound as Japanese troops searched the field for him. They came as close as five yards, but they did not find him. They did, however, find another wounded Raider not far away and tortured him for hours while Clusker lay nearby, unable to do anything to stop it. Finally, the screaming ceased and the jungle lay silent.

The next day, Raiders found "the disfigured, mistreated corpse of Private Owen Barber. His face was slashed horribly, and his testicles had been cut off and shoved into his mouth. . . . [T]he tortured form of Private Barber had a transformative effect on the Raiders. They knew what to expect if captured and most resolved not to take prisoners themselves anymore."

"I remember seeing him there," Private Lathrop Gay said in 2008. "He was a young fellow. I think only seventeen. That made us decide,

OK, no prisoners. We really didn't have a chance to catch that many before, but after this. . . ."

The Raiders had two Japanese prisoners who had been taken earlier back at headquarters at Binu. When Carlson returned there after seeing Barber's mangled body, he asked some Raiders nearby if any of them had lost a buddy in the fighting the day before. "When a few raised their hands, Carlson pointed to the prisoners and told them to take care of them The men led the prisoners into the jungle, killed them, and left their lifeless bodies to rot in Guadalcanal's heat."

Carlson later told Jim Lucas, a Marine Corps combat correspondent, "We never take a prisoner. That's not our job. I tell my men to kill every Jap they meet—lame, halt, and well."

Seventeen

Pale Ghosts

The native scouts did not take prisoners. They killed every Japanese they found, using knives, swords, and machetes, as well as rifles they took from the dead. The Raiders had been fighting the Japanese on Guadalcanal for only two weeks, but the natives had been at war with them for six months, ever since they brutally occupied the Solomon Islands in May.

"The natives hated the Japanese," Lowell Bulger wrote, "and were 100 percent loyal to their British Government and the American Marines. . . . Any stray Jap was killed." And with good reason. They had plundered native villages, molested and raped the women and some children, commandeered pigs and chickens, and stripped their food gardens bare. Instead of climbing up papaya trees to get the fruit, they cut the trees down, leaving nothing for the local population. By the time the Raiders went into the jungle, most of the villages had been abandoned, and the women, children, and elderly had fled into the mountains.

Many of the younger men stayed behind, and when the Americans came—first with the invasion in August, then the landing of the Raiders in November—they did everything they could to help. It was their way of fighting back against their hated occupiers. The Long Patrol might not have succeeded as well as it did, or perhaps not at all, without the help of the local scouts and bearers.

The most courageous, and a loyal friend of the marines until his death more than forty years later, was retired forty-two-year-old Sergeant Major Jacob Charles Vouza of the Solomon Island Protectorate Armed Constabulary. He had been a policeman from age sixteen until he retired in 1940. But after the Japanese came, and his four younger children died of disease and malnutrition, he sent his wife and two remaining children into hiding in the mountains. And when the Americans came, Vouza went to war.

He was in charge of Carlson's native scouts, under the command of the Australian army major, John Mather, who understood the native language and served as interpreter for the Raiders. Vouza was a scout for the marines who landed in Guadalcanal in August and had been fighting ever since. One marine had been so impressed with Vouza and grateful for his help that he gave him a tiny American flag, which nearly got him killed.

Vouza was stopped one day by a Japanese patrol. When they found the flag, Vouza was taken to Colonel Ichiki Ishimoto for interrogation. Where were the Americans? Vouza was asked. When he refused to answer, the Japanese tied him to a tree in the sun and beat and tortured him over several hours, but he revealed nothing. "The soldiers smashed his face with rifle butts, slashed him with a sword, and made him lie on a nest of red ants; still he did not answer. They then hung him in a tree until he passed out from wounds and exposure. At dusk, they took him down, tied his wrists, and . . . bayoneted him repeatedly and left him for dead." Years later, Vouza said about his refusal to tell the Japanese the location of the marines, "Better me die plenty than give Solomon Islands to Japan."

Miraculously, Vouza lived, and he crawled through the jungle for almost three miles before reaching American lines. Martin Clemens, the coast watcher, was one of the first people to see him, and he said, "He was an awful mess, and unable to sit up. I could hardly bear to look at him."

Vouza expected to die, but he managed to give vital information on a pending Japanese attack and to dictate to Clemens a message of farewell to his wife and children. Clemens wrote it down using only one hand while holding one of Vouza's hands with his other. After getting a massive blood transfusion and having his wounds treated, Vouza reported back for duty twelve days later and went on to prove himself invaluable to Carlson's Long Patrol.

Vouza was awarded the Silver Star for his refusal to reveal information about American positions under torture. The medal was presented to him by then-Brigadier General Vandegrift. He also received the US Legion of Merit for his service with Carlson's Raiders. In 1979, he was knighted by Queen Elizabeth and became Sir Jacob Vouza.

He also kept in touch with the marines with whom he had served. In 1968, he was the honored guest at the annual meeting of the 1st Marine Division Association. In his home, he kept two small flags on display in a glass case: an American flag and a US Marine Corps flag. The Raiders set up and continue to support a scholarship fund in Vouza's name and helped to establish the Sir Jacob Vouza Community High School in Guadalcanal.

In 1962, Vouza sent a message to his former marine comrades in arms: "Tell them I love them all. Me Old Man Now, and me no look good no more. But me never forget."

On the night of November 12, 1942, as Carlson and his Raiders fanned out around Asamana, they came across messages the Japanese had left. "We found notices written on paper and tacked to trees," Carlson noted in his after-action report, "indicating where various companies were to go. . . . [O]ur outguards on both the east and west flanks began shooting enemy messengers who attempted to enter [Asamana] apparently thinking the position was occupied by their own people." During the night, twenty-five Japanese soldiers wandered into the marines' position and all were killed.

There was rarely a day when there was not some contact between the Raiders and the Japanese, with the marines almost always coming out on top. On November 13, E Company, on duty in Asamana, was attacked from all sides by the enemy. "I was plenty scared," Bill Lansford wrote, "until I looked up and saw our C.O., Captain Richard T. Washburn, West Hartford, CT, standing in an open glade, calmly shaving his face, while bullets were whistling around. Our leaders bravery were most reassuring to us nervous privates."

On that same day, Carlson moved C Company from Binu to Asamana to bolster his forces there. He also received word that some Japanese troops were hiding out in the jungle at a certain location and ordered Captain Wild Bill Schwerin to find them and wipe them out. Schwerin, carrying a 12-gauge shotgun with his two .45s on his belt, led his men to a narrow gulley that was the only way to get to the Japanese position. There was a guard at the entrance, so they waited patiently and quietly in the jungle for three hours until he left his post and went back to the Japanese camp he was supposed to be guarding. It was time for lunch, and he must have been hungry.

Schwerin led his men slowly forward until he spotted two groups of Japanese sitting down on the ground eating rice balls, with their rifles neatly stacked against tree trunks, all of them out of reach. "'When you hear my shotgun,' Schwerin told his men, 'that's the signal to give 'em hell.'" They did, and in less than one minute, the Raiders had cut them all down. Not a single Japanese soldier had been able to reach his weapon. When the firing died down, Jacob Vouza's scouts went around the clearing slitting the throats of any Japanese still alive.

Captain Peatross's B Company killed sixteen of the enemy in just two days of skirmishes and small-unit actions. On the afternoon of the thirteenth, he was standing under a tall tree talking with two of his men when a lookout he had posted up high in the tree yelled down that he saw a column of Japanese soldiers marching toward them through the tall grass in an orderly column.

Peatross could not believe they would expose themselves like that, so he climbed up the tree to see for himself, only to find it was true. It was one of four similar attacks the Japanese tried that day. Peatross wrote that "closer inspection through my binoculars showed that it was a massed column of Japanese soldiers, each camouflaged with shrubbery from head to toe. The column would advance about 100 yards, halt, crouch down, wait a few minutes, and repeat the process, slowly but surely closing in on our position."

But not for long. Peatross notified Carlson, who called for an artillery barrage, and when it ended, the remaining Japanese troops were seen running back the way they had come. The supposed masters of jungle warfare were turning out to be no match for Carlson's Raiders. Over the next several days, Carlson launched more and more patrols, killing small bands of Japanese stragglers who had lost their units.

By November 15, he began to see that the Japanese were much more on the defensive and were being chased farther away from Asamana. His guerrilla tactics learned from his days behind the Japanese lines in China were working on Guadalcanal, just as he had thought they would. But the fighting and dying on both sides was far from over.

When one Raider patrol ended, Ben Carson "started walking back and I came past this Japanese soldier laying there on the trail. [Another Raider] had taken his rifle and put the bayonet on it and run it right through his chest. And he was laying there with his hand on the wound and there were bubbles coming out. He wasn't dead yet. They had missed his heart. He looked up at me and I lived with that."

Carlson's guerrilla tactics, which he had not had a chance to put into practice on Makin, were improvisational, spontaneous, and daring. Historian John Wukovits wrote that Carlson relied on essentially the same tactics, with modifications for individual situations, throughout the Long Patrol. "From his base camp, Carlson fanned out patrols to explore nearby trails, jungles and fields. When one portion of his patrol encountered the enemy, they formed a defensive line to hold the Japanese in place while Carlson swung his other units toward the fighting in a flanking or an enveloping maneuver."

He ordered his patrol commanders to contact him every two hours, or whenever they met the enemy. He prided himself on always having complete knowledge of exactly where his various units were; in a sense, tracking them in his mind. "They would put up a front," Sergeant McCullough said years later, referring to a defensive line, "but then there'd be a circling action. While they were keeping [the Japanese] busy at one place, they'd hit 'em at another."

The Raiders' tactical skills and confidence were also helped by Carlson's presence on the line as much as possible. He knew how important it was for him to be at his command post in order to be able to coordinate the movements of his units, but he also recognized the value of his presence among them for their morale. When he appeared at the head of a column urging them on to greater speed and seemingly unconcerned by enemy fire, they felt that if he could do it, so could they. They did not want the Old Man to show them up. He led them by example and inspiration, and they would follow him anywhere. And did.

Another important ingredient of the Raiders' success on Guadalcanal was the speed of carrying out actions. The men had been trained to move extremely fast, no matter what the terrain was like. They had made very rapid attacks, done their job, and withdrawn into the jungle before the enemy had time to bring up reinforcements. Their unpredictability was also a factor in their success. They would appear where the enemy did not expect them, then withdraw to positions where the Japanese did not expect them to go, such as even more inhospitable terrain.

Many Raiders came to believe their success was also guided by Carlson's seemingly instinctive and intuitive knowledge of where the Japanese were and what they were going to do. "Carlson had a talent for that I've never seen anybody else with," Frank Duesler said. "He was right across the very front of a long stretch of us guys. And he'd go like this [raising his hand] and we'd all stop. And he'd say, 'There's two or three Japanese back in there watching us.' And he said, 'When we go up past them a ways, I want a squad to come back down and nail them.' How he knew they were there, nobody ever figured out. But he knew and he was right."

While the Raiders began to feel increasingly confident that they were winning the battle against the Japanese, as the days wore on another enemy—the jungle—was taking a terrible toll on them. They were being worn down physically more and more every day by insects, tropical diseases, the extreme wet heat, and undernourishment. "Malaria moved in on us like flies on a dead horse," Carlson's biographer later quoted a Raider as saying. "Two hundred and twenty-five men got dengue fever, dysentery, malaria, ringworm, and other illnesses which the docs and corpsmen called jungle rot. . . . [W]hen we were sick, so sick we couldn't stand, we reported it—and were sent back to Aola. The Old Man kept telling us, 'If you can't make it, don't go on. We'll send you back. There's no disgrace.'"

In the overall battle for Guadalcanal, more than five hundred marines were treated for combat fatigue. The American Psychiatric Association labeled this syndrome "Guadalcanal Disorder." However, only one Raider was ever sent to the rear for psychiatric reasons, perhaps because of the intense training the Raiders received before going into battle.

After two weeks in the steaming jungle, never getting a chance to change their clothes or get themselves clean, being constantly soaking wet from sweat, rain, and muddy rivers and swamps, they were getting weaker by the day. Private Bulger wrote that "jungle rot and fungus, fevers, jaundice, and dysentery ran rampant through our ranks and nearly every Raider suffered one or more malady."

Carlson insisted that only the healthiest men could stay at the front. If those who were the sickest did not turn themselves in, Carlson urged their buddies to do it for them. He argued that those weakest from disease would hold them back and risk the lives of others. It was easy enough to see who were the most sick—there were telltale signs that were difficult to hide from the others. Dean Winters had so much jungle rot that, "I had to stop every three or four miles to dump the blood out of my shoes. It was running down from my crotch."

Strong, tough Raiders broke down in tears when Carlson ordered them back. They felt as though they were letting down the others. The number of men sent back against their will was six times the number killed (sixteen) or wounded (eighteen) during the course of the Long Patrol. There was no escaping the millions of insects, particularly the mosquitoes and the diseases they brought with them. Private Ervin Kaplan counted sixty mosquito bites in one day—just on his right forearm. And if a man scratched the bites—and it was impossible not to, they itched so badly—a single bite became an open running sore that would not heal in the jungle. And every man was bitten hundreds of times every day and night.

Two of every three Raiders on Guadalcanal became ill with some kind of gastrointestinal disorder, diarrhea and dysentery, and even hookworm from drinking unsanitary stagnant water. They were warned repeatedly to boil any water taken from a river or a swamp, but many did not have the time for such a luxury. Or they simply forgot in the stress of combat. Some did not use their water purification tablets for the same reasons, and also because the pills gave the water a bitter taste. Ben Carson remembered wading up a river to take up the point position ahead of the patrol. He was in a hurry and he was also thirsty:

> On my way up, I stopped and scooped up a cup of water out of the River. There was about 50 pairs of dirty feet up ahead of me but I was so thirsty I was going to have a shot of that. Dr. MacCracken was walking along behind me and came up and put his hand on my shoulder and said, 'how many times do I have to tell you to put halizone [water purification tablets] in that cup?' 'OK, doc,' and I threw it off and hooked the canteen cup back up because I couldn't take time to find the halizone tablet. We rounded a curve in the river and there were bloated, dead Japs caught in the willows there. I reached over and said, 'Doctor, does that halizone take care of that too?'

The Raiders were always hungry on Guadalcanal. "The awful hunger was a bad dream of its own," Carlson's biographer wrote. "For a month, it was raisins, tea, bacon, salt, sugar, rice. Ah, rice! That was a worse dream than the running pain in the empty belly. Polished rice, unpolished, coarse Jap rice, rice boiled, rice fried, rice raw, rice mixed with salt, rice with sugar, rice with bacon, rice with chocolate, rice with tea, rice with rice!" Well into old age, Raiders kept saying they never wanted to see rice again.

When anyone complained to Carlson about being hungry all the time, he reminded them that he had told them often enough during training that the time would come when the only thing they would have to eat would be whatever they could scavenge from the "bodies of dead Japs!"

The men lost weight, particularly during the first ten days of the patrol, when they had to get by on only the four days of rations they had brought with them into the jungle. After that they were able to get a daily chocolate bar, since some rations began to be delivered by air and sea. The men also resorted to eating what they could find in the jungle: raw vegetables, roots, fruits—even tree lizards when they were able to catch them. "When we finished the mission," Brian Quirk said, "we looked like pale ghosts. We were a skinny beat up bunch."

The men grew so desperate at one point that one of them, whose name was never known, stole a tin can. In the jungle, a tin can was worth its weight in gold because a man could use it to boil water and heat his rice. Everybody was furious at the breakdown of the Gung Ho spirit. And no one was more furious than Carlson.

"Here's what I'm going to do," he told them. "The next man accused of stealing a tin can I'm going to bring up before the men in his company. I'm not going to court-martial him. You are. We'll get the facts and the evidence. If you tell me to shoot him, I'll shoot him." Nothing was ever stolen again.

Captain Schwerin shot two wild native cows. The men butchered them, hung the great slabs of meat from trees, and quickly ate it all. Within hours, everyone became violently ill with even worse diarrhea than some already had. In one of the food shipments, they received a rare delicacy: canned New Zealand corned beef. That made them even sicker than the wild cows. Some men had such violent reactions and persistent bouts of diarrhea that they simply slit the seats of their pants open and let it happen, to the dismay of those walking single file behind them.

Rumor had it that some raiders "dined on mongoose and an unfortunate cat," according to Private Kaplan. He also remembered what happened on Thanksgiving Day when the traditional holiday dinner was sent to them courtesy of the US Navy, "all secure in stainless steel cylinders. Refrigeration not being one of the Guadalcanal conveniences, when opening the containers, we found our dinner in an advance state of decomposition. There is always salt pork and rice!!"

On November 17, Carlson, while several miles away from his command post, received an urgent message to report to Major General Vandegrift, commander of all Marine forces on Guadalcanal, for new orders. By the time Carlson and those on patrol with him made it back at top speed to his command post still at Asamana, they were "hot, sweaty, dirty, and worn out." But that did not stop Carlson, or even slow him down, from quickly briefing his officers on the result of the twelve-mile patrol he had just made and heading off for a six-mile hike to the beach. From there, he took a Higgins boat and then a jeep, arriving at Vandegrift's headquarters just before dark.

"Calling in Evans Carlson," Vandegrift later wrote, "I asked him to include the Mount Austen area, mopping up where he could and destroying some batteries of the enemy if possible." Mount Austen was a fifteen-hundred-foot-high ridgeline of one rocky hill after another about nine miles west of Carlson's location at Asamana. But those were nine miles as the crow flies, and as at least one Raider had already pointed out to the colonel, his men weren't crows.

The meandering route through the jungle to Mount Austen was much longer than nine miles. The Raiders would have to follow treacherously narrow and winding trails, and equally difficult rivers that wound back and forth in such contorted patterns of flow that they would cross the same river at different places many times or more in one day. And then, of course, there were the Japanese, who would be pushed back onto an ever-smaller body of land with the Raiders closing in on one side and the 1st Marine Division's troopers around Henderson Field only about nine miles away on the other side.

Vandegrift gave Carlson three specific missions: (1) find a suspected trail behind Mount Austen that intelligence officers believed the Japanese were using to bring in supplies and reinforcements, (2) find and destroy Japanese artillery pieces, collectively and colloquially known as "Pistol Pete," which kept being moved to different locations on Mount Austen and firing on Henderson Field, and (3) find out how large the Japanese troop strength was south of Henderson Field.

On the day before the Raiders headed out for their new missions, Carlson ordered seventy more of his men back for rest and medical treatment. Five days later, on Thanksgiving Day, forty more were sent back, and two days after that, sixty more men were told they were too sick to continue.

A few of the men not ordered back felt they could no longer go on and tried to get sent back. Two told their sergeant that they were ready to shoot themselves in the foot, saying they just could not take it anymore. The sergeant told them that if they did that, he would personally shoot them in the other foot, and leave them there, helpless, for the Japanese to find. Both men changed their minds and left with the rest of the Raiders as they headed out the next morning for the last phase of the Long Patrol.

Eighteen

The Proudest Moment

"Saddle up," the sergeants yelled. The Raiders moved into their familiar positions, heading single file toward the west, with the native scouts going ahead of the squad serving as the point that morning. Other scouts and Raiders trailed behind the main force serving as a rear guard, making sure no one was able to take them by surprise from behind. When they reached patches of open land, those assigned to guard their flanks automatically took up positions fifty yards out on either side of the column.

More often than not, Carlson was out in front, with usually only one Raider ahead of him, setting the pace for all those much younger men. The Raiders worried about the Old Man being up front like that, exposed to more danger than they were, but there was nothing they could do about it. Only one man, Platoon Sergeant Rhel Cook of F Company, seemed capable of talking back to Carlson, who called him Cookie. The colonel seemed more amused than offended by Cookie's attempts to protect him.

"I made him leave the point," Cook said, in 2008. "As soon as he'd come up I'd stop the point. I'd tell him, 'Get out of here, Colonel. This is no place for you. I'm not moving the point until you get back to the main body.' He'd say, 'Cookie, I want to see what's going on.' I'd say, 'Well you just get back to the main body, and we'll make sure you know what's going on.' He'd go mumbling off by himself." But he would not stay behind for long, and they'd go through the same routine again.

The Raiders made good progress over the next two days, moving rapidly to keep the pressure on the Japanese. They were constantly on the alert and were not caught by surprise as they had been on their first foray into the jungle. The enemy was retreating to keep ahead of the Raiders and in their haste they left behind piles of equipment, even weapons—more evidence that they were on the run and getting weaker.

By November 21, the marines were at the base of Mount Austen. To their surprise and relief, Carlson announced that they would have a four-day break. The men washed their clothing and themselves in the muddy waters, cleaned their weapons, and got first-aid treatment for foot blisters and jungle rot. The rest period brought them even more food. When he had been at General Vandegrift's headquarters, Carlson had arranged for a supply of B-rations, which consisted of uncooked foods that did not need refrigeration, and enough canned goods to last for five days. It was the most food the men had seen in a week.

Carlson received a visit from an old friend from the 1st Marine Division who was fast becoming a Marine Corps legend. Colonel Lewis Burwell Puller, better known as "Chesty," had served with Carlson in China and Nicaragua. "While Carlson chain-smoked and Puller puffed on his pipe, they exchanged views on the Guadalcanal campaign, looking for all the world like Chinese warlords planning their next foray," Captain Peatross wrote later.

Chesty Puller, like Carlson, was a maverick, an unorthodox bender of rules, and so was not well accepted by the tradition-bound officers of the 1st Division. Peatross wondered if that was the reason why, when they were within Jeep-riding distance of the Henderson Field headquarters, Puller was the only officer to visit Carlson. It was typical, Peatross thought, of how the officer corps viewed him, and it did not bode well for Carlson's future commands or ultimate career. Nor for Puller's. He would advance no higher than his present rank of colonel during all of World War II and was not promoted to general until the Korean War.

———

By Thanksgiving Day, November 25, three weeks after landing at Aola Bay, Carlson and his Raiders had moved twenty-five miles west through what had been Japanese-held territory. The Raiders were entrenched near the Lunga River at the base of Mount Austen with its fifteen-hundred-foot-high warren of ridges and ravines, craggy, rock-strewn heights, and thick jungles.

A patrol from Peatross's B Company got lucky; it came across some one hundred weapons the Japanese had been storing no more than two miles from Henderson Field. The men rushed over to "gawk at the weapons like a flock of tourists," Peatross wrote. "The rifles were in stacks of four, as if a company had halted, dressed ranks, and stacked arms, and fallen out to take a break from which it never returned. As we crowded together around the neatly stacked rifles, laughing at the peculiar ways of the Japanese, and completely oblivi-ous of our surroundings, the sudden sharp crack of an Arisaka [Japanese rifle] from surprisingly nearby brought everyone back to earth, literally, as we instantly hit the deck."

As the men tried to burrow into the ground, waiting for more shots, Peatross blamed himself for being so careless as to not have posted proper security. He had violated a basic rule of survival in the jungle: always be on the lookout. But no other shots were fired. Peatross immediately sent out a patrol to scour the area, but the shooter was never found. The captain commented that "the Lord does indeed look after drunks and fools, ranking myself as the biggest of the latter."

Later the patrol found a cache of hundreds of rounds of ammuni-tion and a box containing seven pistols. Each man carried one of the captured weapons and some ammunition in addition to his own as they made their way back to their new camp. The enemy rifles, along with some captured earlier, were enough to arm the native scouts.

There was some opposition at first to arming them, particularly from Major Mather, the Australian coast watcher. He was concerned because the scouts had never used guns before, only bows and arrows, knives, and machetes. Mather insisted that Sergeant Major Vouza train them in the use of rifles, above all emphasizing safety in carrying them through the jungle so the weapons would not be fired accidentally.

"No safe, no have!" Mather told Vouza, who set up a training program for the native scouts. They turned out to be diligent students, proud to possess the rifles and more safety conscious than some of the Raiders.

A patrol from E Company also went out on Thanksgiving Day. Its mission was to find the trail between two major rivers, the Lunga and the Tenaru, which ran roughly parallel courses from the area around Henderson Field to the sea. The patrol traveled mostly through water rather than jungle, Private Ervin Kaplan wrote. "There was no trail up the Tenaru, the seven or eight mile hike and return was a wade. We crossed the Tenaru 110 times by my count." They discovered an artillery piece of the kind the marines around Henderson Field called Pistol Pete, and destroyed it.

When Kaplan and the rest of that patrol returned to their base, they found the stainless steel cylinders the navy had sent with their traditional Thanksgiving dinners that made them all sick. Thanksgiving Day also saw the long-awaited arrival of A Company, which had remained behind on Espiritu Santo for the last three weeks.

It was easy to spot the newcomers. They were clean and well fed, with no jungle rot, and wore parade-ground-neat uniforms. They brought the common items, such as toothbrushes, which the others had not seen in weeks. The jungle Raiders drew straws to see who would get one. Those who lost had to keep using mud on their fingers to clean their teeth.

Private J. Leon Vanlandingham remembered that "our company received about a half a dozen toothbrushes. Our radio squad received one toothbrush, so that six of us shared the use of the toothbrush. I haven't been that close friends with anyone since then, not even my wife."

The new arrivals also acted differently. Private Werner Heumann wrote, "When A Company joined us, we got some decent food for a couple of days. One new Raider took a piece of bacon, cut off the rind and threw it away. Six guys jumped on it, cut it into six pieces, and roasted it over the fire." For those who had been in the jungle all those weeks, bacon rind was a rare delicacy.

Almost every day thereafter was marked by a battle, a skirmish, or the discovery of discarded Japanese supplies, even as the enemy was beaten farther back. On the twenty-sixth, a patrol of six Raiders, led by Corporal John Yancy, found a Japanese telephone wire and followed it to a clearing where some one hundred soldiers were resting. Their weapons were neatly stacked nearby but out of their reach. The Raiders opened fire with BARS and submachine guns. They killed seventy-five; the rest ran into the jungle. "Later," historian Christopher Miskimon wrote, "native scouts and a few Raiders moved among the Japanese, ramming their bayonets into any who yet drew breath. The bodies were dumped into a mass grave. Carlson was proud of the young corporal for showing such initiative, calling it 'the most spectacular of any of our engagements.' For his actions, Yancy was later awarded a Navy Cross."

A patrol led by Captain Peatross found a trail on the eastern slope of Mount Austen that clearly had been used by Japanese troops. The Raiders easily spotted Japanese footprints, and farther up the slope they saw two emaciated bodies of Japanese soldiers. There were no gunshot wounds on the bodies, or any other sign of violent death. But their field packs were full of leaves that a scout identified as poisonous. Apparently the Japanese had been reduced to living off the jungle vegetation. Their food supplies were gone, and they had been so hungry that they chose the wrong plant to eat.

Peatross led his men higher up the mountain for a time and then back down to reach camp before dark. They were exhausted by then, but perked up instantly when they heard hand grenades exploding not far ahead from the perimeter of the area assigned to D Company.

"As we approached the camp," Peatross said, "I had mixed emotions about what I saw, being at first angry and then pleased. Aside from the men in the security outposts, the entire company . . . seemed to be having a picnic. Small groups were gathered around campfires cooking what seemed to be fish, and everyone was laughing and living it up. . . . My first inclination was to raise holy hell, but they were so unabashedly happy, I just couldn't bring myself to be a party pooper."

The men had been throwing hand grenades into the river, killing the fish. Peatross and his men joined in the fun for a while and then left for their own camp, having enjoyed their best meal in quite some time.

On November 28, Captain Wild Bill Schwerin led F Company up the Tenaru River and from there began to climb up Mount Austen. Schwerin's executive officer, Captain James Davis, wrote, "Up in the mountains, there were no mosquitos, and it was cold at night, we were hot on the trail of the fleeing enemy, as the landscape and trails were littered with Jap equipment and some dead Japs. The route was torturous. . . . We waded in the river, crossing and recrossing the Tenaru for one whole day."

Their mission was to find more Pistol Petes, the artillery pieces the Japanese had used to shell Henderson Field. The next day, the patrol was successful, but it was rough going. Captain Davis described how "we climbed that damn mountain in a steady rain. We had to use ropes to pull each other up the wet slippery cliffs. I remember losing my footing and sliding backwards carrying several Raiders back down the hill. One of those vicious fish-hook vine tendrils whipped across my face, tearing open my nose and Adam's apple. . . . But I staunched the blood and re-scaled the cliff."

When they reached the top of the mountain, the Raiders found three Japanese howitzers guarded by two soldiers, whom they shot down immediately. The artillery pieces had a clear open range of fire onto Henderson Field, which the Raiders could see in the distance. They disassembled the guns and scattered the pieces down into the ravines and gullies. Every patrol on Mount Austen during the last days of November found more evidence that the Japanese were increasingly malnourished and less well equipped and organized, worn down by the ever-increasing pressure from Carlson's men.

But the Raiders were being worn down as well. On the night of November 29, when the patrols returned to base camp on the Tenaru River, Carlson made an announcement. He told his men that many of them were no longer physically fit for action and were to be sent back. That would leave the Raiders short of men, since others had been sent back previously. One company, which had begun the Long Patrol with more than one hundred men, was reduced to a mere twenty-three.

Of course, this meant greater demands on those who remained, Private Bulger said. "Each healthy Raider who remained was given extra gear to carry forward . . . a machine gun tripod, or barrel; a mortar round or two, a radio or a belt of machine gun ammo. This is in addition to our own weapons, packs and unit of fire . . . when every ounce of weight presented us with more cutting shoulder straps, and one more exhausting challenge to the undaunted survivors."

The next day, the Raiders who were still fit started up the mountain again. "You dragged your ass all the way," Private Ray Bauml said later. "Christ, it was raining, of course, when didn't it rain in the hills? We climbed up on this hill; well you couldn't walk up it. It was almost perpendicular. We'd tie the rope to a small tree, boost the guys—we got over."

Bauml was the point man, out in front of the others with a native scout nearby. Suddenly, the scout said in his pidgin English, "I smell'm Jap." Bauml froze until another man told him to go check it out. He crawled up the hill over a floor of dead leaves, every one of which seemed to make a loud crackling noise. He finally reached the top and found an abandoned Japanese camp with a half dozen foxholes. He saw some meat that was just starting to rot, a sign that the camp had been recently occupied. Bauml knew the Japanese could still be around, maybe hiding in the trees or behind rocks, taking aim at him.

"I'm looking around, I'm the only one there, there's no one backing me, no one protecting my butt—that's what bothered me," Bauml said. "I'm looking around at all these foxholes, stepping lightly. My weapon went into the foxhole first, and I'm thinking, 'Why the hell am I doing this?'"

But that did not stop him. He walked from one foxhole to the next, checking each one, scanning the rough terrain around him, making sure there were no Japanese soldiers lying in wait so that when the rest of his outfit came forward, they would not be wiped out by an enemy he had failed to see.

He knew he was expendable, out in front to trade his life to save the lives of his patrol. Because of such individual acts of dedication to duty, for which medals were rarely given, the Raiders finished another long day scouring Mount Austen without losing a single man. The Japanese lost at least eighty.

Food fell from the sky at six o'clock in the morning on December 1. The rain had stopped and the morning sun was bright as an olive drab DC-3 circled over the Raider camp in a clearing along the Tenaru River. At first the crew threw containers with parachutes out the side door, but the winds blew them too far into the jungle to retrieve. The pilot brought the plane down low and slow while the crew tossed out one-hundred-pound containers of rice and raisins, tea and fatback. The Raiders retrieved most of them, but one man was killed by a Japanese sniper when he wandered too far into the jungle searching for one. December 1 was also a day of rest, a chance to clean up, eat, and relax, as much as anyone could with Japanese troops still around.

It was back to war the next day, with patrols fanning outward and upward. Captain Peatross led a group along the winding Lunga River, which they had to cross seven times while heading in a more or less straight line. Shortly after the last crossing, they saw ten Japanese soldiers sitting around a campfire. They did not seem to have posted any guards.

Peatross positioned his men around them, less than fifty yards away, so quietly that the Japanese were unaware they were in danger. On his command, the Raiders opened fire. Within seconds, nine of the enemy were dead where they sat. One staggered a few steps before being cut down. Not a single shot was fired in return.

The condition of the dead men reinforced what they were discovering about the state of the Japanese defenders. "They were a pitiful sight," Peatross said, "emaciated beyond words, pale and sickly looking; one had a crutch, and another had a crude homemade splint on his leg. Their uniforms were in rags, and although each had a rifle, not one had a full clip of ammunition. That notwithstanding, had they pooled their cartridges and placed a single marksman at the top of the gorge, he could have picked off every man in our patrol. On the other hand, perhaps none of them any longer had the physical strength to scale the steep walls of the gorge."

A growing number of the Raiders were also reaching the point where they no longer had the strength to climb the rugged heights of Mount Austen. They had been fighting on Guadalcanal for a month, and they were ready to see it end. They had gotten the idea that the Long Patrol was supposed to have finished on December 1, and that they would be heading to the Marine encampment around Henderson Field.

Carlson called his men together that afternoon. About six hundred Raiders were left, "half-starved, sick men with layers of mud on their combat dungarees. We were tired, we wanted to get the hell out of the jungle; we thought he was going to tell us that the time had come for us to return to our base; that it was all over. He looked like a scarecrow when he stood up to talk. He looked like we looked. We waited for the Old Man to say, 'Now we go home!'"

Carlson told them that there were two ways to get to Henderson Field: the most direct and easiest was over the Tenaru River; the difficult, challenging, and dangerous way was over Mount Austen. The men knew for sure which way they wanted to go, but something told them the Old Man had the hard way in mind.

He told them that a patrol had found a strongly fortified Japanese position on top of the mountain. He paused and all was quiet until suddenly there was a loud crack. Everybody reached for their weapons, but it was only a tree limb. Carlson waited, letting the tension build up, and then he shouted, "The Jap position is unoccupied!"

The Raiders knew that a position on top of Mount Austen had a clear view of Henderson Field. If they could reach that position before the Japanese could reoccupy it, they would relieve the pressure on the field and its defenses. This would mean a quicker end to the fighting on Guadalcanal. Reaching the top of the mountain "would be a good thing, wouldn't it?" Carlson asked his men.

They silently nodded, agreeing that it would, indeed, be a good thing, but no one asked the question foremost in their minds: why the Raiders? They had already been behind enemy lines for a month. Why did they always have to be the ones going up the mountain?

"It is a good thing," Carlson insisted, before answering their unspoken question. "We're going to do it because it's important, because we're fitted to do it and in a position to do it." Then he gave them some good news. Three companies—C, D, and E—would leave for Henderson along the Tenaru River route. They had been in the jungle the longest, and had lost more men to combat and disease. The other companies—A, B, and F—would take the mountain route with Carlson. The rumor spread quickly that Carlson had told Captain Washburn that he was determined to go over the mountain to get to Henderson even he had to do it by himself.

Carlson thanked them all for their service, and as the companies lined up in formation, he called out, "Let's sing 'Onward Christian Soldiers.'"

"It was right," one man said. "That's what we wanted. We didn't care or not if the Japs heard us. We felt good singing."

"To those of us who were there," Lowell Bulger wrote thirty-six years later, "it was the proudest moment of our young lives."

Nineteen

Gung Ho Is Dead

S hortly after Carlson led the three companies of Raiders to the top of Mount Austen on December 3, Ray Bauml was startled by two figures "crashing through [the jungle] like a herd of elephants." He whirled around and raised his weapon to fire, but at the last possible instant, he recognized Lieutenant Jack Miller and his runner. Miller had missed the Makin raid because he had broken his arm during training but was more than making up for it on the Long Patrol.

Miller headed off to where he thought the rest of the Raiders were, with Bauml right behind him. "We took two steps," Bauml wrote, "and a Jap machine gun went off and almost blew his entire head off. All his teeth were knocked out, and his tongue was like strips of liver; his whole lower jaw was almost missing. I said, 'Lay low.' It's amazing how you react, and I said, 'Lay low, Lieutenant.'"

The Japanese opened up with more machine guns and injured Miller's runner, severing his arm. Bauml's life was saved by some iron-wood trees, so named because they were like iron and could stop any kind of bullet from passing through. Bauml lay there firing back while gently patting Miller's leg and telling him to lay still. "I don't know if he heard me or not."

Victor Maghakian, who had been shot in one arm on Makin, was hit in his other arm in the fight on the mountaintop. He came barreling down from the crest of the hill, cursing wildly.

"I got hit in my f—— arm!" he yelled.

"Is it the same arm again?" the Old Man asked.

"No, the other one! Why don't I learn not to point?"

"It wasn't funny," one Raider said after the war, "but those who heard him laughed."

No one was laughing when Maghakian found out that his close friend Jack Miller was severely wounded. Maghakian knelt beside him and heard Miller whisper his nickname, Transport. He sounded delirious, and it did not appear that he would pull through. Maghakian was wild with rage. "I seen red," Maghakian wrote to Miller's parents years later. "I got sore and went after the machine gun nest because we were having a lot of trouble from it and there was a sniper up in a tree and we could not tell where he was."

Maghakian stood up and ran toward the machine gun nest with a grenade in his good hand. He was sure the sniper would get him but he no longer cared. He wiped out the machine gun nest, but the sniper got him in the wrist. The shot gave away the sniper's position, and other Raiders blasted him out of the tree with their Tommy guns.

"I made a human target out of myself but I did the job," Maghakian wrote, "and I did not care if I never came out of it because I knew I could save lots of lives if I knock it out and besides I seen everything in the world. I have been to China and the Philippines so I did not care as long as I revenged Jack."

He refused to leave the battle despite his bullet-shattered wrist. Years later, doctors would find the mainspring of his wristwatch twisted around an artery. He kept on fighting until he lost so much blood that he had to be helped off the field. The battle of the mountaintop raged for two hours before the Japanese were finally driven back.

The Raiders found twenty-five Japanese dead when it was over. They suffered four wounded and one killed—Miller—who died the next day. The two doctors treating him thought they might be able to save him if they could get him down the mountain to the 1st Division base hospital. Carlson faced a tough choice; in the end, he decided the risk was too great for the rest of the men to rush down to the camp to try to save one.

Over the coming months, a number of officers and men of Carlson's Raiders wrote letters to Jack Miller's parents back in Texas. "We gave him a decent burial on the side of the trail," Sergeant Maghakian wrote, "and I am not ashamed to admit I cried like a baby which I have never done in my life. I am supposed to be pretty tough. . . . I wish they had more men in the Marine Corps like your son—he was tops and he led his men with plenty of skill in a fight. . . . Well that is the way everything goes. I will never forget him." Two years later, the Navy launched a new destroyer escort, the USS *Jack Miller.**

After the battle in which Miller was hit, Carlson, along with Gunnery Sergeant Sam Cone and Captain Peatross, roamed over the area where the Japanese dead lay sprawled. They were looking for anything that could be useful for intelligence purposes. They found some papers and also large chunks of beef the soldiers had been carrying.

"As I stood over one of the thought-to-be dead Japanese," Peatross wrote. "I suddenly saw his eyes flicker open and just as quickly close, almost like the shutter of a high-speed camera. I stooped down to feel his pulse and found a strong regular beat coming through." The Japanese soldier leaped up, threw a chunk of beef at Peatross, and reached for his rifle.

"Shoot the bastard!" Carlson yelled.

Peatross dodged the hunk of meat, raised his shotgun, and fired. The Japanese fell a few inches from Peatross's boots and stared at him before fading away. It was a close call. If Peatross hadn't taken him out so quickly, the Japanese might have killed Carlson.

Peatross searched the body and found photos of what must have been the man's wife and children. "A feeling of deep sadness suddenly engulfed me," Peatross wrote. "For the very first time, I saw my

---

*Victor Maghakian survived his wounds and went on to win more than two dozen awards, including the Silver Star and the Bronze Star for his heroic actions in other Pacific island campaigns. Actor Lee Marvin, who had been a marine, described Maghakian as the toughest marine he had ever met. Maghakian retired as a captain in 1946 on 60 percent disability from his wounds and later worked in security for a Las Vegas hotel. He died in 1977.

'enemy' not as a ravening beast but as another human being, and I felt sorry for him and his loved ones."

The next morning, December 4, the Raiders started down the mountain, toward Henderson Field and a break from their month of combat. They moved about five hundred yards along a trail, with Corporal Albert Hermiston among those taking the point. He sensed something up ahead and signaled to those following him. Suddenly a Japanese machine gun opened fire, killing him and another man and wounding a third.

Ben Carson was close behind with his buddy, Private First Class Cyril Matelski and another Raider. Carson and Matelski had fought together on Makin and spent the week at the Royal Hawaiian Hotel having a grand party. "We all three saw someone in a G.I. helmet," Carson said. "Matelski hollered, 'Ahoy Raider.' . . . It was a Jap in the American helmet and that son-of-a bitch dropped Matelski with a shot right between the eyes."

Corporal Orin Croft crawled forward, opened up with his BAR at fifty feet, and blew the machine gunner away; the brave action would earn him a Silver Star. And those were the last shots fired on the Long Patrol. The wounded men were brought on stretchers to the front of the column. As one was carried past Peatross, the man looked at him and asked, "Captain, how am I doing now?" It was Private Stuyvesant Van Buren, one of the men Peatross had gotten out of jail in Honolulu after he and others had stolen a trolley bus.

Peatross had said then that Van Buren would get a promotion if he behaved for the next three months. Now Peatross smiled and said, "'Hold onto your stretcher. It's all downhill from here.' When I last saw him, he had a big smile on his face." He died of his wounds the next day, having not received a promotion.

By the middle of the afternoon, the three companies of Raiders coming down from the mountain reached the perimeter of the defensive line around Henderson Field. They still had eight more miles to march to reach their new camp, but the terrain was level, and there were no enemy soldiers waiting to ambush them.

Carlson ordered his men to straighten up and march smartly. An officer greeting them offered to bring up trucks to take them to their camp, but Carlson said, "The Raiders walked in. The Raiders will walk out." They looked awful—with uniforms in tatters, blood oozing from jungle-rot sores, unkempt beards and matted hair, filthy, skinny, and grimy. "We were basket cases," said Captain Washburn, who had lost thirty pounds. "I really felt lousy."

Carlson led them across Henderson Field while hundreds of marines looked on. Private Bulger remembered how long and difficult that march was, "if you could call that drag-ass limping marching, . . . but we held our heads high." The marines cheered them on, handing out food and precious Cokes. "My God, walking skeletons!" one man commented. "Everyone who saw us said, 'There goes Carlson's Raiders.' We felt very tired, but also very good."

The men of Carlson's Raiders did not know it yet, but the most famous and celebrated special operations unit of World War II had fought its last battle. They would win even more fame and acclaim than they had after the Makin raid and be celebrated and glorified all over again as national heroes, as men who were winning the war against the Japanese. It was that glory and adulation—and all the bitter resentment and anger it generated among others—that would lead to their downfall.

Once again, only four months after the Makin raid, the Raiders found themselves in the headlines of newspapers all over the United States and in the lead stories in radio news broadcasts and newsreels. Reporters crowded around them, first on Guadalcanal and then back at Camp Gung Ho when they returned to Espiritu Santo.

Carlson was awarded a Navy Cross, and many Raiders received a variety of medals, honors, and awards. General Vandegrift issued a rare unit citation, commemorating their heroic service and sacrifice, which he read aloud in person to them and which was liberally quoted in the *New York Times* on December 26, 1942. "For the consummate skill displayed in the conduct of operations, for the training, stamina, and fortitude displayed by all members of the battalion and for its commendably aggressive spirit and high morale, the commanding general cites to the division, the commanding officer, officers and men of the raider battalion."

The only other Marine unit to have been honored thus far with a citation was the force on Wake Island, which had held out for weeks before being forced to surrender to a far superior force. Vandegrift had given Carlson and his men a major honor, which would alienate them even further from other Marine outfits, still struggling on Guadalcanal after six months of brutal combat. Those included Colonel Merritt Edson of the 1st Marine Raider Battalion. Although Edson would be awarded the Medal of Honor, neither he nor his unit would receive anywhere near the public accolades that Carlson and his men did.

When Carlson held a solemn memorial service for the Raiders lost on the Long Patrol, none other than Admiral Nimitz told a reporter after the service that Carlson's eulogy was "the best sermon he had ever heard." The *New York Times* quoted much of Carlson's sermon verbatim as part of a glowing tribute to the Raiders. The United States Office of War Information, the official American propaganda outfit during World War II, broadcast Carlson's memorial speech to American troops around the world and then had it translated into more than a dozen languages for transmission to other countries, including Japan and Germany. It was a hit, Carlson was a star, and the Raiders once again became celebrities.

His old friend from China, Agnes Smedley, wrote a long column glorifying the man and his achievements that was reprinted in newspapers all over the country and read by millions. "Carlson is one of those dangerous men of lean and hungry look. He's a throwback from our own distant revolutionary past—a mixture of Tom Paine, John Brown—with a touch of Lincoln. But all of him is New England—craggy and grim in appearance, yet kindly and philosophical."

The stories in the press gave the impression that Carlson and his men were beating the Japanese all on their own. No other outfit on Guadalcanal was given a fraction of the publicity the Raiders got. Some correspondents compared him to Lincoln, as Agnes Smedley had done, while others went all the way and compared him to the then popular actor Gary Cooper. One reporter, in a piece in a New York paper proclaimed that Carlson "writes books, kills Japs, plays his harmonica, and speaks Chinese. He can deliver polished lectures on Asiatic problems, swim an ice-flocked river naked and exist on a half-sock of rice a day."

Evans Carlson had become one of the most beloved and idolized figures in America. The man could do no wrong. The whole nation loved him and his Raiders. But for some others still fighting on Guadalcanal and those in the Marine Corps hierarchy, it was too much glory and too much publicity. They began to ask, what about all the other marines who had been on that godforsaken island of Guadalcanal for so long and who seemed to be forgotten men? A backlash was building within the corps.

One unidentified Raider wrote: "Things were much too good for us after Guadalcanal. Everybody made a fuss over us and we were crossing our fingers. Sooner or later, the payoff must come. We had crowded our luck too far."

On December 16, 1942, twelve days after the end of the Long Patrol, the Raiders boarded the USS *Neville* and sailed back to Espiritu Santo. It was a happy time aboard ship, with as much food as they could wolf down, even ice cream, as well as soft mattresses and pillows to sleep on for as long as they wanted. Captain Peatross said he slept through the night and most of the next day, and when he got up, he ate everything he could find. But reality set in when they docked at Espiritu Santo on December 20 and marched back to Camp Gung Ho.

The place was a wreck. Everything was covered in mildew and rust; tall grass had grown so high that it was hard to see the tents, much less get into them. It took the men three days of hard work to make the camp livable again. For the first time in over a month, the men got mail, including a number of Dear John letters, notifying them that their wives or girlfriends had found someone else.

Many got Christmas packages from home, including a large ham that had been sitting so long in the tropical heat that it looked to be alive with maggots. Of course, being Raiders, they were used to making do with what they had, and so the recipient simply scraped off the top layers of ham, picked off all the maggots, and made four sandwiches out of what was left. Life was good.

The Raiders' outlook got even better two months later when they sailed to Wellington, New Zealand, for a month of R&R. They were given four months' back pay. They were beginning to regain at least some of their health and were returning to civilization, to a city with bars and women. It lived up to all their expectations and then some.

"Never before in the history of the Corps," Captain Peatross wrote, "had Marines been welcomed so graciously and treated so kindly as by the citizens of Wellington. On the streets, in bars and restaurants, in hotels, in private homes, and in churches, New Zealanders treated Marines as heroes and defenders of their county." When the Raiders went to the movies, they were startled to hear "The Marines' Hymn" being played right after the New Zealand national anthem.

Wellington was clean and attractive, the people took them into their homes, and no one would let them pay for their drinks in a bar. And there were no signs of a jungle. Many Raiders said they felt like they had died and gone to heaven. And the best part was that they planned to enjoy it for a whole month. Unfortunately, after only one week, they were loaded aboard a transport and taken back to Espiritu Santo. Their holiday was over.

Carlson told them it was for "military reasons," but they found that hard to believe. They were too undermanned, and still in too poor health and physical condition to undertake another campaign. Some were still suffering from malaria, dengue fever, jaundice, and other tropical diseases. They had not had nearly enough time to recover from the ravages of the jungle and their malnutrition and undernourishment. A few men went AWOL and missed the boat back, and there was a growing feeling of bitterness, anger, and intense disappointment at not being given more time to build themselves back up again.

"There was hell in the ranks," Carlson's biographer wrote. "The one thing which shattered the men most was that it seemed to them that other outfits who had done less than they had were getting *their* period of rest. . . . No one liked the Raiders, they concluded, because the Raiders had done so well and therefore had received more publicity than other units. Their record, their fame, their spirit, their morale, their Gung Ho was being held against them."

Many men came to see the shortened leave as the first step in a deliberate campaign of revenge and retribution for getting all the glory. It was, in fact, the beginning of the end for Carlson's Raiders.

The reluctant Raiders reached Espiritu Santo on February 23, 1943, and started in immediately on a new training schedule that was just as demanding as the ones they had gone through when they were in better shape. As the days wore on, a growing number of men had to be sent to the hospital for malaria, dysentery, and other lingering ailments from their days on the Long Patrol.

They became even more severely undermanned. Finally, in late February, they received replacements who created their own set of problems. None of them had any training beyond the basics learned in boot camp. They would require much more training to come up to Raider standards.

Worse, many of the new men were rejects from other commands; discipline problems their former COs wanted to get rid of. Captain Peatross received twenty-nine new men in his company and found that every one of them had been court-martialed for one offense or another, usually for going AWOL. In spite of these problems, the training continued, including landing on beaches from submarines, as they had done at Makin.

Marine combat correspondent Jim Lucas went along on one of the exercises and watched as Carlson, still rail thin and frail, came close to being swept overboard by a wave. Corporal Ira Lind grabbed hold of him by the shoulder and yanked him back. "Goddamn it, colonel," Lind shouted, "stand clear. What would become of us if anything happened to you?"

By the second week in March, the daily sick call of men too ill to continue their training got so big that a staff surgeon had to be flown in from New Caledonia, five hundred miles away, to investigate the problem. He examined each of the Raiders and declared that none of them could be classified as medically fit for combat. The men of the

2nd Marine Raider Battalion were in bad shape. And so were their equipment and their morale.

Carlson came to believe that the Marine Corps high command had embarked on a deliberate campaign of ignoring his requests for new equipment and was laggard in supplying the basic equipment and supplies needed to keep the outfit going. Ever since Makin, for example, Carlson had been requesting a different outboard motor for the landing rafts to replace the kind that rarely worked in the rough seas off Makin. Despite repeated requests to the overall Marine commander in the Pacific, Major General Clayton Barney Vogel, Carlson never received the newer and better motor.

The same problem occurred when Carlson tried to get better radios for his men, so that isolated units could stay in contact. He did not want a repeat of what had happened on Makin when almost all the radios failed. But once again, his requests were either refused outright or simply delayed in getting through the chain of command. Carlson was getting so frustrated and angry with the situation that he wrote an angry, daring, and dangerous letter to General Vogel:

> It is my belief that any officer, having knowledge of obstacles or conditions which mitigate against the vigorous and intelligent prosecution of the war, is remiss in his obligations as an officer and a loyal citizen if he does not do all within his power to remove such obstacles and correct such conditions. It is in this spirit that I write. Pride, prejudice, sentiment, and even considerations of personal security cannot be permitted to stand in the way of an efficient and economic war effort.

He went on to say that he was willing to make any sacrifice, even accepting a court-martial for insubordination, if that would result in getting the right equipment needed to fight the war. Men had wrecked their careers by treating their commanders in such a taunting and even threatening manner. Carlson knew, however, that no general wanted to be involved in court-martialing a man who was regarded as a national hero. The press would cover every word of such a hearing and would make Carlson an even greater hero than he already was. After all, he was fighting to get his men the right equipment they needed to continue fighting the war.

There would be no court-martial, no public reprimand, but there were more subtle ways of getting back. The anger and resentment against Carlson reached all the way to Marine headquarters in Washington. It was bad enough, the members of the high command felt, that Carlson had gotten so much more acclaim than any other outfit, but now he was threatening one of their own, Major General Vogel, with public disclosures of what Carlson saw as unfair and incompetent leadership. Something had to be done. Carlson's biographer wrote:

> None of this was official. No one sat down in Headquarters and wrote a report to the effect that Carlson's Raiders had better be 'handled.' But the word got around nevertheless. Carlson and his men knew that word was getting around. They had heard officers say that the goddam Raiders were getting too goddam arrogant; that they thought they owned the Corps; that they were all a bunch of publicity hounds, and sooner or later they would have something done to them. . . . Carlson saw it coming.

It started in small ways, with everyday matters such as routine requisitions for ordinary supplies. Carlson watched new units arrive on Espiritu Santo from the States and be given lumber to build mess halls and to put down floors in their tents, as well as pipes and plumbing for real showers and toilets. Every other outfit on the island had those things, but not the Raiders. He wanted post-exchange (PX) facilities made available to his men, and a film projector so they could watch movies like everyone else could.

Carlson could no longer ask Jimmy Roosevelt to contact his father and get them what they wanted, a privilege some still held against Carlson. The president by then was far too involved with the larger war effort, and he and Carlson had not exchanged letters in a long time. Carlson's Raiders were being discriminated against because they had been too good, and were made too much of in the press. Now they had to pay the price.

The men saw what was happening—how much better other units were being treated—and some blamed Carlson for it. They demanded to know why he was not providing for them the way other commanders were for their men. Bitter words and angry accusations were hurled at him at Gung Ho meetings, but Carlson never told them how hard he had tried, how his requests and requisitions were ignored. It was not his way to blame others, to "pass the buck up."

They were his men, he was their leader. It was his job to provide for them. He silently took the blame and became depressed and dispirited. But there was nothing more he could do or say to those above him, or to his own men. It was unfair to him and ultimately to them all, but if he realized his mistake in not telling them what was happening, he never admitted it publicly. And, as it turned out, there was very little time to brood over it, or to try to change it.

On Monday, March 15, 1943, Carlson was ordered to report to headquarters on Espiritu Santo, where he was formally relieved of his command of the 2nd Marine Raider Battalion. He was made executive officer, second in command, of the newly formed 1st Raider Regiment, which would consist of the four Raider battalions that had been formed by then. Forty-year-old Lieutenant Colonel Alan Shapley, a graduate of the US Naval Academy and a career man of the old school, was placed in command of what had been Carlson's Raider Battalion.

The Raiders were devastated, despite their anger at Carlson over the lack of supplies. Jim Lucas, the combat correspondent, was with them that day as they returned from another submarine training exercise and got the word about the change in command. "Tragedy awaited us," Lucas wrote a year later. "On shore we learned that Colonel Carlson was to leave his men. I stumbled with them up the beach, tears in their eyes, and heard them curse the fate that had robbed them of their old man. I sat in their tents and heard them cry like babies."

Six days later, on March 21, Carlson formally turned his command over to Shapley. He looked even more gaunt than usual. His malaria was coming back, along with a high fever, and he said very little at the ceremony.

"I have been relieved of my command here. Lieutenant Colonel Alan Shapley will be your new CO. I hope you will give him the loyalty you gave me." Shapley spoke briefly, but he said enough for the men to know they were no longer going be the same kind of outfit. He made it clear that things would go by the book from then on, and he closed by saying that he wanted them to straighten out their tent rows. The tents were not in perfect alignment, the way regulations called for.

"I want this camp to look like a Marine camp," he said.

One of the Raiders said quietly, "Gung Ho is dead."

Epilogue

Thank God, He's Gone

E vans Carlson, one of the most famous battlefield commanders of World War II, never commanded men in combat again. And he never again served with his beloved Raiders, though he continued receiving letters from them until the day he died. He left Espiritu Santo sick in body and dispirited in mind.

He followed the progress of his old outfit from its invasion of Bougainville in November 1943, through to its absorption, along with the other Raider battalions, into larger units. The war in the Pacific had grown to such a large scale that it was thought that commando-type raids were no longer needed. As a result, the special-ops units were broken up and distributed through the Marine Corps in early 1944. That decision was made by the newly appointed commandant of the corps, Lieutenant General Alexander Vandegrift. It was one of the first changes he introduced into the corps, just two months after he took command.

It was the end of the elite within the elite, the last of the small, mobile, independent fighting units, and it left the men resentful of the loss of their unique identity and special status. A Raider in one of the other battalions wrote a poem expressing how they felt:

> *Here's some news to make you hot,*
> *They're doing away with the best they got.*
> *And throwing us in with the common lot,*
> *For we're the last of the Raiders. . . .*
> *So throw away your Raider schemes,*

And throw away your Raider dreams. We're going to join the
4th Marines,
For we're the last of the Raiders.

"Carlson became a very sick man," his biographer wrote. "His malaria was complicated by jaundice and complete nervous exhaustion. The loss of his battalion and the defeat of Gung Ho depleted him more than did Makin and Guadalcanal." And so the 2nd Marine Raider Battalion, whose maverick commander was too far out of step with every other officer in the corps, was effectively eliminated by being made part of more traditional units. Major General Merrill B. Twining, who had known Carlson in the years before the war, wrote in 1996, "Evans Carlson was worthy of a more generous treatment than he received." Twining considered Carlson's Long Patrol to be "The most perfectly planned and executed mission of the Guadalcanal campaign."

He left Espiritu Santo shortly after he was relieved of command and went to the San Diego Naval Hospital for medical care and rest. When he checked in, he told his doctors that he did not want any visitors for two weeks. He was in no condition to talk to the press, or even to close friends and colleagues. He needed time to come to terms with what had happened, and to figure out how much of it was his fault.

He wrote long, heartfelt letters to his friend the radio commentator Raymond Gram Swing, venting his despair and frustration. "Suffice to say that the work of the last year has been washed out by the top-side of the Marine Corps." He told Swing that his battalion had been turned over to an "orthodox" officer who would destroy the Gung Ho spirit he had instilled and turn his outfit into a unit like all the others. And, he added, he had lost all the authority, discretion, and independence he once had, and no longer commanded anything. All that he had worked for and achieved, he said, were gone.

After two weeks of treatment, Carlson left the hospital and went to Washington, DC, to see about the possibility of getting an active combat command again. He had lunch with President Roosevelt and told him how valuable his son, Jimmy, had been on the Makin raid, how courageously he had served, and how highly his men thought of him, but apparently Carlson did not bring up his own situation.

Then Carlson went to Marine headquarters to see the corps commandant, Lieutenant General Thomas Holcomb, who had been a marine for thirty-eight years. Holcomb listened politely to Carlson's argument for continuing the special-ops units in the Pacific and passed him on to the Plans and Policies Section, where he made his case again. He received no agreement with or commitment to his plan for keeping the Raiders going. He also received no response to his request to be sent back to combat.

He knew he was simply being passed on from one office to another. Holcomb even sent him to General Wild Bill Donovan to see about a clandestine mission for the Office of Strategic Services. As far as the Marine high command was concerned, any assignment would be better than putting him back in command of his own unorthodox outfit in the Pacific—or anywhere else. But Carlson turned down the shadowy mission to China that Donovan offered him.

One of the other key people Carlson saw in Washington was a friend from his Nicaragua days, fifty-nine-year-old Brigadier General Robert Denig, who was in charge of public relations for the Marine Corps. Whether by chance or design on Holcomb's part, another man was in Denig's office when Carlson arrived. He was Lucien Hubbard, a Hollywood legend for writing or directing dozens of films from as far back as 1919.

Hubbard was discussing with Denig a movie he wanted to make about the raid on Makin. He planned to call it *Gung Ho*. The producer would be the well-known Walter Wanger, and the star of the film would be Randolph Scott, who would play the tall, thin, dynamic leader of the raid, a Lieutenant Colonel Thorwald, who had served in China. General Denig suddenly proposed that there was no one better qualified to serve as technical adviser than Evans Carlson. And it would keep Carlson out of the way for several months.

Carlson liked Hubbard's script. It was loosely based on the two lengthy *Saturday Evening Post* magazine articles written by Sergeant Wilfred LeFrancois, who would also serve as an adviser, along with Transport Maghakian. The Raiders in the movie would be played by real Raiders, albeit ones still training in San Diego: James Roosevelt's new 4th Marine Raider Battalion.

One of those Raiders, Robert Stech, said, "It was fun helping to make the movie, but we had a price to pay. After being in the water [Pacific Ocean] for two and a half days making landings from rubber boats for the cameras, our weapons got so rusty we failed inspection and liberty call. Boy, you should have seen us! Out came the steel wool . . . and we finally got our weapons clean and got our liberty hours late."

Another of the real marines, Mel Heckt, told a reporter, "His job in *Gung Ho* was to run and hit the barbed wire fence and then everybody would run over his back. A young [real] actor, lying on the fence next to him, cut his finger. . . . [T]he actor received immediate medical attention while, Heckt said, 'I was bleeding like a stuck hog.' He added 'that was part of being a Raider.'"

Carlson, in addition to advising on script changes, also brought the spirit of Gung Ho to the living arrangements of the cast and crew. He and Randolph Scott and the other actors and directors had been given private hotel rooms, while the workers and extras, including large numbers of Mexicans who were playing Japanese soldiers, were housed in bunks in a makeshift temporary building. This did not suit Carlson's beliefs.

"If this picture is going to be about 'Gung Ho,'" he said, "the people who make it ought to try living it."

He got his way, and everyone involved in the movie—cast and crew—moved into the same bunkhouse to provide an extraordinary example of working together that had never happened in the movie industry before. Stagehands and other workers talked about it for years afterward.

Carlson's friend Helen Snow later wrote that the whole idea of being made the central heroic figure in a Hollywood movie was in keeping with Carlson's air of flamboyance. "Evans lived a theatrical life," she said, "and he was aware of it. He did things with style and had a flair for the dramatic. . . . He knew how handsome and commanding he looked in his blues on parade. He loved it when the movie 'Gung Ho' was made in 1943 with Randolph Scott taking his part."

The reviews of the movie were favorable, and most mentioned Carlson not only as a technical adviser but also as the real-life star of the battle shown in the movie. One review in the *New York Times* on January 26, 1944, described it as "a sizzling war film. . . . It possessed all the elements of the suspense of sudden and concentrated action, and of heroic accomplishment against odds."

The film was a big success for the movie company, as well as for the Marine Corps and for the image of Evans Carlson. *Gung Ho* was a very effective tool for getting more young men to join the Marines. The lines at Marine recruiting offices always got longer when the movie came to town. The film added immensely to the already huge celebrity status of Carlson, which, of course, further displeased the top brass of the Marine Corps. They were annoyed enough at him already over all the publicity he had received after Makin and Guadalcanal. Now he was getting even more.

The movie was also good for the morale of the American people. "All things considered," the editor of the Raiders Association newsletter wrote in 2005, "*Gung Ho!* was, and still is, a rip-roaring, shoot em up film that a victory hungry America needed. Even if it was filled with inaccuracies." The movie was so popular that Hollywood made another one a year later called *Marine Raiders*, without Carlson's help, that was not nearly as successful. A wise reviewer wrote, "Miss it if you can."

The men of Carlson's Raiders did not think much of *Gung Ho!*. In fact, most of them hated it for its gross inaccuracies. Ben Carson said he came close to walking out of the theater when he saw it. He felt "belittled and embarrassed" by it. "It was pure Hollywood. . . . There was one scene where the Raiders were painting an American flag on the top of a building. Like we carried buckets of red, white, and blue paint with us on the raid."

When Carlson finished his movie career, he went back on duty in a staff job shuffling papers at Camp Pendleton in California. "He was restless and still depressed," his biographer wrote. "Only when he received letters from some of his old men, or read some article which plugged *Gung Ho*, did he feel that he had not failed completely."

In fall 1943, Carlson learned about a planned invasion of Tarawa in the Gilbert Islands. He tried to join in the assault, at least in a staff position, but his requests were turned down. Finally he was allowed to participate in the landing on November 20 as an observer with no official duties. He came ashore in one of the early waves in what turned out to be a costly operation, with the Marines losing over three thousand killed and wounded in three days of fierce fighting.

Despite not having an active command, Carlson stayed in the thick of the fighting. When it was over, he told war correspondent Robert Sherrod, "This was not only worse than Guadalcanal. It was the damnedest fight I've seen in thirty years of this business."

"I've been in many battles now," he wrote to his father, "and I've had a lot of lead and steel thrown in my direction. But I don't believe that more lead was ever flowing around me at one time than during the first two days at Tarawa. How I got through is a miracle."

Ten days after the battle was over, Carlson flew back to California and promptly got into more trouble when he spoke to a group of one thousand Marine officers at Camp Pendleton. He was very blunt in criticizing the quality of leadership on Tarawa. "Our greatest weakness," he said, "is the caliber of our officers. . . . Tarawa was won because a few enlisted men of great courage called out simply to their comrades, 'Come on, fellows. Follow me!'"

Carlson was angry at the lack of leadership he had seen on Tarawa, and also at the lack of initiative and resourcefulness on the part of many enlisted marines. "What if they had been trained not to wait for orders," he asked his audience, "what if all had been trained to act by themselves, and to take the initiative as he had trained his Raiders?" So many fewer men would have been lost, he said.

Carlson wrote to his father that he believed his mission was not yet finished but that he still could not get an active command. Nor could he persuade the brass to implement any aspects of his unique approach to training men for combat. His career was at a standstill, and there was no reason to think his situation would improve. But his personal life changed for the better: he fell in love.

Her name was Peggy Tatum Whyte; she was the daughter of an army colonel and the divorced mother of a six-year-old son who liked

Carlson immediately. She was quick-witted, bright, and articulate, but she was unhappy about the way her life had turned out. He asked her to marry him and she agreed, but first he had to go back to the Pacific for the invasion of Kwajalein. He was allowed to participate in the planning of the assault, but again, he was only allowed to function as an observer during the battle. When it was over, he flew back to California, where he and Peggy were married on Leap Year Day, February 29, 1944, a date he chose deliberately.

"With malice aforethought," Carlson said. "We like the idea of having a wedding anniversary only every four years." The bride's son served as the best man. Not long after, Carlson flew to New York alone to speak at a meeting to honor Sun Yat-sen. Another featured speaker was the well-known black actor, singer, and political activist long accused of being a communist sympathizer, Paul Robeson. Speaking in such a setting with Robeson only served to further inflame those who insisted that Carlson was a communist himself.

He went back to California to be reunited with his bride and then left the following day to help plan another invasion. This time it was Saipan, and Carlson eagerly threw himself into the work. His biographer wrote:

> He was tired. The last two years—it was now the end of March, 1944—had depleted him. He had been through Makin, Guadalcanal, Tarawa, and Kwajalein. He had crossed the Pacific eight times, the [US] continent four times. Malaria still fevered and froze him. He had had no rest, little chance to recapture the ceaseless outflow of energy. And now on him was placed the heavy responsibility of helping to plan an invasion.

Carlson had always been excited and eager to go into every battle he had faced, but less so at Saipan. He told a friend (who would later write his biography) that he wished he was not going on this one. He had a premonition that something was going to happen to him. On June 2, 1944, eight days after the landing on Saipan, Carlson was in the fighting even though he still commanded no troops. He was with Lieutenant Colonel Justice Chambers and a twenty-one-year-old radioman from Brooklyn, New York, Private First Class Vito Cassaro.

As they moved forward, a Japanese machine gun opened fire and hit Cassaro in his thigh, knocking him to the ground. He could not move himself out of the line of fire because he had heavy radio equipment on his back. Carlson picked him up, with machine-gun bullets whizzing all around him, and started carrying Cassaro to safety. He did not make it. Bullets struck him in the arm and leg after he had gone only a few yards.

Seconds later, a medic and two stretcher bearers reached the two fallen men and started to place Carlson on the stretcher. He refused and told them to take Cassaro first because he had been hit first. "They don't come any better than the colonel," Cassaro later said about Carlson. "He has won the respect and admiration of all who have served with him. I know if he hadn't carried me away from that spot I would certainly have been hit again and probably killed."

Carlson was bleeding badly when he was taken to the aid station. All through those first hours and days of being wounded, he said he experienced a profound sense of gratitude. It was not just that he was still alive, he said, but that getting wounded meant he would be able to stay out of the war for a while. Perhaps, he thought, he might even survive the war. Just then, Japanese mortars began firing shells at the old stable that had been made into an aid station. Shells exploded all around the place, and everybody there expected to be blown to bits any second. But Carlson was certain that it was not going to happen.

"I remember thinking at the time that if the Japs couldn't hit me up front, they weren't going to hit me back there."

By July 1944, Carlson was back in the San Diego Naval Hospital where he had been sent a year earlier after being relieved of command of the Raiders. This time his mood was better, and he did not impose any restrictions on visitors as he had the last time. His wife was there, and friends in the Marines stopped by, as did James Roosevelt, then on staff duty, who had been promoted to full colonel almost a year before Carlson would be.

The visitors who caused the most excitement for Carlson and everybody else at the hospital were Franklin and Eleanor Roosevelt. The visit also occasioned more bad feelings among the high command

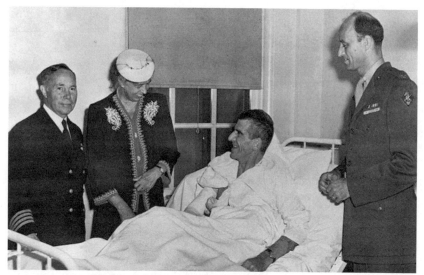

Eleanor Roosevelt visits Evans Carlson at the San Diego Naval Hospital on July 20, 1944, where he was recovering from wounds received at Saipan. James Roosevelt is at right and navy doctor Morton D. Willcutts is at left. (© *Bettmann/CORBIS*)

when Mrs. Roosevelt wrote about the visit in her very popular newspaper column, "My Day," in which she mistakenly referred to him as "General Carlson." The Marine Corps was not pleased at his "promotion" and immediately notified the press that Carlson, "whatever his deserts, still had two jumps to make before becoming a general officer."

Carlson was kept quite busy with many other less famous visitors, a great many interviews with reporters, and hundreds of letters from former Raiders, as well as others he had served with on Saipan and elsewhere, in addition to sad letters asking about lost loved ones.

His wounded arm was not healing well and needed still more surgery a month later. When surgeons opened the wound, intending to repair a piece of bone shattered by a Japanese bullet, they discovered that it was infected and that adhesions had formed, extending his pain to his shoulder and elbow. He would have to wait for corrective surgery.

Carlson and his wife were living in a home nearby, and a month later, he was operated on again. A piece of his shin bone was taken out and grafted onto the bone in his right arm. He was suffering a great deal of pain, but, as always, he did not let that stop him. He traveled to Chicago to give several talks, one on a radio program that was broadcast nationally.

He was still restless and began to long for an active role in the war again. In March 1945, he was finally promoted to the rank of colonel, far later than those of similar age and experience. Along with the promotion came an assignment in the headquarters staff of the 5th Amphibious Corps based at Pearl Harbor.

A month later, on April 12, 1945, he and the rest of the nation were stunned by the unexpected death of the man who had been their president the past twelve years. "The news of the President's passing has hit me hard," Carlson wrote to a friend. "I was privileged to serve him and was honored by his friendship and confidence. . . . At the moment I feel like a ship without a rudder."

Two months later, he had to go back to the Naval Hospital in San Diego to undergo still more surgery on his arm. The bone graft had not worked. The new and old bones were not knitting together the way the surgeons had said they would. Now they were going to have to try it again.

Carlson did get some good news when he got back to California. His elderly father and his sister were waiting for him, having driven across the country to see him. They told him there were going to move nearby. He was further delighted to find that they got along well with his wife, Peggy.

Carlson continued to suffer from constant pain in his arm, but he was very happy to have his family together, and he was delighted for his fellow marines when the Japanese surrendered on September 2, 1945. No more marines would have to give their lives for their country. But of course, the end of the war left a vacuum in his life. What would he do now?

Carlson stayed on sick leave for months after the war ended, still in great pain, undergoing more bone grafts. He nevertheless went on extended and very tiring speaking tours. He received so many invitations that he could be selective in which ones he accepted. On the other hand, he did not like to cause disappointment, particularly to those whose cause he was in sympathy with.

In early December 1945, he flew to New York to talk to the American Veterans' Committee, and then to an audience of twenty-two thousand at a meeting of the Independent Citizens' Committee of the Arts, Sciences, and Professions. It was held at Madison Square Garden and attended by Henry Wallace, US vice president from 1941 to 1945; Julian Huxley and other well-known scientists; Helen Keller; and the head of the United Automobile Workers, one of the most powerful labor unions.

When Carlson stood and made his way to the podium in full dress uniform, wearing his medals and decorations, the audience stood up and shouted, "Gung Ho! Gung Ho!" Carlson smiled and waved at the crowd with his good arm. The size of the audience and the illustrious people on the podium with him that day was a measure of just how highly regarded, famous, and well-connected Evans Carlson was.

Invitations to give more speeches kept pouring in. Carlson's status as a war hero and a notably good speaker for good causes had not dimmed. Two days after the Madison Square Garden event, he spoke to a group trying to raise money for China. The next day, he flew to San Francisco to give a talk at a large union meeting and then to the Press Club. Both speeches were about China.

He flew home to San Diego but left two days later for another demanding week of talks that would have worn out a man half his age who did not have a painfully wounded arm. He gave speeches about war, about China, about working together, and he joined in public debates over one of his favorite topics: the peaceful uses of atomic energy.

He met with many wealthy and powerful people, but also with veterans, union members, and the poor and disadvantaged. Along the way he also met a large number of celebrities at all levels of life, from Thomas Mann, the noted German writer and Nobel laureate, to one of his favorites, Bill Mauldin, the famous World War II cartoonist. Mauldin told him that there were only two "brass hats" whom ordinary GIs respected: Dwight Eisenhower and Evans Carlson.

It was an exhilarating, joyful time for Carlson, but it was wearing him out and worsening the pain in his arm. Back home in California, a number of influential people, including James Roosevelt, were urging him to run for the US Senate. It was a very exciting prospect, perhaps too much so.

After his hectic round of speaking engagements in December, Carlson began feeling sick. He was sure he was coming down with a chest cold. Either that, he told himself, or those new strong chest pains were referred pains from his arm wound. He told no one, not even his wife, about how bad he felt until a few days after Christmas 1945, when he had a heart attack. It would not be his last one.

His doctors told him he had to stop all the frantic activity; indeed, to stop doing just about everything. The only way he could get better, they said, was to essentially stay in bed for at least six months. He could no longer live the way he had been—not if he wanted to keep living.

"I've fallen apart like a one-horse shay," he said, referring to Oliver Wendell Holmes' poem "The Deacon's Masterpiece," in which a "one-hoss shay"—a carriage for two people pulled by one horse—runs perfectly for one hundred years and then one day simply falls apart. That was how Carlson felt: broken—as well as afraid, bitter, frustrated, and angry.

To friends, he adopted a stoical, even cheerful facade. "Don't worry about me," he wrote to Agnes Smedley. "I have just got to keep down until some of these blood vessels are healed. I know a lot of people, including yourself, living with heart ailments for a long time. I'm sorry this came to me at this time, but probably some other time would have been no better."

Evans Carlson retired from the Marine Corps on July 1, 1946, and was moved up to the rank of brigadier general on the retired list, generally referred to as a "tombstone promotion."

He held on for another year, trying, though not always successfully, to stay relaxed. But too many issues still riled him and fueled his temper. "He worried about atomic energy control, rising prices, civil rights, and fair employment practices. He became active in the

Independent Citizens Committee of the Arts, Sciences, and Professions; he was vice chairman of the Progressive Citizens of America. . . . He was called a crank, a pink, a fanatic, a Communist." Similar accusations continued up to his dying day, and well beyond it.

In 1950, at a Senate Foreign Relation subcommittee hearing investigating the alleged spread of communism in the nation, Louis Budenz, a professor at Fordham University and a former communist himself, testified that Evans Carlson "was a communist." As it turned out, there was no evidence that Budenz and Carlson had known each other or ever met. But the testimony was widely reported.

Even James Roosevelt let him down in that regard. In 1972, thirty years after they went to Makin together and twenty-five years after Carlson's death, he told a reporter that Carlson "was married to a lady who was frankly and openly a member of the Communist party . . . and it became known that his political views were not very different from hers." He went on to say that Carlson had run as an "official Communist candidate" for senator in California in 1948. That was one year after Carlson died. Roosevelt updated the charge four years later in a book he wrote about his parents.

For some fighting men it didn't matter. Even though Carlson was only officially allowed to go as an observer following the Guadalcanal campaign, he involved himself so directly in the fighting that Colonel David Shoup (later commandant of the Marine Corps), said, memorably, "He may be red, but he isn't yellow."

Carlson tried to defend himself against the many accusations of his being a communist during the last year of his life. In October 1946, he wrote to *Time* magazine, protesting against the assertion that his political views were similar to those of communist front organizations.

"I am not a member of the Communist Party," he wrote "nor am I an apostle for Communist causes. I am a free American citizen who has spent over 30 years in the armed services, fighting in defense of the right of American citizens to enjoy life, liberty, the pursuit of happiness, and the four freedoms . . . and I am exercising the right, common to all citizens, of expressing my opinions and working for those objectives which I am convinced are beneficial to my countrymen and humanity. . . . I choose now to work for peace."

Carlson did not have much time left to work for peace, or to find it within himself. He was wearing out and wearing down from all his years of hard service, the lingering pain in his arm, and now his damaged heart. He was too weak to continue giving more impassioned speeches around the country, or even meet with reporters and supporters for very long at his home. He moved to a nursing home outside of Portland, Oregon, in the town of Brightwood. He died at Emmanuel Hospital in Portland on May 27, 1947, at age fifty-one.

Henry Wallace, who had visited him a few days before, told a reporter that "he believed the general was subjecting himself to too great a strain by his actions inherent in world affairs." When his former Raiders found out about his death, many said they were convinced he died of a broken heart from having his Raiders taken away from him and never being given another command.

The top brass of the Marine Corps had one last humiliation in store for Carlson, who had expressed the wish to be buried in Arlington National Cemetery, in Virginia across the Potomac River from Washington, in the beautiful site that was once the home of Robert E. Lee. Peggy Carlson was told that her late husband was eligible to be buried there. However, the Marine Corps also told her it had no funds to transport Carlson's body across the country for burial. She had very little money, certainly not enough for the cost of shipment.

When former Raiders and other marines found out, they were furious that one of the war's great heroes was to be denied the honor of being buried at Arlington. The press made much of the story, fueling public outrage, and when James Roosevelt found out, he was mad enough to do something about it.

He contacted some wealthy friends in Hollywood, which had gotten two movies out of Carlson's wartime career, and quickly collected $812.95. That covered the shipment of the body to Washington and Peggy Carlson's expenses to get there and back. Roosevelt wrote, "I didn't have the money either, but I went to friends in Hollywood who provided it. They were liberals, but not Communists. The man had been a patriot, regardless of his politics. His men loved and respected him, and were pleased he received, as he deserved, this burial with honors."

Carlson was buried at Arlington on June 4, 1947, and given full military honors, but not many in the Marine Corps were there, even though a large number of the high command were stationed in Washington. General Vandegrift attended in his role as commandant of the Marine Corps. After the ceremony, Carlson's wife told a reporter for the *Washington Post* that Carlson had "died a disillusioned man."

Merritt Edson, by then a major general, never forgave Carlson for rejecting some of his men who had been sent to him, for claiming that his was the first Raider battalion, and for winning so much more glory than he had. Edson felt that his much longer time spent in combat on Guadalcanal and his heroism in winning the Medal of Honor were relatively ignored in the press, while Carlson received so much more coverage, both during and after the war. He openly refused to lead the memorial service for Carlson, commenting, "I have never been nor am I now an ardent admirer of General Carlson, although I respected his bravery as an individual, I have never agreed with the doctrines and policies he espoused."*

There was no official public praise for Carlson from the Marine Corps and very little official recognition of the event. The press, however, offered as much lavish coverage and praise to Carlson in death as it had when he was alive. Every major newspaper in the country wrote about his death. The *New York Times* published a four-column obituary with the headline "Gen. Carlson Dead: Led Raiders in War/Heroic Marine Officer Buoyed Hopes Early in War."

But the Marine Corps gave no notice to the public of the date and time of the funeral at Arlington. As a result, attendance at the ceremony was sparse. A few of his old friends were there, including Agnes Smedley and Raymond Gram Swing, but they and others felt that Carlson had been denied the final proper respect he deserved. Swing wrote an open letter to the *Washington Post* that was published the day after the funeral.

"May I call attention to the strange absence of public participation in the burial of Brig. Gen. Evans Carlson at Arlington National

---

*Edson retired from the Marines in 1947, became director of the National Rifle Association in 1951, and committed suicide in 1955.

Cemetery," it said. "For this the public was not to blame. No notice of the funeral was given, and most of the friends who appeared—only enough to fill a dozen pews—were notified by the family."

Referring to the service as a "relatively obscure burial," Swing wrote that "one had no sense that a grateful nation was lovingly saying farewell to one of its rarest heroes." On the same day, the *Post* published an editorial with the headline "Honor Slighted." It referred to the lack of official recognition of Carlson's funeral as "shabby treatment."

After the ceremony, before the small crowd left the burial site, Major General William Worton, who had served with Carlson in China, overheard General Vandegrift remark, "Thank God, he's gone."

Notes

EPIGRAPH:
"many [are] eccentrics," "impatient with the petty rules." (Boot, 7, 2)

CHAPTER 1: A TEST OF HONOR
"had hurt her beyond repair." (Blankfort, 90)
"The boy went outside." (Blankfort, 90)
"hymns and grace before meals." (Blankfort, 81)
"The aristocratic attitude of my mother." (Snow, 1940, 2)
"Evans, . . . that isn't the way it's done." (Blankfort, 83)
"cutting away the last excuse." (Blankfort, 93)
"Evans enlisted U.S. Army, underage." (Blankfort, 100)
"The boy has to learn." (Blankfort, 101)
"Years later he told a friend, 'At first I tried to drink." (Snow, 1940, 2)
"I know now, father." (Smith, 29)
"beautiful, clever and resourceful." (Blankfort, 107)
"It is curious that during these last months." (Blankfort, 111)
"Evans Junior, . . . born at 5:30 A.M." (Blankfort, 112)
"It's all past now, Evans." (Blankfort, 114)
"I didn't like to be in an army in peacetime." (Snow, 1940, 7)
"I made money." (Snow, 1940, 7)
"He had failed." (Blankfort, 119)

CHAPTER 2: HOW'S THAT FOR GUTS?
"Well, I'm back in the service." (Blankfort, 121)
"Always friendly and helpful." (Twining, 140)
"We went hungry." (Twining, 140)
"He made his protocol calls." (Blankfort, 128)
"lovely Southern girl." (Farnsworth, 46)
"an excellent hostess." (Personal communication from Gail and Glenn Everett, 2013)
"I took her over to headquarters." (Blankfort, 130)
"Failure is hard to take gracefully." (Blankfort, 132)

"I never took an arbitrary attidude." (Snow, 1940, 9)
"Where else in the world do they send Marines?" (Blankfort, 134)
"silent Chinese." (Blankfort, 138–139)
"combined with the steaming sultry Shanghai summer." (Blankfort, 146)
"I didn't know anything about intelligence work." (Snow, 1940, 10)
"I met Nicaraguans as equals." (Snow, 1940, 11)
"So he [Carlson] got himself a mule." (Berry, 113–114)
"When I knew him in Peiping." (Blankfort, 168)
"The editorial was 250 words." (Gomrick, 3)
"when soldiers are given information." (Blankfort, 169)

CHAPTER 3: DIRECT TO THE WHITE HOUSE
"Shall we go into the dining room?" (Blankfort, 171)
"Carlson was prouder of his relationship." (Peatross, 6)
"I have a background." (Persico, 60)
"In the next two weeks." (Blankfort, 170)
"nothing, not even having dinner with FDR." (Blankfort, 172)
"I understand you are going out to China." (Blankfort, 173)
"Father never gave a hoot." (Roosevelt, *My Parents*, 184)
"My chief loves your letters." (Wukovits, 14)
"I am devoted to him." (Wukovits, 14)
"We need all the trained observers we can find." (Blankfort, 183)
"It was a grand scene." (Blankfort, 185)
"They were in love with each other." (Blankfort, 207)
"found Agnes 'grand, attractive, alive.'" (Price, 323)
"A single candle lighted the room." (Alley, 219–221)
"most self-restrained, self-disciplined army." (Wukowits, 13)
"knew why he was fighting." (Carlson, "Marine Raiders," 20)
"The Chinese have two words for working together." (Blankfort, 25)
"I have a responsibility to tell." (Alley, 213)
"You're crazy, Evans." (Blankfort, 251)
"I feel deeply that I can be more useful." (Wukovits, 15)
"If Carlson wanted it, so then did she." (Blankfort, 289)
"He cannot see things clearly ahead of him." (Farnsworth, 355)
"Carlson, isn't it about time you came back?" (Blankfort, 287)
"All leaves cancelled, sir." (Blankfort, 281)

CHAPTER 4: WE GIVE NO MERCY
"At last I have received a break." (Blankfort, 8)
"The Donovan affair is still uppermost." (Smith, 25)
"Daddy, I want to be a Captain, too." (Berry, 117)
"Jimmy!" the president said. (Smith, 26, from Morgan, *FDR*, 463).

"It was ridiculous, really." (Patch editor, "What Sort of Man," 8–9)

"Development within the Marine Corps." (Wukovits, 30)

"The plan," he wrote, "was rather revolutionary." (Patch editor, "What Sort of Man," 9)

"I'll never forget my first entry into that place." (Carson, 2)

"Doctor, what about my finger?" (Carson, 2)

"some nutty major." (Carson, 3)

"I just hated the idea of anyone attacking." (Voight, 2)

"He just said that he would rather have a sister." (Voight, 3)

"The first to fight." (Winters, 10)

"there was a ninety-nine percent chance." (Winters, 11)

"We were afraid the war would be over." (Orrick, 20)

"We didn't want to miss it." (Orrick, 20)

"where things are happening." (Thomason, 2)

"I'd scrounge around the area." (Wukovits, 39–40)

"Jack decided he wanted to be one of them." (Maghakian, 2)

"Went AWOL." (McCarthy, "Wayward Warrior," 6–7)

"I saw on the bulletin board." (Murphree, 7)

"[They] rejected me over and over." (*Carlson's Raiders*, 2)

"Roosevelt had a great sense of humor." ("Carlson of the Raider Marines," 105)

"Expect no favors." (Smith, 48)

"Jim Roosevelt interviewed me." (Voight, 5)

"'Can you march?'" (Carson, 3)

"Can you cut?" (Blankfort, 12)

"I told him if anybody else could, I could." (Wukovits, 43)

"I won't take a man." (Blankfort, 11)

"I promise you nothing but hardships and danger." (Blankfort, 12)

CHAPTER 5: CLOSER TO WAR

"Rarely has a person combined." (Wukovits, 2)

"As you were, boys." (Blankfort, 19)

"The first thing we're going to do." (Blankfort, 19)

"We'll live as you live." (Blankfort, 21)

"The Jap is a wily and rugged enemy." (Blankfort, 22)

"Full of manure and rattlesnakes." (Carson, 4)

"We hoped the food would get a little better." (Carson, 4)

"lived out of a pup tent." (Wukovits, 48)

"marching five, eight, ten miles." (Richardson, 5)

"'See that mountain over there?'" (Smith, 56)

"Gradually, . . . individuals were converted into units." (Peatross, 16)

"a boot nut." (Carson, 4)

"This is my rifle." (Rupertus, 1)

"We had tremendous firepower." (Carson, 5)
"You can never enforce discipline." (Fry, 4)
"we weren't allowed liberty." (Duesler, 11)
"we were close knit." (Voight, 10)
"When I was a Raider, I was with friends." (Winters, 24)
"Ahoy Raiders!" (Blankfort, 32)
"claimed to be an Eskimo." (Peatross, 14)
"We used to hold discussions." (Sherrod, 36–37)
"I had never seen an abalone in my life." (Carson, 6)
"had reached a morale peak." (Peatross, 17)
"I feel now that those months of experience." (Zimmerman, 8)
"I am delighted to have your letter." (Frank, 707)
"This battalion is now headed." (Smith, 35)
"It'll probably take me the rest of my life." (Peatross, 19)
"A lot of marching." (Voight, 6)
"After a long hike." (Peatross, 19)
"To the last man and last bullet." (Peatross, 20)
"This time, Carlson, it sticks." (Blankfort, 38)
"If there really were." (Smith, 88)
"We had no doubts." (Peatross, 48)
"Jimmy was a hell of a good Marine." (Berry, 117)
"a liability to my own group." (Smith, 90)
"Look, my son's an officer in that battalion." (Berry, 117)

CHAPTER 6: TO MAKIN ATOLL
"told to find a place to sit down." (Carson, 10)
"Everything was thrown together." (Blair, 317)
"You feel like you're in a tomb." (Wukovits, 94)
"We never did take our clothes off." (Carson, 10)
"barely enough oxygen to light a match." (Smith, 9)
"They trained me to flush toilets." (Winters, 12–13)
"It was a criminal case if you got caught." (Carson, 10)
"The sleeping accommodations." (Smith, 97–98)
"It was hot and humid." (Peatross, *Bless 'em All*, 51)
"I remember I never did sleep in my bunk." (Carson, 10)
"We became buddies." (Smith, 101)
"After spending hours." (Peatross, *Bless 'em All*, 52)
"Hell," one man said, "I know this atoll." (Blankfort, 39)
"If a man needed to challenge someone." (Wukovits, 94)
"'now this thing [about prisoners].'" (Carson, 9)
"Not one Raider had a direct route." (Peatross, *Bless 'em All*, 53)
"Even under ideal conditions." (Peatross, *Bless 'em All*, 53–54)

"they could expect tank resistance." (Smith, 106)
"I had thoughts." (Smith, 106)
"I looked through the periscope." (Carson, 10)
"palm trees, a sandy beach." (Peatross, *Bless 'em All*, 54)
"'At best,' one man said to the other." (Peatross, *Bless 'em All*, 51)
"Colonel," he said, "I've got some bad news for you." (Blankfort, 46)

CHAPTER 7: EVERYTHING LOUSY
"God, it was a mess up there." (Wukovits, 99)
"Rain was coming down in torrents." (Peatross, *Bless 'em All*, 54)
"When you blow those rubber boats up." (Carson, 12)
"It was pitching." (Carson, 12)
"If I miss the jump into the boat." (Wukovits, 101)
"If I miss the boat, I'm going straight down." (Wukovits, 101)
"Corporal Ben Midulla . . . got his foot stuck." (Smith, 111)
"I had this miserable can of gas." (Carson, 12-13)
"They were useless hunks of dead weight." (Smith, 112)
"banged his right cheekbone." (Wukovits, 102).
"Captain," Peatross shouted back. (Peatross, *Bless 'em All*, 55)
"The resulting confusion." (Carlson, "Operations on Makin," 1)
"It was raining like hell." (Wukovits, 103)
"We didn't get tipped over." (Wukovits, 105)
"I came up then." (Waddell, "Raider Tells," 5)
"And on that snap." (Carson, 13)
"the landing was all mixed up." (Smith, 116)
"Communications by voice radio." (Haines, 3)
"Things were pretty fucked up." (O'Donnell, 28)
"Vern Mitchell was trying to chamber a round." (Carson, 13)
"Jesus, they can hear that in Tokyo." (O'Donnell, 29)
"They might as well just blow the bugle." (Wukovits, 107)
"I wonder if I am ever going to." (Waddell, "Raider Tells," 3)
"I would bet that there's not one of us." (Peatross, *Bless 'em All*, 56)
"Everything lousy." (Smith, 116)

CHAPTER 8: LET 'EM HAVE IT!
"It was a shootout at the OK corral." (Carson, 14)
"Everybody was on his own." (Carson, 14-15)
"Situation expected to be well in hand shortly." (Smith, 116)
"At first, we didn't see anything." (Smith, 117)
"I immediately directed Lieutenant Plumley." (Carlson, "Operations on Makin," 2)
"You hit the nail on the head, Colonel." (Blankfort, 43)
"A group of tall, well-built native men." (LeFrancois, pt. 1, 109)

"We knew you come." (Blankfort, 44)

"The native police chief." (Karig and Purdon, 6)

"Two small Jap transports." (Blankfort, 44)

"Direct hits." (Blankfort, 46)

"Isn't Peatross with you?" (Blankfort, 35)

"Orders came to move up the road." (LeFrancois, pt. 1, 109)

"Without regard for his own safety." (LeFrancois, pt. 1,109)

"I could see the Japs creeping toward us." (LeFrancois, pt. 1, 109)

"Let 'em have it." (LeFrancois, pt.1, 109)

"There was about four minutes of inferno." (LeFrancois, pt. 1, 109)

"I worked my way over to him." (LeFrancois, pt. 1, 109)

"for conspicuous heroism and intrepidity." (Thomason, 3)

"It didn't work!" (Peatross, *Bless 'em All*, 56)

"Without command and almost as one." (Peatross, "The Raid on Makin," pt. 1, 5)

"burst of fire completely surrounded the bicyclist." (Peatross, *Bless 'em All*, 57)

"We are all now dying in battle." (Wukovits, 109)

"as if it were payday." (Peatross, *Bless 'em All*, 57)

"Through sheer good fortune." (Peatross, *Bless 'em All*, 58)

"For Carlson." (Blankfort, 47)

"Snipers and machine gun fire." (Carlson, "Operations on Makin," 2)

"I'll lose control." (Wukovits, 113)

"I never regained control of my platoon." (Wukovits, 113)

"Nobody ever told us to look up." (Smith, 129)

"Here we get ashore." (Carson, 13-14)

"When they fired that Arisaka rifle." (Carson, 14)

"I felt sure that two of the enemy snipers." (LeFrancois, pt. 1, 109)

"We were taught to use arm signals." (Carson, 14)

"He kept pointing up into this tree." (Carson, 15)

"had to piss real bad." (Smith, 125)

"a Jap sniper in a tree shot Johnson." (McCarthy, 7)

"He got me good in the side." (Faulkner, 1)

"Somebody shouted from my right." (LeFrancois, pt. 1, 109)

"and for the first time I realized." (Wukovits, 112)

"He was looking for me." (Smith, 125)

Chapter 9: A Free-for-All

"It happened a lot of times." (Blankfort, 48)

"Hya Colonel." (Blankfort, 51)

"Carlson seemingly had no fear of dying." (Wukovits, 120)

"I remember a walkie-talkie was shot." (Roosevelt, *My Parents*, 271)

"cool as the proverbial cucumber." (Wukovits, 121)

"We had been issued this model." (Peatross, *Bless 'em All*, 58)

"struggled close enough to the enemy." (Peatross, "The Raid on Makin," pt. 1, 6)
"holes in my shirt." (Peatross, "The Raid on Makin," pt. 1, 6)
"like a rabbit flushed from cover." (Peatross, "The Raid on Makin," pt. 1, 6)
"When we were about 50 yards from him." (Peatross, *Bless 'em All*, 59)
"It seemed like there was no end to them." (LeFrancois, pt. 1, 110)
"They would yell and holler." (Carson, 15)
"My arm went dead almost immediately." (Wukovits, 112)
"It seems to get you mad." (Wukovits, 112)
"There is no doubt in my mind." (Wukovits, 113)
"I poured almost twenty precious slugs." (LeFrancois, pt. 1, 113)
"I'll get those heathen by myself!" (Wukovits, 116)
"like a madman," "The fellows told me afterward." (Wukovits, 116)
"We had Japs in front of us." (Smith, 122)
"free-for-all. Every man was trying to move up." (Spotts, 14)
"the Japanese were near perfect." (Spotts, 14)
"One of the boys crept up to me." (LeFrancois, pt. 1, 110)
"Frenchie," the doctor said. (Smith, 128)
"could have ordered a rapid advance." (Wukovits, 115)
"They were on an island." (Blankfort, 49)
"They were both knocked out." (Winters, 15)
"That old ship is still there today." (Carson, 16)
"There is no doubt in my mind." (Stidham, 15)
"Our light machine guns opened up." (Inman, 9)
"They strafed and bombed us." (LeFrancois, pt. 2, 28)
"I was with Lieutenant Peatross." (Blankfort, 51)
"We've got another two hours." (Blankfort, 51)
"Jimmy," Carlson said. (Blankfort, 51)
"It seemed to us." (Peatross, "The Raid on Makin," pt. 1, 7)
"It appeared that Carlson." (Wukovits, 126)
"waved, shouted, whistled." (Peatross, *Bless 'em All*, 60)
"We were running out of steam." (Peatross, *Bless 'em All*, 60)
"In that bush, we didn't know," "on an individual mission there." (Wukovits, 117–118)
"There were quite a few guys." (O'Donnell, 39)
"All of a sudden." (Carson, 16)
"No one was apprehensive." (Carlson, "Operations on Makin," 3)

CHAPTER 10: GETTING OFF THE ISLAND
"We walked the boat out." (Carlson, "Operations on Makin," 4)
"and we lost all of our weapons." (Winters, 15)
"I figured I was on the island." (Winters, 15)
"God in heaven!" (Blankfort, 57)

"Some of the men paddled." (LeFrancois, pt. 2, 28)

"dead weights," "to try to get a good night's rest." (LeFrancois, pt. 2, 29)

"flipped the boat over." (Peatross, *Bless 'em All*, 61)

"We were so exhausted paddling." (O'Donnell, 31)

"We got overturned." (Wukovits, 131)

"Getting off the island." (Smith, 146)

"It got dark." (Carson, 16)

"Raiders would stick with the wounded." (Peatross, *Bless 'em All*, 79–80)

"It was kind of like being in a football game," "the toughest thing I've ever done," "You could see them about popping out." (Wukovits, 130)

"Wading and pushing," "In all of our training," "That way, Sam." (Peatross, *Bless 'em All*, 60)

"They all looked to be pale shadows," "Some had their eyes fixed." (Peatross, *Bless 'em All*, 61)

"operational low point." (Carlson, "Operations on Makin," 5)

"The situation at this point." (Carlson, "Operations on Makin," 5)

"Someone else had a rifle," "bottomed out in the absolute depths of despair." (Wukovits, 137–138)

"Carlson was extremely upset." (Peatross, *Bless 'em All*, 80)

"Don't say I didn't warn you, boys." (Smith, 151)

"Peat," Haines said. (Peatross, *Bless 'em All*, 63)

"It was darker than the inside of a black cow." (Carson, 16)

CHAPTER 11: SURRENDER

"To the Commanding Officer." (Smith, 155; Wukovits, 139; Wiles, 28; Peatross, *Bless 'em All*, 81)

"Lieutenant Peatross contended." (Peatross, "Raid on Makin," pt. 1, 16)

"had told him that we should re-write." (Peatross, *Bless 'em All*, 82)

"Let's surrender!" (Blankfort, 60)

"had to accept the unpleasant fact." (Wiles, 47)

"forget about the surrender note," "Carlson told me not to say anything," "There was a tacit agreement." (Smith, 156–157)

"Carlson would never think of [surrender]." (Wukovits, 140)

"I heard about the note." (McCullough, "Reflections," 2)

"I didn't learn about it," "As far as I know." (Wukovits, 135)

"see Carlson's side too." (Smith, 158)

"That night we voted on survival." (Roosevelt, 272)

"As far as I have been able to determine." (Smith, 153)

"shaken by the recent firefight." (Smith, 154)

"to arrange for the surrender." (Smith, 154)

"was a really savvy guy." (Carlson 17)

"He was most unhappy." (Peatross, *Bless 'em All*, 81)

"Bill [McCall] said that was the biggest mistake." (Carson, 17)

"a popular Japanese history." (Peatross, *Bless 'em All*, 81–82)

"The word started," "not many of us accepted," "The most terrible message." (Peatross, "Raid on Makin," pt. 2, 17)

"the most disheartened." (LeFrancois, pt. 2, 29)

"Few men enjoyed any sleep." (Wukovits, 141)

"a bunch of native women." (Winters, 16)

"and he gave me three hand grenades." (Winters, 16)

Ben Carson and his rear guard. (Wiles, 29)

"What's going on back there?" (Peatross, *Bless 'em All*, 63)

"Peat," Haines said, "that crusty old boss of yours." (Peatross, *Bless 'em All*, 65)

"We are going to stay here." (Peatross, *Bless 'em All*, 65)

"I had to lay the law down." (Wukovits, 143)

"big as a barn door," "I don't recall anyone uttering." (Wukovits, 143)

"Getting back aboard." (Spotts, 16)

"I pleaded that [the skipper] wait." (Roosevelt, *My Parents*, 272)

"The planes concentrated on the subs." (LeFrancois, pt. 2, 41)

CHAPTER 12: WE NEVER SAW THEM AGAIN

"She would have gone straight on down." (Peatross, *Bless 'em All*, 66)

"Had they been depth charges." (Peatross, *Bless 'em All*, 66)

"My duty," he wrote. (Carlson, "Operations on Makin," 5)

"They were all wondering." (Smith, 166)

"This was fired by shooting." (Carlson, "Operations on Makin," 7)

"He sought out [Joe] Miller." (Blankfort, 64)

"I was sitting cross-legged." (LeFrancois, pt. 2, 43)

"In years, if not in experience." (LeFrancois, pt. 2, 43)

"Lieutenant," McCall asked. (LeFrancois, pt. 2, 43)

"I had brought a small camera." (Spotts, 15)

"Soon our raiders were wearing this stuff." (LeFrancois, pt. 2, 43)

"Lamb's Ark." (Smith, 168)

"I was in this coconut tree." (Waddell, 4; Peatross, *Bless 'em All*, 83)

"requested by blinker." (Karig and Purdon, 7)

"Squeegie Long." (Peatross, *Bless 'em All*, 83)

"Start the motors." (LeFrancois, pt. 2, 48)

"Can you imagine." (Wukovits, 150)

"I could see that Carlson was concerned." (Smith, 172)

"So, they cut loose," "I realize that sixty-four years." (McCullough, "Makin Raid," 2)

"We hung on to one another." (LeFrancois, pt. 2, 48)

"Never before or since." (Peatross, *Bless 'em All*, 84)

"utterly dazed." (LeFrancois, pt. 2, 48)

"I think I just let down." (Wukovits, 151–152)

"finally lost his cool." (Peatross, *Bless 'em All*, 86)
"I was sure glad to get back." (Winters, 17)
"prideful feeling . . . was tempered." (Stidham, 12)
"We are gathered here today." ("Makin Island Raid Brief" 1977, 14)

CHAPTER 13: TO HONOR THE SOULS
"Over his head." (Hillenbrand, 174)
"Nine Marines Marooned." (Hillenbrand, 175)
"They weren't left behind." (Wukovits, 172)
"There was an Italian priest." (Carson, 18)
"We were surprised." (Wiles, 52)
"good friends." (Wiles, 67)
"an administrative nuisance." (Smith, 228)
"to honor the souls of those executed." (Wiles, 66)
"The Japanese dug holes." (Wiles, 63)
"in order to prevent." (Wiles, 66)
"I ordered a thin woven straw mat." (Peatross, *Bless 'em All*, 88)
"I stayed a week." (Zamperini, 288)
"the whereabouts of the raiders' remains." (Wiles, 128)
"were so outraged." (Wiles, 128)
"I was billeted in the same room." (Stidham, 13)
"The party at the Royal Hawaiian Hotel." (Smith, 185)
"We changed clothes." (Voight, 9)
"I didn't want to go back." (Wukovits, 170)
"Peanuts, popcorn, Navy Crosses." (Smith, 188)
"The Colonel wants to see the captain." (Peatross, *Bless 'em All*, 122)
"I had never before in my life." (Peatross, *Bless 'em All*, 123)

CHAPTER 14: ANOTHER ONE OF THOSE ZERO HOURS
"Apparently," Peatross wrote. (Peatross, *Bless 'em All*, 124)
"Once again," Peatross said. (Peatross, *Bless 'em All*, 124)
"we were able to assemble." (Peatross, *Bless 'em All*, 124)
"the ultimate development." (Peatross, *Bless 'em All*, 125)
"The flies were terrible, terrible." (Wukovits, 175)
"jungles were cleared." (Archibald, 2)
"The Seabees built a ramp." (Archibald, 1)
"Consequently," Peatross wrote. (Peatross, *Bless 'em All*, 126)
"I miss you keenly," "was a good man." (Wukovits, 178)
"We thought we'd never see action again." (Blankfort, 295)
"I certainly hope so." (Smith, 193)
"If Carlson was disappointed." (Smith, 193)

"The bow plunged." (Bulger, Nov., 7)
"We had no idea." (Wukovits, 181)
"Another one of those zero hours." (Blankfort, 293)
"We thought we would have to fight." (Wukovits, 181)
"I say, what kept you chaps?" (Bulger, Nov., 8)
"Nips, of course." (Clemens, 277–278)
"I made the decision to suffer." (Kaplan, 2)
"a crocodile ranch." (Carson, 18)
"drenching rains, eerie jungle noises." (Bulger, Nov., 9)
"We saw no more of that crocodile." (Bulger, Nov., 9)

CHAPTER 15: THE LONG PATROL
"This is a very unusual set of circumstances." (Duesler, 15)
"Great reliance was placed on these scouts." (Carlson, "Report on the Operations,"
2)
"Next morning, we started." (Lansford, 2)
"I was in a machine gun squad." (Wukovits, 216)
"We who lived through Guadalcanal." (Blankfort, 296–297)
"simply could not move." (Bulger, March, 11)
"had been giving us one of his lectures." (Berry, 123)
"When you first go out." (Carson, 19)
"I put my pouch down." (Carlson, 20)
"A strange stillness." (Bulger, May, 2)
"He stopped like a man." (Bulger, May, 3)
"As I stood guard." (Bulger, May, 3)
"The image of the young soldiers." (Wukovits, 186–187)
"Now we were miles from nowhere." (Peatross, *Bless 'em All*, 135)
"Oh," the man said. (Peatross, *Bless 'em All*, 137)
"he was no great shakes as a speaker." (Wukovits, 202)
"telling how proud they were." (Blankfort, 299)
"We shouldered our packs." (Lansford, 3)
"Hold on," he told his patrols. (Lansford, 4)

CHAPTER 16: HE KNEW HE WOULD DIE
"Man, I never heard so much." (Bulger, May, 6)
"The whole platoon got clobbered." (Bulger, May, 8)
"We charged full speed ahead." (Bulger, May, 13)
"The realization that we were alone." (Bulger, May, 13)
"creeping and crawlin'," "We felt naked as a jaybird." (Bulger, May, 13)
"'Let's stand up,' Bulger said." (Bulger, May, 13)
"I found 'C' Company in a bad state of disorganization." (Carlson, "Report on the
Operations," 4)

"Like a Civil War outfit." (Tutt, 1)
"For us, time had lost all meaning." (Lansford, 4)
"Like a mile-long snake." (Lansford, 5)
"For the Japanese." (Keene, 6)
"They were rightfully surprised." (Tutt, 1)
"they still held Asamana." (Lansford, 8–9)
"He knew he would die." (Wukovits, 197)
"He used his head." (Wukovits, 201)
"Finally, the word was passed." (Bulger, Sept., 12)
"Finally, in desperation." (Bulger, Sept., 12)
"amazed at how haggard." (Peatross, *Bless 'em All*, 140)
"Although Carlson usually did not let his features show." (Peatross, *Bless 'em All*, 140)
"quite hysterical and exhausted." (Wukovits, 199–200)
"for incompetency." (Carlson, "Report of the Operations," 6)
"was as impulsive as Washburn was prudent." (Lansford, 4)
"Over here, Yankee, over here." (Wukovits, 204)
"the disfigured, mistreated corpse." (Miskimon, 66)
"I remember seeing him there." (Wukovits, 204)
"When a few raised their hands." (Wukovits, 204)
"We never take a prisoner." (Wukovits, 205)

CHAPTER 17: PALE GHOSTS
"The natives hated the Japanese." (Bulger, 1981, March, 11)
"The soldiers smashed his face." (Clemens, 209–210)
"Better me die plenty." (Bartlett, 2)
"He was an awful mess." (Clemens, 209)
"Tell them I love them all." (Bartlett, 4)
"We found notices." (Carlson, "Report of the Operations," 6)
"I was plenty scared." (Bulger, 1981, Sept., 12)
"'When you hear my shotgun.'" (Wukovits, 209)
"closer inspection through my binoculars." (Peatross, *Bless 'em All*, 152)
"started walking back." (Carson, 2)
"From his base camp." (Wukovits, 211)
"They would put up a front." (Wukovits, 212)
"Carlson had a talent for that." (Duesler, 17)
"Malaria moved in on us." (Blankfort, 300)
"jungle rot and fungus." (Bulger, 1981, Sept., 16)
"I had to stop every three or four miles." (Winters, 20)
"On my way up, I stopped." (Carson, 20)
"The awful hunger." (Blankfort, 298)
"bodies of dead Japs!" (Blankfort, 298)

"When we finished the mission." (Waddell, "Kwajalein Visit," 2)

"Here's what I'm going to do." (Blankfort, 300)

"dined on mongoose and an unfortunate cat." (Kaplan, 6)

"all secure in stainless steel cylinders." (Kaplan, 7)

"hot, sweaty, dirty, and worn out." (Peatross, *Bless 'em All*, 156)

"Calling in Evans Carlson." (Keene, 7)

CHAPTER 18: THE PROUDEST MOMENT

"I made him leave the point." (Wukovits, 217)

"While Carlson chain-smoked." (Peatross, *Bless 'em All*, 158)

"gawk at the weapons." (Peatross, *Bless 'em All*, 158)

"the Lord does indeed." (Peatross, *Bless 'em All*, 158)

"No safe, no have!" (Peatross, *Bless 'em All*, 158)

"There was no trail up the Tenaru." (Kaplan, 6)

"our company received." (Vanlandingham, 19)

"When A Company joined us." (Bulger 1981, Nov., 10)

"Later," historian Christopher Miskimon wrote. (Miskimon, 67)

"As we approached the camp." (Peatross, *Bless 'em All*, 159)

"Up in the mountains." (Bulger, 1981, Nov. 10)

"we climbed that damn mountain." (Bulger, 1981, Nov., 10)

"Each healthy Raider who remained." (Bulger, 1981, Nov., 11)

"You dragged your ass all the way." (Bauml, 1)

"I smell'm Jap." (Bauml, 1)

"I'm looking around" (Bauml, 2)

"They were a pitiful sight." (Peatross, *Bless 'em All*, 164)

"half-starved, sick men." (Blankfort, 301–302)

"The Jap position is unoccupied!" (Blankfort, 302)

"would be a good thing, wouldn't it?" (Blankfort, 302)

"It is a good thing." (Blankfort, 302–303)

"Let's sing 'Onward Christian Soldiers.'" (Blankfort, 303)

"To those of us who were there." (Bulger, 1981, Nov., 13)

CHAPTER 19: GUNG HO IS DEAD

"crashing through [the jungle]." (Bauml, 2)

"We took two steps." (Bauml, 2)

"I don't know if he heard me or not." (Bauml, 2)

"I got hit in my." (Blankfort, 304)

"I seen red." (Maghakian, 2)

"I made a human target out of myself." (Maghakian, 3)

"We gave him a decent burial." (Maghakian, 4, 5)

"As I stood over." (Peatross, *Bless 'em All*, 165)

"A feeling of deep sadness." (Peatross, *Bless 'em All*, 165)

"We all three saw someone." (Bulger, 1981, Nov., 14)

"Captain, how am I doing," "'Hold onto your stretcher.'" (Peatross, *Bless 'em All,* 166)

"The Raiders walked in." (Wukovits, 249)

"We were basket cases." (Berry, 125)

"if you could call that drag-ass limping." (Bulger, 1981, Nov., 14)

"My God, walking skeletons!" (Blankfort, 305)

"For the consummate skill." ("Carlson Men Win," 1)

"the best sermon he had ever heard." (Blankfort, 308)

"Carlson is one of those dangerous men." (Smith, 206)

"writes books." (Wukovits, 258)

"Things were much too good for us." (Blankfort, 308)

"Never before in the history of the Corps." (Peatross, *Bless 'em All,* 173)

"There was hell in the ranks." (Blankfort, 309–310)

"Goddamn it, colonel." (Lucas, 103)

"It is my belief that any officer." (Blankfort, 311)

"None of this was official." (Blankfort, 310)

"Tragedy awaited us." (Lucas, 105)

"I have been relieved of my command." (Blankfort, 315)

"I want this camp to look like a Marine camp," "Gung Ho is dead." (Blankfort, 316)

EPILOGUE: THANK GOD, HE'S GONE

"Here's some news to make you hot." (Peatross, *Bless 'em All,* 294)

"Carlson became a very sick man." (Blankfort, 318)

"Evans Carlson was worthy," "the most perfectly planned." (Twining, 146)

"Suffice to say." (Wukovits, 267)

"It was fun helping to make the movie." (McCarthy, *Gung Ho, the Movie,* 8)

"His job in *Gung Ho* was to run." (Waddell, *Kwajalein Visit,* 2)

"If this picture is going to be about 'Gung Ho.'" (Blankfort, 323)

"Evans lived a theatrical life." (Wukovits, 271)

"a sizzling war film." (Crowther, 1)

"All things considered." (McCarthy, 9)

"Miss it if you can." (McCarthy, 2)

"belittled and embarrassed." (Smith, 213)

"He was restless and still depressed." (Blankfort, 323)

"This was not only worse." (Sherrod, 109)

"I've been in many battles." (Blankfort, 331)

"Our greatest weakness." (Gaines, 4)

"What if they had been trained." (Gaines, 4)

"With malice aforethought." (Blankfort, 336)

"He was tired." (Blankfort, 337)

"They don't come any better." (Richardson, 8)

"I remember thinking." (Blankfort, 341)

"whatever his deserts." (Blankfort, 342)

"The news of the President's passing." (Blankfort, 351)

"I've fallen apart like a one-horse shay." (Blankfort, 356)

"Don't worry about me." (Blankfort, 356)

"He worried about atomic energy control." (Marder, 4)

"was a communist." ("Late Gen. Carlson," 1)

"was married to a lady," "official Communist candidate." (Fry, 1)

"He may be red." (Smith, 214)

"I am not a member of the Communist Party." (Marder, 4)

"he believed the general was subjecting himself." ("Gen. Carlson Dead," 1)

"I didn't have the money either." (Roosevelt, *My Parents*, 277)

"died a disillusioned man." (Marder, B3)

"I have never been." (Hoffman, 400)

"May I call attention." (Swing, 12)

"shabby treatment." ("Honor Slighted," 12)

"Thank God, he's gone." (Thomas, 268)

Bibliography

Alley, Rewi. *Six Americans in China*. Washington, DC: International Culture Publishing, 1985.

Aquilina, Robert V. "Who Was Left Behind on Makin?" *Fortitudine* 19, no. 1 (1989).

Archibald, Sasha. "Million Dollar Point." *Cabinet Magazine* 10, 2003 (Spring).

"Armistice Day: Carlson's Raiders: November 11, 1942." Posted March 5, 2001. *Lt. Col. Evans F. Carlson of the Raider Marines Forum*. http://www.network54.com/Forum/54215/.

"Atabrine." *Raider Patch*, Nov. 1986. US Marine Raider Association.

Ballard, J. G. *Miracles of Life: Shanghai to Shepperton*. New York: Liveright Publishing, 2008.

Bartlett, Tom. "Sir Jacob Vouza." *Leatherneck: Magazine of the Marines,* May 1944.

Bauml, Ray. "The Marines on Guadalcanal." In Patrick O'Donnell, *Into the Rising Sun: In Their Own Words, World War II's Pacific Veterans Reveal the Heart of Combat*. New York: Simon and Schuster, 2002.

Berry, Henry. *Semper Fi, Mac: Living Memories of the US Marines in World War II*. New York: Arbor House, 1982.

Blair, Clay, Jr. *Silent Victory: The US Submarine War against Japan*. Annapolis, MD: Naval Institute Press, 1975.

Blankfort, Michael. *The Big Yankee: The Life of Carlson of the Raiders*. Boston: Little, Brown, 1947.

"Bloody Plains Brief, Asamana, Guadalcanal." *Raider Patch*, May 1980. US Marine Raider Association.

Boot, Max. "After Abbottabad: Navy SEALs and American Security," *New Republic*, Oct. 19, 2012. Review of Mark Owen, *No Easy Day: The Firsthand Account of the Mission That Killed Osama Bin Laden*. New York: Dutton, 2012. http://www.newrepublic.com/article/books-and-arts/magazine/108762/after-abbottabad-navy-seals-and-american-security.

Bulger, Lowell. "The Second Marine Raider Battalion on Guadalcanal." *Raider Patch*, Mar., May, Sept., Nov. 1981 (4 parts). US Marine Raider Association.

"Butaritari Island." *Raider Patch*, May 1989. US Marine Raider Association.

Carlson, Evans. "Operations on Makin, August 17-18, 1942. To: The Commander, Submarines, Pacific Fleet." PAC-90-wb. A16(6). Aug. 21, 1942. National Archives.

————. "The Raid on Makin Island by the Second Marine Raider Battalion. To: Commander, Submarines, Pacific Fleet." No date. CINPAC File No. Pac-90-wb. A16(6). National Archives.

————. "Report of the Operations of This Battalion on Guadalcanal between 4 November and 4 December, 1942. To: The Commanding General. 1st Marine Amphibious Corps." Dec. 30, 1942. Record Group 127, Records of the US Marine Corps. Reports of the 2nd Raider Battalion: Records Relating to the Operations in Guadalcanal, Entry A1 1051. National Archives.

————. "Report of the Raid Against Makin, 17-18 August, 1942. To: The Commanding Officer, U. S. Marine Corps." Sept. 2, 1942. CINPAC File No. Pac-90-wb. A16(6). National Archives.

Carlson, Evans F. "Marine Raiders." *Raider Patch*, May 1993. US Marine Raider Association.

"Carlson Men Win Blanket Citation." *New York Times*, Dec. 27, 1942.

"Carlson of the Raider Marines." Gunny G's Marines Websites. www.angelfire.com/ca/dickg/carlson.html.

"Carlson Raider Gung Ho Knife." *Raider Patch*, Nov. 1980. US Marine Raider Association.

Carlson's Raiders: [Bill] Lansford and [Pete] Arias. Sept. 2007. WETA/PBS, Washington, DC, and American Lives Film Project. Pbs.org/thewar/detail_5375.htm.

Carson, Ben E. Interview, Sept. 21, 2001. "Pacific D-Days Symposium." Fredericksburg TX: Admiral Nimitz National Museum of the Pacific War, Oral History Program.

Clark, Curt. "Raiders and the Deep Blue Sea." *Raider Patch* 107 (2009). US Marine Raider Association.

Clemens, Martin. *Alone on Guadalcanal: A Coastwatcher's Story.* Annapolis, MD: Naval Institute Press, 1998.

Corbett, John R. "Awards and Citations." *Raider Patch*, no date. US Marine Raider Association.

Courtier, Jerry A. "Ollie North's War Stories to Focus on the Missing in Action." *Raider Patch* 104 (2008). US Marine Raider Association.

Crowther, Bosley. "'Gung Ho!' A Lurid Action Film about the Makin Island Raid." Movie review. *New York Times*, Jan. 26, 1944.

Duesler, Frank. Oral History Interview. Madison: Wisconsin Veterans Museum Research Center, 2002.

Durdin, F. Tillman. "The Roughest and the Toughest." *New York Times*, Nov. 8, 1942.

English, R. H. "Report of the Raider Expedition Against Makin—comments on. To: Commander Submarines, Pacific Fleet." Sept. 3, 1942. CINPAC. File No. Pac-90-wb A16 (6). National Archives.

Everett, Gail. E-mail message to the author, Mar. 29, 2013.

Everett, Glenn. E-mail message to the author, Mar. 29, 2013.

Farnsworth, Robert M. *From Vagabond to Journalist: Edgar Snow in Asia, 1928–1941*. Columbia: University of Missouri Press, 1996.

Faulkner, Sgt. James. "Navy Cross, Makin." *Raider Patch*, Mar. 1997. US Marine Raider Association.

Ford, Regina. "Soldier Returns Lost Dog Tags to WWII Arizona Vet [John Joseph Keker]." *Raider Patch*, June 2012. US Marine Raider Association.

Frank, Benis M., and Henry I. Shaw. *Victory and Occupation: History of US Marine Corps Operations in World War II*. Vol. 5. Washington, DC: Government Printing Office, 1968.

Fry, Amelia. *General Evans Carlson: Mao Militarist and California Politician*. Interview with James Roosevelt, 2011. Regional Oral History Office, University of California, Berkeley.

Gaines, Dick. "Carlson of the Raider Marines." Aug. 1999. angelfire.com/ca/dickg/carlson.html.

"Gen. Carlson Dead." *New York Times*, May 28, 1947.

"Gen. Carlson Is Buried." *New York Times*, June 5, 1947.

Gomrick, Kathleen. "Gung Ho, Raider! The Philosophy and Methods of Brig. Gen. Evans F. Carlson, Marine Corps Raider." Research report, April 1999. Air Command and Staff College, Air University, Maxwell Air Force Base, Alabama.

Haines, John. "Report of Marine-Submarine Raider Expedition. To: Commander, Task Force 7." Aug. 24, 1942. CINPAC File No. Pac-90-wb. A16(6). National Archives.

Hamilton, John Maxwell. *Edgar Snow: A Biography*. Bloomington: Indiana University Press, 1988.

Haughey, David W. "Carlson's Raid on Makin Island." *Marine Corps Gazette*, Aug. 2001.

Heinl, Robert Debs. *Soldiers of the Sea: The United States Marine Corps, 1775–1962*. Annapolis, MD: Naval Institute Press, 1962.

Hepburn, Francis. (1993, Nov.). "Recovery of the Remains of Marine Raiders Killed on Makin Atoll." *Raider Patch*, Nov. 1993. US Marine Raider Association.

Hillenbrand, Laura. *Unbroken: A World War II Story of Survival, Resilience, and Redemption*. New York: Random House, 2010.

Hoffman, Jon T. *Once a Legend: "Red Mike" Edson of the Marine Raiders*. New York: Presidio Press, 1994.

"Honor Slighted." *Washington Post*, June 5, 1947.

Hoyt, Edwin P. *Raider Battalion*. Los Angeles: Pinnacle, 1980.

Inman, Calvin. Interview. *Raider Patch*, Sept. 1988. US Marine Raider Association.

"James Roosevelt Dies at 83." *New York Times*, Aug. 14, 1991.

Kaplan, Ervin. "A Personal View of the Guadalcanal Long Patrol." US Marine Raider Association. usmarineraiders.org/longpatrolview.htm.

Karig, Walter, and Eric Purdon. "The Makin Island Raid at 70." *US Naval Institute Proceedings*, Aug. 2012.

Keene, R. R. "Gung Ho: The Long Patrol." *Leatherneck: Magazine of the Marines*, Nov. 1992.

Lansford, William Douglas. "The Battle at Asamana." *Leatherneck: Magazine of the Marines*, Nov. 2007.

"Late Gen. Carlson and Barnes, Editor, Accused by Budenz in Inquiry as Reds." *New York Times*, July 18, 1950.

LeFrancois, Wilfred. "We Mopped Up Makin Island." Parts 1 and 2. *Saturday Evening Post* 216, no. 23 (Dec. 4, 1943): 20–21, 109–110, and no. 24 (Dec. 11, 1943): 28–29, 41, 43, 45, 48.

Lewis, Jack. "The Remains of Marines Who Died in the August 1942 Makin Atoll Raid Arrive in Hawaii." *Leatherneck: Magazine of the Marines*, March 2000.

Lucas, Jim. *Combat Correspondent*. New York: Reynal and Hitchcock, 1944.

Maghakian, Victor. Letter to Henry Miller, June 12, 1943. Jack Miller Collection, DeGolyer Library, Southern Methodist University.

"Makin Island Raid Brief." *Raider Patch*, May 1977 and July 1980. US Marine Raider Association.

Marder, Murray. "Raider Carlson: Maverick Marine." Obituary. *Washington Post*, June 1, 1947.

"Marine Raiders." *Sacramento Bee*, September 17, 1992. Reprinted in *Raider Patch*, May 1993, 20. US Marine Raider Association.

"Marines Learn to Hit Below Belt." *Raider Patch, Sept. 1991*. US Marine Raider Association.

McCarthy, John. "Gung Ho, the Movie." *Raider Patch* 94 (2005). US Marine Raider Association.

———. "The Legend: Evans F. Carlson." *Raider Patch* 94 (2005). US Marine Raider Association.

———. "Makin Raiders Return to Paradise." *Raider Patch*, July–Sept. 2006. US Marine Raider Association.

———. "The Wayward Warrior: The Intriguing Double Life of a Raider Hero [Howard Craven/William Murphree]. *Raider Patch*, May 1997. US Marine Raider Association.

———. "Why the Marines? Why the Raiders?" *Raider Patch* 94 (2005). US Marine Raider Association.

McCullough, Kenneth L. "The Makin Raid." *Marine Corps Gazette*, Aug. 2006.

McCullough, K. L. "Reflections of a Carlson's Marine Raider." Aug. 18, 1942. US Navy. http://www.public.navy.mil/surfor/lhd8/Pages/RaiderReflections.aspx.

Merillat, Herbert Christian. *Guadalcanal Remembered*. New York: Dodd, Mead, 1982.

Miskimon, Christopher. "Carlson's Long Patrol." *WWII History*, Fall 2012.

Moore, Arthur C. "From a Raider 11-6-1942." Poem. *Raider Patch* 117 (2012). US Marine Raider Association.

Morgan, Ted. *FDR: A Biography.* New York: Simon and Schuster, 1985.

O'Donnell, Patrick K. *Into the Rising Sun: In Their Own Words, World War II's Pacific Veterans Reveal the Heart of Combat.* New York: Free Press, 2002.

Orrick, Bill. Interview. *Sacramento (CA) Bee,* Sept. 17, 1992.

Patch editor. Article by Col. Evans F. Carlson, CO 2nd Raiders. *Raider Patch,* May 1993. US Marine Raider Association.

———. "Boot Camp: The Making of a Marine and Future Raider." *Raider Patch* 108 (2009). US Marine Raider Association.

———. "Carlson's 3-Man Fire Team Concept Becomes Reality in the Pacific War." *Raider Patch* 112 (2012). US Marine Raider Association.

———. "Elite Marine Corps School Receives Raider Name." *Raider Patch* 91 (2005). US Marine Raider Association.

———. "What Sort of Man Was the President's Son?" *Raider Patch* 102 (2007). US Marine Raider Association.

Peatross, Oscar F. *Bless 'em All: The Raider Marines of World War II.* Irvine, CA: Review Publications, 1995.

———. "The Raid on Makin Island." *Leatherneck: Magazine of the Marines,* Parts 1 and 2. Sept. 1992 and Aug. 2002.

Persico, Joseph E. "FDR's China Syndrome." *World War II,* July/Aug. 2012.

Price, Ruth. *The Lives of Agnes Smedley.* New York: Oxford University Press, 2005.

Quirk, Brian J. "Marine Veteran." Obituary. *Chicago Tribune,* June 1, 2010.

Ragland, Janet. "Lt. Jack Miller Biography." University Park, TX: Southern Methodist University World War II Memorial Plaza website, no date. smu.edu/cul/memorial/.

"Raider Cleary's Plaque to be Placed on USS *Makin Island.*" US Marine Raider Association. www.usmarineraiders.org/makin.html.

"Ralph H. Coyte 1914–1998."(1999). Ancentry.com. http://boards.ancestry.com/localities.northam.usa.states.colorado.counties.lari.

Richardson, Herb. "Giants of the Corps: Evans Carlson." *Leatherneck: Magazine of the Marines,* Mar. 1997.

"Robert B. Maulding." Posted Aug. 17, 2001. Arlington National Cemetery website. www.arlingtoncemetery.net/rbmaulding.htm.

Roosevelt, James. Interview (no date). "California Democrats in the Earl Warren Era: General Evans Carlson." Berkeley: Regional Oral History Office, University of California, 2011.

———. *My Parents: A Differing View.* Chicago: Playboy Press, 1976.

Roosevelt, James, and Sidney Shalett. *Affectionately, FDR.* New York: Harcourt, Brace, 1959.

Rupertus, William. "My Rifle." *Raider Patch,* Sept. 1985. US Marine Raider Association.

Schultz, Duane. "The Breaking Point: Combat Fatigue Took Its Toll on the Fighting Men During World War II." *WWII History*, June 2013, 8–11.

Shawlee, Ralph. "Salty Sea Story." *Raider Patch*, May 1989. US Marine Raider Association.

Sherrod, Robert. *Tarawa: The Story of a Battle*. New York: Duell, Sloan and Pearce, 1944.

Smith, George W. *Carlson's Raid: The Daring Marine Assault on Makin*. Novato, CA: Presidio, 2001.

Snow, Helen. "Autobiography of Evans Carlson: Reminiscences Told to Helen Snow in China, 1940." MSS 2219, Box 98, Folder 4, Helen Foster Snow papers, 20th Centry Western and Mormon Manuscripts, L. Tom Perry Special Collections, Harold B. Lee Library, Brigham Young University.

———. *My China Years: A Memoir*. New York: William Morrow, 1984.

Spotts, Melvin J. "Makin Island." *Raider Patch*, July 1980. US Marine Raider Association.

Stidham, Buck. "Comments on Returning from the Makin Raid." *Raider Patch*, Jan. 1988 and Jan. 1993. US Marine Raider Association.

Swing, Raymond Gram. "Evans F. Carlson." Letter to the editor. *Washington Post*, June 5, 1947.

———. *Preview of History*. Garden City, NY: Doubleday, 1943.

Thomas, S. Bernard. *Season of High Adventure: Edgar Snow in China*. Berkeley: University of California Press, 1996.

Thomason, Clyde. "Medal of Honor Citation." *Raider Patch*, March 1977. US Marine Raider Association.

Trumbull, Robert. "Foe Belted on [Makin] Isle." *New York Times*, Aug. 22, 1942.

———. "Marines Wiped Out Japanese on Makin Isle in Hot Fighting." *New York Times*, Aug. 28, 1942.

Tutt, Bob. "Guerrilla-like Carlson's Raiders Rode to the Sound of the Guns." *Houston Chronicle*, July 1, 1995.

Twining, Merrill B. *No Bended Knee: The Battle for Guadalcanal: The Memoir of Gen. Merrill B. Twining, USMC*. New York: Presidio Press, 1996.

Ulbrich, David J. *Preparing for Victory: Thomas Holcomb and the Making of the Modern Marine Corps, 1936–1943*. Annapolis, MD: Naval Institute Press, 2011.

Vandegrift, A. A. *Once a Marine: The Memoirs of General A. A. Vandegrift*. New York: W. W. Norton, 1964.

Vanlandingham, J. Leon. Interview. *Raider Patch*, Sept. 1984. US Marine Raider Association.

Voight, Dean S. Oral History Interview. Madison, WI: Wisconsin Veterans Museum Research Center, 1995.

Vouza, Jacob. "Solomon Island Hero." *Solomon Times*, Sept. 22, 2008.

Waddell, Jan. "Kwajalein Visit Brings Back Memories of War." Interviews, 2003. Dan Marsh's Marine Raider Page. usmcraiders.com/KwajInterviews1.htm.

————. "Raider Tells of Three-Man Teams and Airfield Strike." *Kwajalein Hourglass,* Nov. 14, 2003. http://www.smdc.army.mil/KWAJ/Hourglass/issues-archived/03Issues/hourglass11_14_03.pdf.

"War Criminal." *Raider Patch*, Sept. 1989. US Marine Raider Association.

Wells, Edward F. "FDR and the Marines." *Fortitudine* 2, no. 11 (1981).

Wheeler, Richard. *A Special Valor: The US Marines and the Pacific War.* New York: Harper and Row, 1983.

Wiles, Tripp. *Forgotten Raiders of '42: The Fate of the Marines Left Behind on Makin.* Washington, DC: Potomac Books, 2007.

Williams, Hugh. *The Old Corps: A Portrait of the U.S. Marine Corps between the Wars.* Annapolis, MD: Naval Institute Press, 1982.

Winters, Dean. Interview, July 17, 2001 (tape no. 404). Salt Lake City: Oral History of Utah's World War II Veterans, Fort Douglas Military Museum and Marriott Library, University of Utah.

Wukovits, John. *American Commando: Evans Carlson, His WWII Marine Raiders, and America's First Special Forces Mission.* New York: NAL, 2009.

Zamperini, Louis. *Devil at My Heels: A World War II Hero's Epic Saga of Torment, Survival, and Forgiveness.* New York: William Morrow, 2003.

Zimmerman, John. "Inspection of the Records of the Trial for Murder of Vice Admiral Abe." June 30, 1947. National Archives.

Zimmerman, Phyllis A. "Braiding the Cord: The Role of Evans F. Carlson's 2d Marine Raider Battalion in Amphibious Warfare." *Marine Corps Gazette,* Nov. 1994.

Acknowledgments

Anyone trying to write about events that occurred more than seventy years ago owes a debt of gratitude to many individuals and organizations whose work involves keeping memories alive. I am grateful to the archivists, librarians, website developers, veterans' associations, oral history collections, and historians who made available information about Evans Carlson and his band of Raiders. They are the keepers of history who allow the rest of us to go back in time.

Many such keepers of history not only generously supplied material I had requested but often suggested other sources for me to pursue. Thanks to Cindy Brightenburg, Reference Assistant, Harold B. Lee Library at Brigham Young University, for sending me the unpublished document entitled, "Autobiography of Evans Carlson: Reminiscences Told to Helen Snow in China, 1940." It is the only known first-person account of Carlson's life. Excerpts from this autobiography have been printed in Chapters 1–3 and the Epilogue with permission of the L. Tom Perry Special Collections: MSS 2219, Box 98, Folder 4, Helen Foster Snow papers, 20th Century Western and Mormon Manuscripts, L. Tom Perry Special Collections, Harold B. Lee Library, Brigham Young University. Also thanks to Cynthia Franco, librarian at the DeGolyer Library at Southern Methodist University in Dallas. Excerpts from the letter from Sergeant Victor "'Transport'" Maghakian to Henry Miller on July 12, 1943, have been reprinted in chapter 19 with the permission of DeGolyer Library, Southern Methodist University, Dallas, Texas (A2004,0001).

Other archivists and librarians who provided valuable help are Nathaniel Patch, archive specialist, Archives II, Reference Section, National Archives, College Park, MD; Reagan Grau, archivist, National Museum of the Pacific War, Fredericksburg, TX; Julia Huddleston, senior library specialist, J. Willard Marriott Library, Special

Collections, Manuscript Division, University of Utah, Salt Lake City; Virginia Lewis, archivist, Franklin D. Roosevelt Presidential Library, Hyde Park, NY; and Rachel Telford, processing specialist, Veterans History Project, Library of Congress, Washington, DC.

Useful websites for research on Carlson's Raiders include the US Marine Raider Association and Foundation at www.usmarineraiders. org. This is the official website of the Marine Raider Association, which includes material on all four Raider battalions. It is very well organized and has links to related websites. This site also publishes digital versions of the Marine Raider newsletter, *Raider Patch*, from 1956 to date. This is an extremely valuable source, with articles about the Raiders' experiences, many written by Raiders themselves.

Another helpful site is Dan Marsh's Marine Raider Page at www.usmcraiders.com. It is dedicated to "Keeping the Legacy Alive," and it contains good information on the Raider battalions. Also useful is *Fortitudine*, a USMC historical journal from the Marine Corps Historical Center with issues available online from 1971, at www.mcu. usmc.mil/historydivisin/pages/fortitudine. "Fortitudine," the original Marine Corps rallying cry, is Latin for "fortitude."

Major archival sources include Records of the United States Marine Corps, Historical Files, box 183,370-D-04-1, National Archives, College Park, MD, www.archives.gov/; The Raid at Makin Island, James Roosevelt Papers, Box 761957-58, Franklin D. Roosevelt Presidential Library, Hyde Park, NY; Evans F. Carlson Collection, Marine Corps Archives and Special Collections, Quantico, VA, www.guides.grc.usmcu.edu/archives; and "Gung Ho Raider! The Philosophy and Methods of Brig. Gen. Evans F. Carlson, Marine Corps Raider," research report by Kathleen Gomrick, April 1999, Air Command and Staff College, Air University, Maxwell Air Force Base, Alabama.

I would like to thank the following authors, whose earlier books on Carlson's Raiders provided a wealth of information, including interviews with Raiders who have since passed on: George Smith, author of *Carlson's Raid: The Daring Marine Assault on Makin*; John Wukovits, author of *American Commando: Evans Carlson, His WWII Marine Raiders, and America's First Special Forces Mission*; and Tripp

Wiles, author of *Forgotten Raiders of '42: The Fate of the Marines Left Behind on Makin.*

I am grateful to Bruce H. Franklin of Westholme Publishing for the passion, dedication, and enthusiasm he brings to the publication of his books; to literary agent Robin Rue for her patience and counsel; to consulting editor Ron Silverman for his knowledgeable and thorough approach and his careful attention to detail; to Trudi Gershenov for another striking book jacket design; and to my wife, Sydney Ellen, who still makes everything so much better.

Index